Sam Rice

Sam Rice

*A Biography of the
Washington Senators
Hall of Famer*

Jeff Carroll

McFarland & Company, Inc., Publishers
Jefferson, North Carolina, and London

[LIBRARY OF CONGRESS ONLINE CATALOG]
Carroll, Jeff, 1977–
   Sam Rice / a biography of the Washington Senators hall of famer / Jeff Carroll.
      p.   cm.
   Includes bibliographical references and index.

   ISBN-13: 978-0-7864-3119-9
   softcover : 50# alkaline paper ∞

   1. Rice, Sam, 1890–1974. 2. Baseball players — United States — Biography. 3. Washington Senators (Baseball team : 1886–1960) — History. I. Title.
   GV865.R427 C37   2008
   796.357092 B — dc22   2007029501

British Library cataloguing data are available

©2008 Jeff Carroll. All rights reserved

No part of this book may be reproduced or transmitted in any form or by any means, electronic or mechanical, including photocopying or recording, or by any information storage and retrieval system, without permission in writing from the publisher.

On the cover: Sam Rice, 1916 (National Baseball Hall of Fame Library, Cooperstown, N.Y.)

Manufactured in the United States of America

McFarland & Company, Inc., Publishers
  Box 611, Jefferson, North Carolina 28640
    www.mcfarlandpub.com

Acknowledgments

This book took about two years to complete, though the bulk of the work was done over a whirlwind three-month span from August through October of 2006. There were days when the book seemed like it would never be completed, but every time I came across a new and interesting fact about Rice, it spurred me on for at least a few more days until, one afternoon, I looked around and found nothing else to add. I believed in his story and believed that the world needed a full Rice biography.

Thanks go to, first of all, my former sports editor at *The Times of Northwest Indiana* and one of my best friends in the business, Mike Clark, who acted as excited as I was when I first discovered Rice's story, and cleared out a mountain of prime Sunday newspaper space for me to introduce Sam to our readers. My current editor, *Irish Sports Report*'s Bob Wieneke, never questioned me when I had to scamper off for a couple hours to sift through microfilm at the South Bend Public Library, or come in a couple of hours late while I took advantage of a quiet house. Former and current colleagues George Castle, Bill Bilinski, Jason Kelly and Eric Hansen have all written books, and helped with both moral support and tips on the process.

The Michigan City Public Library and the University of Notre Dame Library were two places where I was able to dig up much of the research used in the book. The Baseball Hall of Fame also had many of the materials I was seeking. Thanks also go out to the faceless army of researchers who have built an awe-inspiring database of baseball references online.

I'm not sure I would have been able to finish this project and retain my sanity had it not been for the tremendous, tremendous help of Society of American Baseball Research member and fellow Sam Rice buff Stephen Able. Able wrote the Rice biography that appears online at the SABR Baseball Bio Project.

For no personal gain, he copied dozens and dozens of newspaper articles and mailed them to me. Filling in Rice's minor league days would have been a difficult task had Able not tread that ground before me. This book would not have been possible, in its current form, without his help.

Bill Birely, one of Rice's friends as well as his investment broker during the later years of his life, wrote me out of the blue, graciously sharing his memories of Sam.

Andrew Sharp, another SABR member, took the time to take down and email me a transcript of an on-camera interview Rice gave at the old Griffith Stadium. Margaret Robinson helped a great deal by directing me to sources where I might find out more about Rice's post-baseball life. That and her enthusiasm for the project were both helpful.

Finally, perhaps the largest thank you of all goes out to my wife Kelley, who never questioned me when it was seventy degrees and sunny out and rather than rake leaves, grill out, throw toys for our two dogs in the yard or tend to whatever else needed to be done around the house, I spent the time hunched over a computer, sifting through baseball box scores and articles from eighty years ago.

Table of Contents

Acknowledgments — v
Preface — 1
Prologue: Induction Day — 5

1. Too Terrible to Relate — 7
2. In the Navy — 16
3. Man o' War — 27
4. The War in Europe — 40
5. Roaring into the 1920s — 54
6. Bush League Manager — 66
7. Streaking to a Pennant — 80
8. To the Brink — 92
9. Party Town — 103
10. Another Pennant Run — 112
11. The Catch — 124
12. Back to Earth — 144
13. Grandpap of the Potomac — 160
14. End of the Line — 171

15. Reunion in Cleveland	183
16. Life on the Farm	190
17. Thirteen Hits	198
Epilogue	213
Appendix: Sam Rice by the Numbers	215
Chapter Notes	219
Bibliography	233
Index	237

PREFACE

Browsing a bookstore one afternoon a few years ago, I came upon a book called *Walter Johnson: Baseball's Big Train*, written by Henry W. Thomas. After purchase, it sat in closets for at least two years before, for whatever reason, I finally decided to give it a read.

Besides being thoroughly impressed by the exhaustive research and annotation performed by Thomas, the legendary pitcher's grandson, I was particularly intrigued by the story, touched upon briefly, of Johnson's Washington teammate Sam Rice. And not just because he had grown up less than an hour south of me.

A Hall of Famer himself, Rice had lived quite an eventful life already by the time he first set foot on a Major League Baseball diamond at age twenty-five. Most startlingly, a northern Indiana natural disaster wiped the slate of his life clean and forced him to begin anew, with an unthinkably heavy heart, at age twenty-two. And while many of his peers would go on to know the horrors of war when it broke out in Europe later in the decade, Rice had already participated in battle, at Veracruz, Mexico, before he ever earned a real paycheck playing baseball.

Thomas's biography of Johnson was valuable because it opened a window, ever so slightly, on the life of Sam Rice. But it also taught a lesson of sorts.

So often, in what seems like an attempt to streamline our knowledge base, to make order out of chaos, it is our habit to distill entire bygone eras into overriding themes. And it's typically not a far leap from there to tab a few key figures to embody those themes. Thus baseball of the "Roaring 1920s" is forever viewed through the boisterous, big-bellied prism that is Babe Ruth. Bombastic in personality and the game's most feared home run hitter in an era that saw the blossoming of the long ball as baseball's preferred offensive weapon, Ruth is without a doubt the most important historical sports figure of the era.

But he wasn't the only one that made an impact.

Along those same lines, Ruth's New York Yankees were, without question, the dominant team of the '20s, winning three World Series and five American League pennants. But again, they weren't the only team having an impact.

The Washington Senators—Sam Rice's Washington Senators—won three American League pennants during his nineteen seasons with the club. Not bad for a franchise often conveniently used as a favorite example of organizational incompetence.

The truth is that baseball once thrived in the nation's capital. Clearly, the powers-that-be running Major League Baseball think it can happen again, moving the Montreal Expos off of life support and into the District's RFK Stadium before the 2005 season.

A few historians have attempted to combat the tired label of Washington as a perennial loser. Mark Gauvreau Judge, like Thomas a relative of one of the Senators of the era, wrote an account of the 1924 World Series championship season, rescuing one of baseball's best postseasons from the dustbin. Thomas' definitive biography of his grandfather brought us a portrait of baseball in the period as seen through the experiences of the dominant pitcher of the time, a somewhat novel approach since almost everything of note penned about the 1920s and '30s revolves around the hitting revolution.

It is, then, little wonder a singles hitter and terror on the base paths, a poor man's Ty Cobb, is so overlooked.

Rice hit thirty-four home runs in his career, 680 less than the Babe. But he finished his career with 2,987 hits—104 more than Ruth. Still, for thirty years, the Baseball Hall of Fame didn't think he merited a plaque on its walls.

Which brings us to the other reason Rice's story intrigued me. In 2004, the comedian Bernie Mac starred in a baseball movie titled *Mr. 3000*. The story's hero, whose name of Stan Ross is uncannily similar to the subject of the book you hold in your hands, is notified soon before his name is to first appear on the Hall of Fame ballot that he didn't finish with exactly three thousand hits, as he thought. He actually remains three hits short.

The movie is, of course, fiction. But the convention that the central plot line depends upon is fairly accurate—in collating its former stars, statistical milestones are paramount to baseball's keepers of the game. Despite a remarkable career, thirteen hits stood between Rice and that drizzle-flecked Cooperstown stage for three decades.

The Bernie Mac character in *Mr. 3000* is an egotistical, loudmouth buffoon. Here he deviates sharply from Rice, like his teammate Johnson a strong, silent type to counter the bluster of the other stars of his era. He is the anti–Ruth.

As baseball changed dramatically, Rice remained the same player. After what he'd already been through in life, who could expect him to be anything other than what he was: a pillar of strength no matter what degree of storminess surrounded him.

"Rice's start in the game was notable for its complete lack of success," a sports writer said near the end of his career.

"He was a left-handed hitter who stood up straight, even with the plate and very close to it, and he took a quick cut at the ball," a journalist wrote upon his election to the Hall. "His stance hardly varied from the time that Washington bought him from Petersburg of the Virginia League in 1915, until he retired after the season of 1934. He seldom argued with umpires, went about his work quietly and was not considered colorful."[1]

Those who knew him well would argue differently. Rice had a burning competitive fire, tackling endeavors after baseball from the conventional, golf, to the more unconventional, pigeon racing. Along the way, he was known to dispense his own brand of horse sense to anyone he knew, well-honed from a life fully lived.

"One of the greatest influences of my life was knowing Sam Rice," says Rice's old friend and investment broker Bill Birely. "He was a wonderful human being. His down-to-earthness, his dignity, he was not at all conceited. He was quite modest. He didn't throw his weight around. A lot of these sports heroes are pretty unruly. Not Sam Rice."[2]

The problem was no one was ever sufficiently able to address what clicked in young Sam Rice that triggered the transformation from decent semi-pro player struggling to make the next step to a reliable cornerstone for three American League pennant winners. No one knew the truth. So for a long time, all accounts of his career were left with a glaring hole.

Initially making the majors as a pitcher, Rice was switched to outfield permanently by the middle of his second season, 1916. (Baseball Hall of Fame)

Prologue: Induction Day

America was different then. When a pair of graying old men stood side-by-side on stage that afternoon, America was a more innocent place. Naively so, one might argue, considering it had been through two World Wars, and considering that even as they stood there, racial unrest was reaching a breaking point in the nation's Deep South. Meanwhile across the sea, American Green Berets continued to train South Vietnamese troops.[1] Trouble, at home and abroad, was brewing for the United States.

That was something, however, America's citizenry would find out soon enough. Before the year's end, it would begin with the sudden and public death of a popular president, with innocence continuing to be chipped away at during a decade of turmoil that followed.

No one knew any of that yet, though. The day belonged to those two men, along with two others who didn't live long enough to enjoy their day on this stage.

The date was August 9, 1963.

A light drizzle fell on Cooperstown, New York. Elmer Flick and Sam Rice, the only living members of baseball's four-man class of Hall of Fame inductees, prepared for the closest thing this nation has devised to the royal and ancient British practice of knighthood. Joining them, posthumously, in the Baseball Hall of Fame Class of 1963 were John Clarkson and Eppa Rixey. Flick and Rice were outfielders. The two late members of the class were pitchers.

It was an eclectic collection and, should a man pry himself away from the modern game long enough to do so, he could trace the evolution of the major league game from some of its earliest days well into the 1930s, by which time its most tumultuous transformations had been completed.[2]

Clarkson was one of the game's early pioneers, a pitching prodigy who exploded out of obscurity to win fifty-three games for Chicago in 1885. Five years later, he nearly reached the fifty-mark again, winning forty-nine games for Boston. By the day of his induction, such a workload was unfathomable. Clarkson had died in 1909, twenty-seven years before the Cooperstown shrine even opened.[3]

Rixey, the class's second pitcher, lived to receive notice of his election. But he didn't make it much longer after that. He died on February 28, just a month after his election. Rixey, in a twenty-one-year career with the Philadelphia Athletics and Cincinnati Reds, had stood fast against all that the explosive hitters of the 1920s could offer him. While others understandably wilted, Rixey, well into his late thirties, reliably provided his teams upwards of three hundred innings each summer.

For younger followers of the game, the cast of inductees lacked the marquee value of the year before, when Jackie Robinson and Bob Feller's images were cast in bronze, ending a six-year drought of selections by the Baseball Writers Association of America. Robinson and Feller were relatively recent retirees. Robinson was a pioneer, credited with breaking baseball's color line (though Rixey's Cincinnati staff mate, Cuban Dolph Luque, was a pioneer in his own right thirty years prior). Feller's fastball, which generated a then-record 348 strikeouts in 1946, was still seared into the recent memory of fans who marveled as he led the American League in strikeouts seven times in the '30s and '40s.

On the other hand, of the 1963 honorees, only the careers of Rice and Rixey could be recalled with anything resembling a similar amount of clarity by even the most wrinkled of baseball fans. Their induction raised to ninety-four the number of men enshrined.

"When I look around the stage and see some of these men who weigh 180 to two hundred pounds, I wonder how I made it so long at 140," Rice said from the podium. "But I'm like Elmer. I don't think there are words to use on a day like this. It's the biggest thing any of us can have."[4]

For Rice, it was a long time coming.

1

Too Terrible to Relate

A driver traveling south on U.S. 41 from Chicago into Indiana may be struck with the sensation that he is steering backward into time.

Leaving Chicago's skyscrapers, twentieth century marvels all, in his rearview mirror, the driver first crosses into the small industrial town of Whiting, Indiana. It is a cozy little city, blossoming around two entities, Lake Michigan and an oil refinery now operated by BP/Amoco, which is the lifeblood of its employment force.

The blue-collar city of Hammond is next, many of its residents driving into the area's famous steel mills every morning to work, followed by Highland and Schererville. In these two suburbs, the twenty-first century bares its teeth on both sides of the road. This is the familiar land of Wal-Marts and Meijers, of shiny new strip malls, of bustling miniature golf courses and clogged intersections, particularly the one where U.S. 41 meets U.S. 30, another main thoroughfare crisscrossing northwest Indiana.

Travel this far without being seduced by Kohl's or by Bennigan's or by a Borders bookstore into pulling off the road, and the years immediately begin to melt away. St. John, Cedar Lake and Lowell are next, in succession, and their snapshots of suburbia are slightly more weathered. Oh, there is the occasional remodeled Pizza Hut or Taco Bell rising from acres of black top, but for now, the locally operated establishments appear to be winning the good fight.

Finally, about sixty miles south of the big city, one crosses the Kankakee River into Newton County and soon one of its larger towns, relatively speaking: Morocco.[1]

This sign greets visitors to Sam Rice's homeown of Morocco, Indiana. (Randy Decker)

Edgar Charles Rice was born here on February 20, 1890, the event today marked by a modest sign, decorated by the image of an old Rice baseball card.[2] And the place has scarcely aged since. This is the Indiana of out-of-towners' mindscapes. It is a place where the corn stalks often stretch as far as the eye can see, much as they did ten years before the turn of the last century, when Charles Rice and the former Louise Newmeyer welcomed their son Edgar into the world.

You know him as "Sam."[3]

Morocco-area residents are aware of something else about their region — it seems to be a sitting target for the best shots nature can deliver.

"One of the uncertainties of life in the Morocco area," writes area historian Gerald Born, "occurs annually during the spring of the year — the cyclone season. It is never known just where or when one may strike, but they come with such frequency that the inhabitants are ever alert to their dangers."[4]

Charles and Louise were married on April 15, 1890, just a few days after Louise turned nineteen and almost two months after Sam's birth. They were farming people, and the boy who would someday come to be known as Sam's birth was just the beginning of their family. There would be four more children, including Mabel, who was born just a few years after Edgar, and another child who died before she reached infancy. Bernadine, a daughter, was born in Newton County thirteen years after her brother. Genevieve was born six years later, in Iroquois, Illinois.[5] The timing isn't clear, but the Rices appear to have bounced around a bit between Morocco and the small, similar Illinois farm communities like Iroquois nearby. Sam, we do know, considered himself a native of the town of Watseka, Illinois.[6]

The little we do know about Sam's earliest athletic days comes from the memories of Ray Webster, a childhood pal of Rice's who recounted those days during the early 1980s, and even his memories were hazy at best. Webster attended Rhode Island Country School in nearby Iroquois County with Rice. Webster said he was a "nice fellow and a good athlete." He also recalled that Rice was a fleet runner.[7]

For most of Rice's upbringing he was known as "Eddie," though once he was of drinking age, bartenders at Giddy Leonard's tavern in Watseka nicknamed him "Rhinegold" after his beverage of choice, the brand of beer he selected over local favorites Radeke, Schlitz and Pabst. Fellow tavern goers like Con O'Shea, Rufe Kendal and "poor old" Frizzy Morris somehow mangled and shortened the nickname to "Rango."[8]

But Rice's good-timing days didn't last too long. Because by the time he was eighteen, he was already ready to settle down.

The girl who captured his heart was Beulah Stam, who was born in Eisle, Nebraska, on April 11, 1892, and moved with her parents to Iroquois when she was just three years old. She and Edgar married on September 17, 1908, when she was sixteen, and they settled in Watseka.⁹

* * *

As much as baseball myth makers seem to enjoy the archetypal fable of a country hayseed rising to prominence against all odds among the sophisticated city boys (*The Natural* springs to mind), Rice's farming background was not unusual in the major leagues of his time period.

Unlike modern times, when a large percentage of major leaguers grow up either in warm weather American states where they can play all year, or Latin American countries where the climate is conducive to the same kind of schedule, Midwesterners like Rice dominated big league rosters of his era. Of the more than five hundred men who appeared in a major league game in 1924, for example, 187 of them were born in the Midwest, more than any other area of the country.

Overall, an estimated one-third grew up on farms, with more than half growing up in small country towns.[10]

His rural upbringing would help Rice fit in particularly well on his own future team, the Washington Senators.

Walter Johnson, the legendary Washington pitcher and one of Rice's close friends later on in life, was idolized not just because of his prowess on the mound, but because of his admirable farming background: "A tall-shouldered farm boy who has set down a pattern for good sportsmanship that every American boy might well follow," read one article.

Johnson, his mother explained, grew up wanting to be a farmer, and owned a cattle ranch in his home state of Kansas in the offseason.

"He likes nothing better," she said, "than to spend hours looking after stock or doing chores."

Johnson and Rice weren't the only country boys on the Washington roster during their era. Leon "Goose" Goslin, a Hall of Fame outfielder alongside Rice, grew up on a farm, as well, in Salem County, New Jersey. Many of Johnson's Washington pitching staff mates, including Tom Zachary and Firpo Marberry, had farming backgrounds, as well.

Pitcher By Speece, a brief member of the '24 title team, was a farmer from the Hoosierland, just like Rice. So, to extend it beyond the Washington club, was Cincinnati outfielder Eddie Roush.

"He and his twin brother took turns at standing in the barn lot batting flies into adjoining fields for the other to chase," one writer said.

"There is no space or occasion to list all the farmer boys who have reached the highest peak in baseball," an article about the phenomenon concluded. "The farm boy has made a place for himself in baseball. He has played hard and clean; and that is the best thing that can be said for anybody in the sport world."[11]

1. Too Terrible to Relate 11

The farming life was painted as the idyllic background for major leaguers, those who grew up that way looked at as All-American kids from proud, traditional American stock.

Rice's experience on the farm would take a sharp, torturous detour, from the ideal, however.

* * *

Sam — Edgar, as he was known then — and Beulah wasted little time beginning their own family in Watseka. In April of 1912, Edgar left the family home to pursue a place on the roster of the minor-league baseball team in Galesburg, all the way on the other side of the state and not far from the Iowa-Illinois border.[12] At the time, the still young couple's first-born, Bernie, was three years old, and Ethel was just eighteen months.[13] Edgar had signed a contract for the Galesburg squad, known as the Pavers, the previous October, and now it was time to fight for a roster spot.[14]

The Pavers played in the Central Association, a very low-level minor league. The regular season was scheduled to begin May 1, and excitement was already beginning to build around the team. In the three weeks between the start of spring training and the first real game, the team's manager, Ducky Eberts, planned to give himself a long look at Rice and the rest of the men so he could make a very informed decision about his final roster, due a couple weeks after the first regular-season game. The hopefuls practiced twice a day at Illinois Park, about three hours per session.[15]

A stiff southwest wind blew on the afternoon of April 15, when the Pavers met nearby Monmouth in an exhibition game. The game nearly wasn't played, as a downpour soaked Monmouth's field the night before, prompting a move to Illinois Park and pushing back the start time to 3:15. That didn't stop about five hundred fans, informed of the event only by fast-spreading word of mouth, from finding their way to the park. April in the Midwest is typically a month of unpredictable, soggy weather. Surely no one thought much of it, just like they didn't think too much about the performance of the future Hall of Famer Rice, who on this day was just one in a long line of wild, rusty pitchers, walking three batters in three innings of work. The Pavers lost 6-2.[16]

By the next time Edgar took the mound, however, the team seemed to be rounding into form. He finished a 19–2 victory over nearby Knox College on April 17, striking out a couple of the college boys.[17]

On April 21, Galesburg had another real test — it would face Monmouth, the same team that had won the exhibition opener less than a week before. As his starter, Eberts selected Russ Smith, but Rice was ready to go, as well.

As it did a week before, the weather made its presence known.

"The wind was blowing a gale even worse than that of last week," an account of the game noted.

No matter. This, again, was April, and to be expected. The game began, the Pavers took a quick 1–0 lead, and Smith held the opposition down for six strong innings.

Eberts sent in Rice to pitch the seventh.[18]

* * *

Edgar had been away for about a week, but Beulah wasn't totally alone in keeping watch over the couple's two children. By this time, Charles and Louise had settled near Donovan, Illinois, about fifteen miles northeast of Watseka, where they lived on a farm owned by the Gard family.[19] The Rices had a difficult go of it from the time they moved onto the property, suffering through, for example, a house fire in 1910 that destroyed most of Charles' belongings. And that was just the latest misfortune that had visited the family. They had also, as previously noted, suffered the death of one of their young children. Charles' livestock had once been wiped out by disease. In 1907, a hail storm destroyed all of his crops, resulting from one of the tornados common to the area.[20]

On the day the Galesburg Pavers were playing Monmouth in that blustery exhibition contest, Charles and Louise and Beulah, along with the four children, left the farm for a while to visit friends. The day was pleasant, and they returned around 6 p.m.[21] Perhaps, spotting a darkening sky, they were trying to beat the weather home.

Working at the house when they returned was hired hand Martin Gray, a twenty-one-year-old from Paoli, Indiana, who Charles and Louise had hired just two weeks before.[22]

The family had just sat down for supper when a tornado, dancing northward across this part of Illinois, began bearing in their direction. It touched down on the property of a Mr. Anderson living nearby, destroying his home.[23] Perhaps hearing the rumbling by now, or noticing through a window the violent turn the weather had taken, the Rices—Edgar's wife, two children, parents and younger siblings—began to seek safety.

But there was, by this point, nothing they could do.

* * *

By 6 o'clock, Edgar Rice had long since finished his outing for the Pavers, and it had been a successful one.

Eberts had sent Rice in to replace Smith in the seventh inning, and Edgar had gone the final three innings, allowing a run in the eighth to cut things closer. But he had also struck out four Monmouth batters.

"Russ Smith and Rice performed for the locals, from the mound, and both handled the pill in an extremely creditable manner," the newspaper account of the game reported.

The game having been completed in an hour and forty-five minutes, Edgar and the rest of the players left the field and retired to the rest of their evenings, doing whatever it was that minor-league hopefuls fighting to earn a roster spot for the summer did in those days. Their biggest worry was making the team.[24]

* * *

Back home in Donovan, the cyclone smashed headlong into the Gard farm with tremendous force. Whatever Charles and the rest of the family had done to find safety was rendered futile. The storm's fury was simply too great.

A swine shelter/tool shed had somehow avoided the tornado's path, but that was about all that remained.

"Everything else on the premises was seized, torn and whirled into fragments and strewn entirely across the farm," the local newspaper reported after later surveying the aftermath.

Most of the house and other structures had been reduced to splintered wood no longer than two feet long, six-to-eight feet at the longest.

Beulah, Edgar's wife, was dead. So were his two children, Bernie and Ethel. His mother, Louise, had also perished in the storm, along with his two siblings, Bernadine and Genevieve. In all, six members of the future Sam Rice's immediate family died in the storm's immediate aftermath.

The hired man, Martin Gray, was killed, as well. The only person alive was Charles Rice, and he was badly injured, recalling how he had been sucked through what he believed to be either a window or a hole in the house created by the storm.[25]

A local newspaper recounted the horrific damage: "Its work there was almost too terrible to relate. The house was blown entirely away, as were other buildings but a tool shed which was untouched. The timbers of the house and barn were scattered for nearly a quarter of a mile to the southeast. The furniture and contents of the house were twisted into shapes that would seem impossible to accomplish, and when the wreck had passed, every member of the family except Mr. (Charles) Rice lay dead either in the yard or adjoining fields. The bodies were found as far as sixty rods from the house, nearly stripped of clothing, bruised and broken."[26]

Charles rushed to the home of a neighbor, Charles Johnson, for help.[27] Together they found one of Charles Rice's children, Genevieve, battered but still breathing. She held on for a short while after the cyclone's destructive rampage. In a ravine on his land, near where the broken bodies of his loved ones had been deposited, he carried the child in his arms. In the chaotic aftermath, though, all he could do was pace frantically before finally the child died, as well.

The tornado would take four more lives before it mercifully left Iroqois, Newton and Jasper counties in its wake. The next two deaths occurred at the farm of Charles Smart. Smart and his family, his wife Anna and three children, tried to outrace the storm in the shelter of their basement. The cellar, however, would provide inadequate protection from the ravenous storm for the Smarts' two daughters, Cassie, fifteen, and Ioleene, age two. As Charles Smart looked on from the bottom of the stairs and his wife, who couldn't scurry down the stairs before the storm hit, looked on, their two daughters were crushed to death between a sill and the brick cellar wall. The storm had pulled the house off of its foundation. Cassie, the older sister, died with her infant sister Ioleene in her arms. They would be buried in the same casket at nearby Murphy Cemetery.

Racked with grief, Anna Smart braved the downpour outside to reach the nearest working telephone, a quarter of a mile away at the home of B.L. Archbald. The Smarts' son, John, also suffered minor injuries in the tornado, but lived. The Smarts had to take on the sad, gruesome task of cutting down a tree, then using it as a lever to extricate the bodies of their two daughters.

In nearby Jasper County, about twelve miles northwest of the town of Rensselaer, thirteen-year-old Robert Schultz was killed when the cyclone ripped through the farm owned by his father August.[28]

As hard hit as the farms south of Indiana's Kankakee River were, the number of casualties were less than half that experienced farther south near St. Louis in the mining town of Bush, Illinois. Eighteen of the community's six hundred people died, while eight more were dead in the unincorporated area just east of town. Plus, "nearly every dwelling in the village was either destroyed or damaged." Five were dead in Willisville, with forty more injured. Three were dead in the town of Campus. Farther south still in Alabama, as many as fifteen were killed when a tornado battered a cluster of mining towns.[29] In all, the storms' destructive swath left seventy-five dead and many more injured.[30]

* * *

In the early morning the next day, Edgar was delivered the news of the tragedy back home via telegram.[31] He rushed home immediately, though there was little to return to. At least his father was still alive, though badly injured.

Charles lived to see the rest of his family buried in a pair of well-attended triple funerals. The first service took place on Tuesday, April 23, two days after the tornado. Held at the Johnson family farm, the memorial for Sam Rice's mother and his two sisters drew more than one thousand mourners.[32] Louise and Genevieve, the last of the seven dead to hang on, were placed in one casket. Bernadine was buried in her own white casket. They were all buried in the Swedish Cemetery near the Rice farm, in one grave, with the Rev. O.G. Sandberg presiding over the 2:30 p.m. service and reading aloud their obituary.

"Mrs. Rice was a kind and faithful wife and mother," he said, "exceedingly devoted to her husband and children, and highly respected by neighbors and friends.

"The two younger children who departed this life with her were the sunbeams of the house, objects of the father's fondest affections.

"Why this disaster should happen we do not know, but we are painfully reminded of life's uncertainty."

The painful burial of Charles Rice's wife and two children was over, but there was more than enough grief to be sufficiently spread over two more days. On Wednesday, services for Beulah Rice and the two infant children, Bernie and Ethel, were held at the home of her parents in Iroquois at the town's Methodist Episcopal Church. The church choir sang, while Grace Nosker provided a soprano solo.

The Rev. Thomas Bartram's sermon "will certainly be always remembered by all who heard it," reported the local paper, "for his tender expressions of sympathy, thought and comfort to the bereaved."

Sam's wife and children were buried in Prairie Dell Cemetery. Martin Gray, the hired man, was buried the following day, Thursday, in Swedish Cemetery. People in town took up a collection to pay for the man's burial expenses, as he had no living relatives to speak of.[33]

The tragedy wasn't over yet, though.

Less than a week later, fifty-year-old Charles Rice would die, as well. Edgar's entire immediate family, except for one adult sister who had not been present for the storm, was now dead.[34]

On May 5, he rejoined the Pavers in Galesburg.[35] Rice pitched in a May 10 game against Burlington, a 6–5 Galesburg loss. But that day Eberts had to turn his final thirteen-man roster into the Central Association. Rice was not on the list, his time away surely hurting his chances, if it was even possible for his heart to still be in the game.[36]

With no job in baseball and nothing to return to back home, Edgar Rice began, as it is frequently reported, "wandering."

2

IN THE NAVY

Racked by grief as he must have been, Rice at least kept himself busy throughout the rest of 1912.

His "wandering" included work at a Louisville, Kentucky, whiskey distillery, as well as work in the wheat fields of the Dakotas and nearby Minnesota.[1] At some point, he worked at a railroad station. Finally, for stability, he turned to the same place many young men turn — the military.

"I had a desire to see the world and I took the first opportunity that offered," Rice later said. "The Navy was making a big campaign trying to get young fellows into the service. One of their grandstand plays was a chance to cruise around the world. That hit me just right."

The location of Rice's enlistment is a matter of some confusion, though the date is known — January 24, 1913. On that morning, Rice marched into a recruiter's office in either Louisville or Norfolk, Virginia, and was enticed by an officer's enthusiastic pitch.

"I walked up to the recruiting office, listened to the glowing accounts of palm trees in the tropics and affixed my John Hancock on the proper line," he said. "I was a full-fledged Navy man."

Rice soon found out that the exotic trips around the world did not take place with the regularity that he had been led to believe. But Rice also discovered a way to at least get himself excused from most of the intense physical labor assignments — baseball.

Assigned to the *U.S.S. New Hampshire,* Rice tried out for the ship's team as a pitcher, and became part of one of the Navy's top squads, one that battled the men aboard the battleship *Louisiana* for the Navy championship.

"I discovered, among other things," Rice said, "that there seemed to be a direct connection between ability as a fireman and my playing ability on the diamond.

"Immediately I rose to the grade of first-class fireman. And I escaped a good deal of the disagreeable work which falls to the lot of the sailor. I never saw a sailor who had any objects to getting out of work.

"So I took my good luck as it came and praised the man who invented baseball."

Rice was playing for the *New Hampshire's* team when, for the first time, a professional baseball team made a play for his services. The owner of Petersburg in the Virginia League, Doc Leigh, noticed Rice's pitching for his battleship squad, and offered to buy him out of his Navy service (apparently an accepted peace-time practice in those days), plus pay him $90 a month.

Rice declined — though he was making just $38 a month from the Navy, he was supplied with room and board, something that would have to come out of his own pocket if he signed a baseball contract. Besides, Rice explained to him, he was still holding out hope that he'd get to see the world as a member of the Navy.[2]

Rice was docked in Norfolk, he and his shipmates peacefully going about their daily duties aboard the *U.S.S. New Hampshire*, when events were turned in motion that would bring him into the dangerous center of one of the United States's most notorious military missteps.

At the time of Rice's enlistment, Mexico was in the middle of a long, ongoing Civil War, the latest turn being the overthrow of president Francisco Madero and rise to power of Victoriano Huerta. Though the U.S. was involved in the overthrow, ultimately President Woodrow Wilson determined that the U.S. government should stand in opposition to Huerta's regime, and tension mounted.

That tension reached a breaking point on the morning of April 9, in the Mexican Gulf Coast town of Tampico. There, while on a routine errand, nine unarmed U.S. soldiers from the *U.S.S. Dolphin* wandered into an area that had been declared a forbidden zone. Mexican forces converged, and the language barrier between the Americans and the Mexicans prevented anything resembling a civil resolution to what amounted to a tense misunderstanding. All nine Americans were arrested.

Back home, the U.S. military immediately voiced its displeasure and, upon finding out what happened, Mexican Colonel Ramon Hinojosa was apologetic and ordered the Americans released.

U.S. Admiral Henry Thomas Mayo was not satisfied, however. Mayo ordered a further Mexican penance: "You publicly hoist the American flag in a prominent position on shore and salute it with twenty-one guns." The Mexican government resisted, fearing the repercussions during the middle of a Civil War if Mexican citizens saw their government as weak and easily pushed into humiliation by the U.S. What seemed like bluster — the *New York Times* predicted that the hostilities would not advance "unless the United States is looking for an excuse to start trouble"—soon turned into something more, however.

Mayo was dead serious with his demands, and soon was able to persuade President Wilson and the United States Senate to his point of view. Five days after the arrests, Wilson ordered seven battleships, including Rice's *New Hampshire*, to head to Mexico.

Wilson's plan was to land at Veracruz, a few miles south of Tampico along the Gulf, and intercept the German cargo ship the *Ypiranga*, a breech of international law that he maneuvered around by not revealing those intentions while seeking approval for a military action at Veracruz. To technically get around the illegality of the action, however, the U.S. planned not to actually take possession of the German shipment, but instead occupy Mexican military installations in the city, then send the *Ypiranga* back home.

The first American ships, which did not include Rice's boat, arrived at about 11 a.m. on the morning of April 21, and U.S. soldiers quickly began scaling the sides of their ships and pouring into Veracruz. The plan was to capture their strategic targets as efficiently and expediently as possible.

All was going well to that end until just after noon, when a shot rang out and a member of the U.S. Navy was killed instantly. Other shots were fired at the American troops in rapid succession, and the surprised Americans began to fire back in self-defense. A situation that had been merely tense had turned violent. Before the day was over, three more U.S. Navy signalmen who had stepped up to take the place of the first man killed had also been shot dead, with other casualties, both soldier deaths and injuries, beginning to pile up, as well.

A shocked and shaken Wilson had to explain what happened to the American people.

"The death of American soldiers and marines owing to an order of his seemed to affect him like an ailment," one reporter wrote. "He was positively shaken."

And things still weren't over with, either.

Rice's ship, the *New Hampshire*, along with the *Arkansas, South Carolina, Michigan* and *New Jersey*, pulled into the harbor at Veracruz very early in the morning on April 22. Admiral Frank F. Fletcher sought out Admiral Charles T. Badger at 2:45 a.m., finding him aboard the *Arkansas*. A little more than an hour later, now under Fletcher's command, Rice and approximately three thousand other men began to climb ashore. No quiet, no false sense of security followed their arrival. Rice and cohorts immediately received fire from snipers.

Though Fletcher had not wanted to occupy more than a couple of areas located at the very edges of Veracruz, the continued fire forced him to send

Rice and the rest of the newly landed troops to begin clearing out every house in Veracruz. This began at about 8:30 a.m., after a last effort to hammer out a truce with a Mexican authority fell through.

It was dangerous work, and the marines involved took to it intelligently and cautiously. Under the direction of W.C. Neville, they displayed patience, blowing holes in walls that connected houses in order to avoid stepping out into the street and opening themselves to possible sniper attacks. They were able to clear out a lot of homes with minimal loss of life or limb.

Rice and his *New Hampshire* shipmates had a much more difficult time, however.

The *New Hampshire's* captain was E.A. Anderson, a thirty-two-year Navy veteran who had built a nice reputation during his three decades of service. There was one problem, though — despite his length of experience, Anderson had no experience fighting on land. Anderson led his men into a flat, open area, declining to send in scouts to scope the area beforehand. From about four hundred feet away, heavy fire rained down. It was coming from a Mexican Naval Academy building, where about forty Mexican soldiers and civilians, shooting from behind makeshift mattress and pillow barricades, began shooting at Anderson's Navy men. Panicked, many of the men retreated.[3]

"It was an exciting day we put in there," Rice told an interviewer during his playing career. "Mexicans were sniping at us from the roofs of the houses.... It was a queer sound to have the bullets humming around and every once in a while spatting near you.

"The Mexicans got twenty-one of us (actually nineteen). But I guess we evened up the score. I am not saying how many of them we got."[4]

Three American ships sitting in the harbor retaliated, ending the resistance and killing about 15 of the Mexican shooters. Anderson and the men, Rice presumably among them, pulled themselves together and continued to march inward. By 11 a.m., the immediate danger had ended — the American forces had control of the city.

But Rice and the rest of the troops at Veracruz weren't completely out of harm's way just yet.

Word filtered out that Mexican General Gustavo Maass had rounded up more than fifteen thousand troops a few miles west of Veracruz. The president called on a force of about 5,200 more troops to join those already occupying Veracruz to help reinforce the Americans in the event of a Mexican attack.

Whipping the city back into livable condition proved to be a dirty task for Rice and the men. Wounded Mexican civilians were gathered and taken to hospitals. Of even greater concern were the dead that still lay in the streets. The American soldiers were forced to burn many of the corpses, with the city's occupants looking on in horror. Occasional shots continued to ring out, and a few days after the initial landing, Fletcher declared martial law in Veracruz.

The Americans raised the flag, lending some symmetry to the ongoing conflict, inflamed just days before when Huerta had refused to raise or salute the stars and stripes.

"We had forcibly seized his principal maritime city and had ourselves wiped out the indignity which had been put upon our country," one soldier later recalled.

Nineteen U.S. soldiers were killed during the Veracruz occupation, including three of Rice's shipmates and fifteen fellow Navy men.[5]

On Capitol Hill, Senator J. Hamilton Lewis of Illinois delivered a stirring eulogy of the men killed aboard the *U.S.S. New Hampshire* and other ships involved in the occupation, while twenty-eight members of the House and Senate were selected to represent Congress at the upcoming state memorial to honor the dead at Veracruz.

"They lived for men," Lewis said, "gave sacrifice to God, and died for country."[6]

For someone like Rice, a man without a rudder in life after the death of his family two years before, involvement with the military must have helped lend some direction and discipline that he had lacked since the vicious storm had wiped out all he had previously lived for. For all the troops on the battlefront participating in the occupation of Veracruz, there was honor in their actions. But much like soldiers of other conflicts that have involved American intervention into foreign interests, including Vietnam and Iraq, the action itself fell under wide scrutiny, both immediately and in hindsight.

Quite simply, history has not judged the Veracruz occupation kindly.

"These actions by the administration confused, startled and mystified the public both in this country and abroad," wrote Woodrow Wilson biographer August Heckscher.

The major criticism of President Wilson's action was that the invasion and occupation seemed to far outweigh the gravity of the offense Mexico had committed against the United States. Out of sheer pride, Wilson had risked involving the country in a potential military quagmire. In the immediate aftermath, Wilson tried to rationalize the maneuver, explaining that it wasn't solely a punitive action against Mexico's Huerta, but rather a precedent-setting move to show that the United States would not tolerate future and perhaps more egregious and damaging insults. Wilson, as he explained it, was only looking out for the long-term interests of the country, and invading Veracruz now would prevent more costly conflicts down the road.

Pundits of the time weren't buying what the president was selling.

"If war is to be made on points of punctillo raised by admirals and generals," said *The Economist* magazine, "it will be a bad day for civilization."

Wilson's reputation for statesmanship took a beating, and even he eventually admitted the error of his ways. The president had been away from Washington, D.C., at the time the decision to move forward had been made, attending to his ill wife Ellen in Hot Springs, Virginia. His divided attention had forced him to go through with a decision without thinking it through, a decision that cost nineteen American lives.[7] Two trusted advisers, Secretary of State William Jennings Bryan and Secretary of the Navy Josephus Daniels had been against the invasion from the outset.[8] When Wilson spoke at a memorial for the fallen men, he appeared to recognize the difficult conditions he had placed them under.

"I fancy that it is just as hard to do your duty when men are sneering at you as when they are shooting at you," he said.[9]

The bottom line was this: Two years after returning to find his family wiped out by a heartland tornado, Rice again had been subjected to what amounted to a senseless loss of human life.

Twice that had happened, and twice, somehow, he himself had been spared. However, things were finally about to turn for him.

By the time the *New Hampshire* finally left Veracruz, Rice's days in the military were numbered. Again the Petersburg owner, Dr. D.H. Leigh, offered Rice a job with the club. And he increased his offer from the last attempt he had made to sign him — this time, he dangled a $135 a month salary in front of him.

The timing and the money were both tempting, considering what Rice had just gone through in Mexico — more adventure than he'd ever hoped for when he enlisted.

"This time I was dead tired of cruising around the world," Rice later joked. "The world as I had found it seemed to consist of the eastern Atlantic seaboard and Mexico."[10]

So while ashore, he signed with the Petersburg Goobers of the Virginia League, a Class C minor league, on July 29.

* * *

Edgar made his professional debut a few days later against Norfolk.

Rice's first appearance wasn't a disaster, nor was it a smashing success. He allowed the winning run to cross the plate in a tie game — however, Rice hadn't put the runner on base, nor was it really his fault he ended up crossing the plate (a fielding error took care of that). Rice had entered the game in the eighth inning, with Norfolk threatening with two runners on and one out. The error occurred on the first batter Rice faced, though he did complete the outing having logged 1⅔ innings without allowing a base hit.

Rice was given a start for his next appearance, but struggled. On August 3, in the opening game of a double header against Roanoke, Rice gave up for runs on seven hits in 4⅓ innings. He was wild, walking three batters and hitting another in a game that Petersburg lost.

He didn't have to wait long for his next opportunity, however — Rice started the second game of the double header played later that day. Perhaps over the jitters of his first two appearances, or simply now past the rust that had accumulated during a year in which his life had been turned upside down repeatedly, Rice looked like the major leaguer he would soon become. He gave up just two runs in the complete-game victory, surrendering seven hits and two walks. His next four starts were successes, as well, all complete-game victories. The first three of those starts, in fact, saw Rice allow just two runs combined.

Leigh, the owner of the Petersburg franchise, realized he had a potential star on his hands, and worked to secure Rice's services permanently. That meant purchasing Rice out of the United States Navy, a deal he was able to swing with the help of Virginia senators Thomas S. Margin and Claude A. Swanson.

Freed from his military obligation, Rice continued to dominate the Virginia League, finishing the 1914 season with nine wins and two losses, making him the winning percentage leader for the league that season. He gave up just seventy-three hits and thirty-eight walks in 123 innings, striking out sixty-two.

And even in part-time duty, Rice proved himself a capable hitter at the Class C level, hitting .310 over seventy-one at-bats as a fill-in outfielder and occasional pinch-hitter.[11]

Rice first got to show his stuff against major league competition in early April of 1915, when the Goobers squared off in an exhibition game against the New York Yankees. The game was the first for the New Yorkers after their exit from their southern spring training base on the way north to begin the season, and from their standpoint, the performance certainly wasn't impressive. Rice and the Goobers beat the major leaguers from the big city 6–2.

"They appeared to find the Virginians unexpectedly strong," the *New York Times* reported, "particularly in the pitcher's box."

Rice was one of three Petersburg pitchers to take the mound against the Yankees and he threw four innings in the game, giving up just two hits (though he did walk four men). He struck out two. Batting in the ninth spot, Rice also picked up a base hit in three at-bats and scored a run.[12]

A beat writer for the Goobers was impressed: "Rice, the ex–Navy man, looks to be the pure goods this season, and (manager) Heine (Busch) has lofty hopes for this youngster. Rice is doomed to go higher."[13]

When the Goobers won seven of their first eight games to begin the 1915 season, Rice was the winning pitcher in three of them. The team began to struggle after that, though, both on the field and at the cash register, prompting rumors that the franchise could fold. Rice compiled an 11–12 record in twenty-nine appearances, but that was misleading — the team behind him simply wasn't providing much in the way of offense (the Goobers would finish the season with 342 runs scored, one hundred less than the next-worst offensive team in the Virginia League, Suffolk). Through it all, Rice remained a staff workhorse, pitching 233 innings (more than eight per outing), striking out 153 and giving up 175 hits and forty-three walks, less than a base runner per inning.

He also batted over .300 again, in limited outfield and pinch-hitting duty (153 at-bats).[14]

Frustrating as Rice's summer may have been, however, things were about to take a turn for the better. The nearby American League franchise had an eye on him. It was late July, 1915. Sam Rice was headed for the major leagues.

* * *

Accounts differ as to the exact amount that D.H. Leigh owed Clark Griffith, manager of the Washington Senators, with various sources reporting it as either a $200, $400 or $800 debt — Griffith himself, in an interview about keeping rookie contracts down during the financial crush of the Great Depression, later stated the figure as $300.[15] Whatever the precise figure, Griffith clearly was able to leverage his credit line with Leigh into something far more valuable, a player who would serve as a cornerstone of the Washington outfield for the next two decades, including the most fruitful period in franchise history. It was an all-time baseball bargain, but to imagine that Griffith was prescient enough to eyeball the diminutive late bloomer and envision the Hall of Famer he would become would be overstating even his considerable legacy as a skilled baseball executive.

And even as early as 1915, Griffith's legacy was definitely considerable, not just in Washington, but across the American League. In fact, the league may not have existed were it not for his impetus.

* * *

Clark Griffith's path first crosses with the path of Washington baseball in 1894, in a relatively historically insignificant, but highly entertaining manner.

Griffith was pitching for the Chicago Colts at the time, and in late August the team visited Washington for a series against the District's National League franchise. Some of the Chicago players had conjectured for some time that it would be possible to catch a ball dropped from the top of the 550-foot Washington Monument obelisk. It was the kind of nonsensical debate, in this case an absurd study in applied physics, that still ferments in baseball dugouts and bullpens.

Griffith entered the monument with baseballs in tow, and dropped them for catcher Bill Schriver to attempt to catch. Griffith's first toss was too wide for Schriver to have a shot at. The second one, as Griffith later explained, was mishandled under some duress.

"The ball carried directly into his mitt, but he couldn't hold it and it plopped out," he said. "It wasn't a catch, no matter what the papers say."

Before Gabby Street finally pulled off the feat in 1908 — this time with local law enforcement's blessing — many people speculated that it was an impossible task. "Any misjudgment of the ball," legendary sports writer Shirley Povich paraphrased the feeling of the time, "would surely produce a broken arm or even fatal injury."

"Schriver was too nervous to hold the ball, and I don't blame him," Griffith said. "He'd have caught one I'm sure if the cops had left us alone."

Years later, Griffith would return to the city with much more serious ambitions.

Griffith became involved with the Senators in the fall of 1911. Jimmy McAleer, the team's manager the previous two seasons, left for an ownership opportunity with the Red Sox after the season's conclusion. It certainly wasn't the worst thing that could have happened for the Washington franchise. McAleer's team finished one step out of the cellar in 1911, with a record of 64–90. For the second year in a row, only the hapless St. Louis Browns (McAleer's previous team) were worse. In McAleer's defense, he didn't exactly inherit a juggernaut to begin with. However, it would soon become apparent how big of a difference a manager could make, particularly one with an eye for talent like Clark Griffith.

He wasn't about to leave his current job with Cincinnati that easily, though. Griffith had managed in the majors for eleven years, beginning in 1901 when he guided the Chicago White Sox to the American League championship in the renegade new league's first year of existence. Griffith also pitched for the White Sox that season. He had limited success in succeeding stints with the New York Highlanders (later, the Yankees) and Cincinnati.

Despite Griffith's three years with the Reds, his heart clearly belonged to the American League.

* * *

In September of 1900, Griffith, Chicago Colts owner Charles Comiskey and businessman/baseball entrepreneur Byron Bancroft "Ban" Johnson met in a Chicago tavern, the West Side's Polk Street Cafe. Johnson had founded the Western League, enjoying some success, but carrying dreams of developing it into another major league. For that, he'd need major league–caliber players, and the National League was not about to give up its primary product, its talented players. At first, Johnson had tried to reach a profitable compromise with the National League. He had two requests. First, he wanted to limit the number of players the National League could "draft" from American League squads. The best American League teams were simply being dismantled in short order because of the contract between the leagues that said the National League could purchase American League players, no bargaining necessary. Also, Johnson wanted to move American League franchises into vacated National League cities, including Washington.

The National League denied his demands, however, setting the stage for a showdown.

Griffith was part of the meeting because of his connection to Comiskey, as well as his role as vice president of the Ball Players Protective Association, a precursor to the modern Major League Baseball Players Association, or the union. For example, he had spent the preceding months attempting to get the National League to increase its maximum salary from $2,400 to $3,000. And he wanted the league to pay for player uniforms. He was interested in joining Johnson and Comiskey on one condition — that the American League pursue major-league status.

Griffith was the trio's link to the players, and by the time the winter was over, he had acquired written pledges from forty National Leaguers. His next step was approaching the National League's power brokers, demanding that they release players from their binding contracts. He carried with him a petition from the players, demanding their freedom, handing it to National League vice president A.H. Soden. Soon after, however, Griffith noticed his petition still in Soden's pocket. The V.P. had reneged on his agreement to distribute it to the National League owners, and Griffith was through with being diplomatic. He called Johnson and Comiskey with the news, yelling into the phone: "There's going to be a new major league if you can get the backing. Because I can get the ball players!" Then he went public with the new league's intentions, as well as what he felt were transgressions by the National League against players, preventing them from bettering their own situation.[16]

The eight-team American League was formed in time for the start of the 1901 season, with Griffith managing and pitching in Chicago. He won twenty-four games for the first American League pennant winners, who beat out teams in Cleveland, Detroit, Milwaukee, Baltimore, Boston, Philadelphia and Washington, D.C., for the title.[17]

* * *

At the time he signed Rice, Griffith was much more enamored of an outfielder he had signed out of the Canadian League named Merlin Kopp.

Griffith found out about Kopp during a trip to Detroit when Doc Reisling, who pitched for the Nationals in 1909 and 1910 and had settled in Michigan afterward, right across the Canadian border, passed along Kopp's name. Kopp played for St. Thomas, and Reisling, playing the role of de facto agent, served as the middleman between Griffith and the outfielder. The negotiations had a cat-and-mouse modern-day feel to them, with the eventual signing following in the wake of stories that the price set on Kopp's head was too high to interest the local management.

"It is said that Kopp has the makings of a great ballplayer," the *Washington Post* reported, "being fast, a good thrower and fielder and a dangerous hitter."

Griffith wouldn't reveal the price he paid to bring Kopp to Washington.[18] In hindsight, that secrecy probably was a good move. He played just sixteen games for the Nationals from his late July signing through the rest of the season, collecting eight base hits in thirty-two at-bats for a .250 average. He wouldn't return to the major leagues again until 1918, when he resurfaced with the Philadelphia Athletics. He batted .234 in an extended look that season of ninety-six games, but when his average fell to .226 in seventy-five games the following season, his time in the big leagues was over. Though Kopp established himself as a stolen base threat with twenty-two in limited action in 1918, his lifetime batting average of .232 in 630 at-bats wasn't enough to earn him another shot.[19]

Even the evaluators with the best eyes for talent win some and lose some in the quest for players. Perhaps Griffith was still sharpening his skills in 1915. A few years later, he'd get on a roll that would make any gambler jealous, with even the most overlooked component parts paying huge dividends at one time or another. Merlin Kopp was one of his misses, but Griffith picked up a couple of decent consolation prizes in 1915. Rice was one. Joe Judge was another.

3

Man o' War

One of the many long-standing myths that has been passed down about Rice, facts be darned, surrounds his sudden name change from Edgar to Sam. According to the tale that has been generally accepted as fact, after Rice reported to the Senators for the first time, a sports writer asked manager Clark Griffith the newcomer's first name.

Griffith, allegedly not knowing the answer, blurted out the first thing that came to his head: "Sam."

According to the myth, the name stuck from that point forward.[1]

In actuality, Rice had picked up the nickname some time before his arrival in the Senators' dugout, most likely during his time with Petersburg. A game account in the Petersburg newspaper a week before Rice's sale to the Senators identifies him as "Sam."[2] Then, on July 29, the paper reported his sale as follows: "Samuel Rice, the leading pitcher of the Petersburg baseball team, was yesterday sold to manager Clark Griffith of the Washington-American Association (sic), to which he is to report Saturday."[3]

The team Rice joined was a first-division club that still managed to find itself too far off the pace by late July to realistically make up the ground needed to challenge for the American League pennant. This, for the Senators, was nothing new. The first year that Griffith took over for McAleer saw an immediate rebirth of a franchise that finished at or near the cellar of the American League standings in all eleven years of it and the league's existence. The Senators had never finished with a record of .500 or better. In 1904, Washington lost 113 games, a hearty 55½ games behind pennant-winning Boston. Nowhere to go but up? Hardly. Five years later, the franchise hadn't progressed at all. The 1909 Senators, despite Walter Johnson's 2.22 earned-run average and four shutouts, lost 110 games. This time, they finished fifty-six games behind first-

Senators manager Clark Griffith, who acquired Rice from a Virginia League squad in exchange for his willingness to forgive the team owner's debt of several hundred dollars. (National Baseball Hall of Fame Library, Cooperstown, N.Y.)

place Detroit. Walter Johnson gave the fans someone to latch onto whenever he took the ball, but his presence couldn't overcome an anemic offense that scored just 380 runs, by far the worst of the sixteen major league teams.

Imagine their glee when in 1912, Griffith's first year at the helm, the Senators went from losers of ninety games the year before to a 91–61 mark and second-place finish in the American League. Griffith turned loose speedster Clyde Milan, who stole eighty-eight bases and energized the lineup. They had begun a new era of competitiveness, but as the middle of the decade approached, the Senators still hadn't really challenged for the ultimate prize, a first-place finish and the glory of a World Series berth.[4]

It was time to retool and begin assembling players around the "Big Train" Walter Johnson who would do more than just compete admirably. Of the ballplayers that Griffith tried, Rice and Judge would yield the best returns. But it wasn't destined to be an overnight success by any means.

Rice reported to the team on July 30. Perhaps not getting a good look, or perhaps still infected with the excitement of decent baseball after years of covering a laughingstock, the *Post* erred laughably with its initial description: "He is a big fellow," the paper gushed. At five-foot-nine and less than 150 pounds, Rice was smallish even on the diamond of the dead-ball era. Washington had a bit of a history of supporting small-framed players, however.[5] One of the franchise's early stars was catcher Connie Mack, who later went on to managerial fame with the Philadelphia Athletics.

"While the players are practicing... Connie won't chase the ball because he is afraid he will lose a pound," the *Washington Evening Star* joked of the wispy six-foot, 160-pound player.[6]

With the resilient Senators playing well after a slow start to the season, it was difficult to work Rice into action right away. A week would pass before he got the call from his manager to take the field in a game. On August 7, the Senators fell behind the Chicago White Sox 5–0 at Chicago. Eddie Murphy, a speedy right fielder, had been struggling when he came over to the Sox mid-season from the Philadelphia Athletics. But the change of scenery from baseball's worst team to a true contender had energized him. On this afternoon, the Senators would pay the price. Hot hitters often seem to catch breaks, and Murphy's came in the form of a bad bounce single over Washington first baseman Chick Gandil's head in the fourth inning that scored two runs. Murphy had four hits in the game, and this one chased usually reliable Bert Gallia from the game in favor of Joe Shaw.

Shaw was suffering from a sore arm, however, and with that acting up, and the game already fairly out of reach, Griffith probably didn't want to risk injury to any more of his veteran staffers. In the sixth inning, he called on Rice to make his major league debut.

Rice performed well in his short outing, hurling $1\frac{2}{3}$ innings of one-hit ball. He didn't walk or strike out a batter, giving way to a pinch hitter. "Rice has a good motion and seemed to have plenty of stuff," the *Post* reported the next day. "He may make a major leaguer with a little more experience."[7]

The White Sox held on to win 6–2, dropping the Senators to 54–46 after one hundred games, 10½ games behind the first-place Red Sox. Even at their torrid pace of the previous month — the Senators had won twenty-one of their last thirty-two games — catching Boston was a pipe dream.[8]

Sam didn't have to wait long for his next appearance, another relief stint, this time against the Detroit Tigers three days later. During the course of his two innings, he set down the four most dangerous hitters in the Detroit lineup in order, including Ty Cobb, who flied out weakly to left.

"Rice ... looked good," noted an account of the game. "Any time a pitcher can dispose of this quartet so easily he must have something other than a glove and a pleasant smile."[9]

It would be nearly another month before he would pitch again, but it was a grand opportunity — a chance to start. On September 7 in Philadelphia, Griffith gave Rice the ball against the Athletics, and he rewarded his manager with his first victory as a major leaguer that afternoon. He beat the Athletics 7–4, though just two of the Philadelphia runs were earned. Rice even struck out four.[10]

By early September, Griffith was thinking youth movement, a drastic measure considering the stability that had contributed to the ballclub's unprecedented success since his arrival. From 1912 through 1915, the Senators had started the same eight position players, a feat of cohesion unmatched in major league history, before or since.

"The Cinderella Eight were a creature of their time," wrote one historian, "building success on steady, tight baseball, speed, opportunism, emphasizing finesse and cunning during the last pre–Ruthian decade."[11]

As admirable as their performance was over the span, however, by 1915 it was clear that the group wasn't the one that was going to lift the Senators to their next step — an American League pennant.

Second baseman Carl Sawyer and outfielder Turner Barber were two of Griffith's most prized youngsters, but he was also planning to use others, like first baseman Joe Judge, in games the rest of the way as he finally looked to the future. And on September 10, Griffith announced that his pitching selection against Cleveland the next day would be Sam Rice, who had impressed him in his last start nearly a month before against the Athletics.

"This youngster is likely to surprise the fans," the *Washington Post* reported. "He looked like a world beater against the (Athletics).... This does not appear much of a feat, even for a young twirler. But when one stops to consider the ability of certain members of (Philadelphia) as hitters, and the way they looked against (Rice), the aspect changes."[12]

It was true. After years of dominating the American League, the Athletics had a terrible record in 1915 as manager and owner Connie Mack had sold off most of his best players, but they could still hit. Amos Strunk and Stuffy McInnis both would finish the season in the top ten in the league, in fact, in hitting.[13] And Rice had held his own.

Against the Indians, however, he looked like the rookie he was. In a game the Senators eventually came back and won, Rice was shaky from the outset. He did manage to battle into the sixth inning, holding tight to a 4–3 advantage. But he walked five men and allowed seven hits before Griffith finally decided to pull him with one out, the game in peril of getting away from the Senators (the bullpen actually coughed up the slim lead before a Washington late rally).[14]

Rice's first season in the big leagues was in the books, and he had pitched very respectably. He had appeared in four games, starting two, and even picking up a victory. Sam displayed some wildness in walking nine men in eighteen innings, but he also showed potential by allowing just thirteen hits and four earned runs.

The season was over, the Senators finishing with an 85–68 record, good for fourth place in the American League.[15] And after years of grieving, "wandering," being shot at and trying to make it to the majors, Sam was going home for the winter.

His demons, of course, awaited. But so did a chance to play a little more baseball.

* * *

Rice entered the majors during a very lucrative period for the players, and it very nearly got him into serious trouble with the American League before he'd even established himself enough to put his hands on some of the money being thrown around.

The catalyst was the formation of the Federal League, an aspiring third major league formed in time for the summer of 1914. Due to the sudden competition for talent, major league salaries jumped from an average of $3,800 in 1913 to $7,300 just two years later, Rice's rookie season. Ty Cobb increased his salary from $10,000 to $20,000. Tris Speaker was awarded a two-year, $36,000 contract. The existence of the Federal League, and the resulting higher salaries, busted up one of baseball's first great dynasties in record time — Connie Mack's Philadelphia Athletics, winners of four American League pennants in five years, went from ninety-nine victories to 109 losses between 1914 to 1915 when Mack refused to pay the going rates.[16]

Tensions between the two established major leagues and the Federal League had reached a boiling point in the fall of 1915, when Rice played in an exhibition game back home in Watseka. He wasn't the only major leaguer on the diamond that day — Chicago White Sox Jim Scott and, finding himself in a bit of trouble that would pale in comparison to that which he would encounter a few years later, Buck Weaver also participated. So did Alex McCarthy of the Chicago Cubs.

Rice was on top of his game that afternoon, pitching a 2–0 shutout and striking out eleven in front of the home folks. But the players involved in the game included Grover Gilmore and Felix Chouinard (a former White Sox, Chouinard had played all of four games in the Federal League in 1915). When American League president Ban Johnson found out about the participation of Rice and the other American Leaguers, he was incensed. Players in his league simply were not supposed to share the field with Federal Leaguers.

"The national commission has issued a ruling which covers this point," he said, "and our players who violate the order are simply playing with fire.

"The commission is unalterably opposed to winter baseball, as it tends to cheapen the game. I believe that at our new annual meeting a rule will be adopted taking the control over the players out of the hands of the club owners. Then, if the players go in for winter games or risk their standings by appearing with or against Federals, they will be dealt with accordingly."[17]

At the time of Rice's exhibition appearance, the Federal League was in the middle of a lawsuit it had filed against the two existing major leaguers. The owners of the upstart league contended that by restricting player movement, the major leagues were in violation of American anti-trust laws. By participating in the game in suburban Chicago, Rice had played in the middle of what was essentially ground zero in the majors' battle with the Federal League. The Federals sued in Chicago's courts, and managed to secure as a judge Kennesaw Mountain Landis, who had found Standard Oil guilty of an antitrust violation a few years before, fining the company nearly $30 million. The Federal Leaguers thought they had discovered a sympathetic ear. But Landis' loyalty to the national pastime outweighed any antimonopoly tendencies he had previously displayed.

"Both sides must understand," he said at the beginning of the case, "that any blows at the thing called baseball would be regarded by this court as a blow to a national institution."

Rather than rule in favor of a monopoly, however, Landis let the case sit in the court system without a final ruling. Forced to, in the meantime, operate under the existing rules, the Federal League quietly went away. Any punishment that Johnson had been considering for Rice became a moot point.[18]

* * *

If there was any aspect of the Senators' game that the club wasn't lacking for heading into the 1916 season, it was pitching. To begin with, the Senators' ace was the best pitcher in baseball, probably the best pitcher in the game's history to that point — and a strong argument could be constructed that Walter

Johnson remains so. The 1915 season had been the sixth straight in which "The Big Train" had won twenty-five games, and also the sixth straight in which he had posted a sub-2.00 ERA.[19] Johnson had been a staple of the Senators' rotation since 1907, when then-manager Joe Cantillon signed him out of an Idaho minor league to great fanfare in success-starved Washington. And unlike many such phenoms, he had delivered many times over.[20]

But Johnson wasn't the only Senator pitcher experiencing success. The team's second starter, Bert Gallia, won seventeen games in 1915 and pitched almost 260 innings. Like Johnson, and unlike Rice, Gallia got his big-league start early. The Texan made his debut as a twenty-year-old in 1912.

Doc Ayers and Joe Boehling were fourteen-game winners in 1915, and even the team's emergency starter, Harry Harper, had posted a 1.77 ERA in limited innings.

Not surprisingly, with that staff, the Senators had led the American League in pitching in 1915.[21] Their spacious ballpark, the future Griffith Stadium, probably didn't hurt matters, either.[22] But ultimately, with all that talent collected on one staff and hitting its prime, there were few innings available for Rice, who at twenty-six years old wasn't getting any younger in baseball terms as he chased a permanent role in the major leagues.

Entering 1916, the Senators were long on pitching and short on hitting, and Rice had proven himself skilled at both when playing for Petersburg.

Plus, a spring training injury threatened to render him ineffective.

"We were training in Charlottesville and working out in the gymnasium," Rice would recall. "I slipped and fell striking on the point of my shoulder.

"My pitching arm seemed to go dead. I hoped it would get in shape, but it didn't seem to. The soreness went away, but I was no longer able to put any stuff on the ball."[23]

Rice always attributed his final decision to switch from the pitcher's mound to the outfield to George Dauss, a Detroit pitcher who tripled off him during a game in early June of 1915. According to the anecdote that Rice himself passed down, Dauss won an extra-inning game with a three-base hit, and Rice swore off pitching forever upon arriving in the Senators' clubhouse after the game.[24]

As the story goes, Rice gave up a triple to Dauss to lose the game — that part was definitely true. On June 4, Dauss batted against Rice in the bottom of the ninth of a tie game. Marty Kavanaugh stood on base with the tying run, and Rice immediately went ahead 1–2 on Dauss.[25]

Dauss had been a workhorse pitcher for the Tigers over the previous seasons, but a putrid hitter, batting just .146 in 103 at-bats in 1915.[26]

Rice challenged him, and Dauss slammed the ball to deep center for a game-winning triple.

"Rice pitched wrong to Dauss," the *Post* reported. "He had the batter in a bad spot, with two strikes and one ball, yet he shot him a fast one right in the groove. He should have pitched him a curve outside and made Dauss go after a bad one."[27]

According to the tale, Sam entered the dugout in despair and announced, "I quit. If that guy can make a (three-) bagger off me, I'm no pitcher. Give me an outfielder's glove." Supposedly, Rice then demanded a knife from team trainer Mike Martin and cut the toe plate off his pitching toe, a terrific little anecdote that provided a symbolic moment in the development of what was to eventually become Washington's championship ballclub.[28]

It may even be at least partially true — it seems plausible that Rice would be frustrated after giving up a hit to Dauss on a pitcher's count, particularly since the game was the Senators' sixth consecutive loss, surely a trying period for everybody.[29]

But Rice did make three more appearances pitching in June after the Detroit game, the first and only loss of his career.[30]

In actuality, June 27 game against the New York Yankees seems to be the date when Griffith seriously began contemplating a Rice position switch. Just a couple of weeks before, the Senators had scored just one combined run in three consecutive losses to the Chicago White Sox, getting shut out twice in a row. The six-game stretch of games in New York that they were currently involved in included double header sweeps by the Yankees on back-to-back days.[31] In the June 27 contest, Griffith sent Rice in to pinch hit for pitcher Joe Boehling in the eighth inning of a game New York led 3–2. Rice singled, yet was stranded.

"Sam Rice is a dangerous pinch hitter," an account of the game noted. "There has not been a time when Griffith has sent him to the bat that he has not hit the ball hard."

The story also noted Rice's speed on the base paths. Clearly, Griffith was noticing the same attributes. Because by the next day, he was beginning to contemplate the move that would alter the course of Rice's career.[32]

"Rice can hit," reported the *Washington Post*, "but it is a question of when his defense will be strong enough to warrant Griffith taking a chance."

Hitting came naturally for Rice, and he was also naturally fleet of foot. Those two facets of his game being in place, Griffith was more than willing to work with him in the mornings before games to help the raw talent learn the nuances of the hidden game.

After a 7–5 loss against the Cleveland Indians on July 17, Griffith decided to convert him to an outfielder permanently. Rice had two hits in the game, and afterward, Griffith told him to be ready to play right field every day.[33] It was a decision born of frustration — over the course of the 1916 season, Griffith would use six different men in right field for at least thirteen games. Two of them, Henri Rondeau and Danny Moeller, never appeared in another major league game after the 1916 season. Howard Shanks, the nearest thing to a productive corner outfielder that Griffith had on the roster, had been forced to play third base because of an injury.[34]

"Rice is worth a most thorough trial," the *Post* said. "He has surely proven this much. Rice is a good pitcher, but Griffith, with his weak-hitting outfield, could spare him from the mound staff and it is believed that Rice will eventually become the most consistent hitter on the team."[35]

Griffith threw Rice right into the fire, batting him cleanup in his first start since being switched to a full-time outfielder. Not only did Rice collect a single and a double at the plate, but he easily tracked down two fly balls, assuaging the bigger worry about the move. The local press, meanwhile, continued to marvel at his potential as a hitter.

"He is bound to be one of the most dangerous hitters in baseball," one account of the game with the Indians, a 3–2 Senators victory, said.[36]

Rice continued to hit well, then suddenly began to slow down. The reason soon became evident — he was suffering from what he believed to be malaria. On August 21, he finally gave up in his battle to play through the ailment, retiring to his bed under a doctor's care. Fear loomed that his illness could develop into typhoid, and it was speculated that he'd be shut down for the rest of the season.[37]

That didn't end up being the case — Rice returned in September to finish out the season.[38] Despite the slump brought on by illness, Rice had put in a strong first season as a position player, batting .299 in 197 at-bats.[39] Griffith had seen all he needed to over the second half of the summer — Rice would be his starting right fielder entering the 1917 season.[40]

Rice later reflected on his training as an outfielder.

"If you have a good arm and a good pair of legs, you ought to be able to learn how to be an outfielder," he said. "At first the long throw bothered me. I was used to throwing speed from sixty feet. In the outfield I had to learn to throw distance much farther than sixty feet. It was something totally different, but I learned it."[41]

* * *

Griffith's decision to switch Rice from the mound to the outfield may seem drastic today, but it was part of a popular trend at the time he broke into the majors. Rice was actually one of three future Hall of Famer position players who broke into the big leagues as position players in 1914 and '15.

George Sisler joined the St. Louis Browns directly from the University of Michigan, making his major league debut as a pinch hitter about a month before Rice was signed by the Senators. Sisler entered that particular game in the sixth inning, then finished the game on the mound. A few days later, he made his first start, winning 3–1. He also beat Walter Johnson 2–1 later in the season (often misreported as Sisler's big-league debut). Sisler would become an everyday first baseman a year later.[42] He had something else in common with Rice—with 2,812 hits, Sisler retired less than two hundred hits short of the magic three thousand mark. His .340 lifetime batting average, along with two seasons at better than .400, helped expedite his Hall of Fame enshrinement, however.[43]

Babe Ruth pulled the feat most famously, and debuted a year before Rice and Sisler. While Rice and Sisler both had very brief careers on the mound before they found their real niche as position players, Ruth's primary role for the Boston Red Sox remained as a pitcher for three full seasons, and he quickly established himself as one of the top hurlers in baseball. Ruth's broke into the majors the year before Rice and Sisler—on July 11, 1914, he beat the Cleveland Indians 4–3. He was removed for a pinch-hitter, Duffy Lewis, in the game.[44]

Others from the era didn't reach the heights of Ruth, Rice and Sisler, yet still carved together very productive careers following the same path as that trio.

Rube Bressler was born just over three months before Ruth, and about four and a half years after Rice. Bressler's path to the majors was much faster than Rice's—he broke in as a left-handed pitcher with the Philadelphia Athletics in 1914 at the age of nineteen. He was an immediate phenom, winning ten games and losing just four while posting a 1.77 ERA. With a depleted defense behind him, as well as arm troubles setting into his apparently overworked young arm, Bressler went 4–17 in his second year with a 5.20 ERA.

He continued to work at that craft for a few years despite continued struggles, and recaptured a little bit of the old magic. But in 1921 Bressler dedicated himself full time to the outfield, playing in more than one hundred games seven times before retiring after the 1932 season with a lifetime batting average of .301.

Reb Russell broke in with twenty-two victories and sub–2.00 ERA as a rookie for the 1913 White Sox, then had a few good seasons on the mound before arm problems similarly derailed his pitching aspirations.

He took the long road back to the majors—making it all the way back in 1922 with the Pirates as an outfielder and batting .368 in sixty games. Russell, an entertainer with a popular wild west/vaudeville show, left baseball soon afterward to pursue that career, more lucrative at the time, instead, or else we may be today lumping in a group with Rice, Ruth and Sisler.

Perhaps the most fascinating player to follow the Rice blueprint played just one season in the majors—Buzz Arlett. The "Babe Ruth of the minor leagues" was a twenty-game winner three times in the Pacific Coast League, sometimes called the "third major league" by its fans, between 1919 and 1922. He was a nineteen-game winner in the other season. Then Barlett's career really got cooking. He hit 432 home runs in his minor league career, including fifty-four during a season in Baltimore of the International League.[45] Yet Arlett only spent one season in the majors, as teams backed away first because of concern about his fielding ability, then because of the expense of signing him, then finally because of worries about his temperament after a brawl with a PCL umpire.[46]

There were several other players who made the pitcher-to-position switch around the same time Rice broke in, including Charlie Jamieson and Johnny Cooney, who also has in common with Rice the fact that he enjoyed a career year at age forty.

The fact that so many players were making the transition around the same time is, in all likelihood, due to the fact that the game was in the final stages of an important transition period at the time. In major league baseball's infancy, rubber-armed pitchers had pitched nearly one hundred percent of their teams' innings. As the game developed, top pitchers shouldered less and less of the workload, though still taking on many more innings than pitchers do in the five-man pitching rotations of today.

Historians pinpoint the period between 1915 and 1920 as the precise time when pitcher workloads had decreased to the point that everyday players, on average, finally became more valuable than top pitchers. Hence, given the choice of where to play multi-skilled players like Ruth, Rice, Sisler and all the others, managers decided more and more often that they wanted their best players on the field every day.[47]

* * *

As the start of the 1917 season neared, Clark Griffith had long since decided that Rice would be an everyday position player, especially after his strong performance at the plate during his second-half tryout in 1916. Where exactly Rice would play was still something he was figuring out, however. Joe Judge, who had received most of the playing time at first base the year before, struggled as a rookie, batting just .220.[48] So Griffith contemplated trying Rice at first. Rice understood the mental aspects of the position. And Griffith was pleased with his arm strength and accuracy in case he needed to make throws to other bases on the diamond. There was one problem, though — Rice couldn't field ground balls. It was an issue that would continue to plague Rice for years in the outfield, but it was much less of a problem for an outfielder than an infielder.[49] Judge stayed at first — a good decision, in hindsight.

Judge would become as much a stalwart for the Senators at first base as Rice was in the outfield. In fact, the pair's eighteen seasons together stood for six decades as the longest continuous time two teammates had spent on the same team.[50]

Rice and Judge came from drastically different backgrounds. While Rice was a Midwest country kid, Judge was city through and through. He was the son of Irish immigrants, and grew up in New York City. By the time he was 16 years old, Judge had dropped out of school and was cashing a paycheck in a Brooklyn semipro league. Clark Griffith discovered him in 1915, the same summer he had landed Rice as repayment of a debt.

Judge was a consistent hitter, like Rice, and would usually bat right around .300. And, as it turned out, first base was the perfect spot for him.

"A genius around that bag," fellow Senators infielder Ossie Bluege would later recall.

Judge set the defensive standard for major league first baseman for many years to come.[51]

Not only would Rice and Judge become longtime teammates, but the bond between the two men of disparate backgrounds extended off the field, as well. They would eventually become neighbors in Washington, D.C., with Judge sometimes bringing his children over to the home of Rice and his wife Edith (the Rices were childless).

"I have just a brief memory of my brother Joe and I going over to their house one day and Mrs. Rice treating us to a bowl of raspberries and cream," Judge's daughter Dorothy recalled. "I remember that he and his wife were a quiet couple."[52]

Judge and Rice were young in 1917, and the Senators' roster still had a long way to go before it would be strong enough to contend for American League supremacy. On July 21, the Senators fell into last place in the standings.[53] At the time, though, Washington's eyes were hardly on baseball at all. Instead, the reality of the raging war in Europe was finally hitting home for Americans, with the beginning of the Selective Service draft.

The United States had attempted to stay out of the hostilities for several years, but it had become more and more difficult. In early April of 1916, the U.S. ship the *Aztec* had taken fire while sailing in the European war zone, killing American John I. Eopolucci. By April 6, 1917, the U.S. could stay out of the fighting no longer. At 1:18 p.m. of that afternoon, President Wilson signed a declaration of war against Germany, which had been approved by landslide votes in both the Senate and the House of Representatives.

The problem was that the U.S. didn't have the military force at that time to participate in a war of the scale of the one going on in Europe, which history knows as World War I. To rectify that, Wilson signed the Selective Service Act on May 18, requiring all males between the ages of twenty-one and thirty-one to register for a possible call to duty.

On July 20, the day before the Senators bottomed out, the "great national lottery" was began. Blind-folded Secretary of War Newton Baker drew the first number, 258, from a glass jar. The draft was underway.[54] And although enthusiasm regarding the war swept the United States as a whole, baseball, its product threatened, would eventually attempt — unsuccessfully — to battle for the exemption of its players.

For now they carried on. The Senators rallied to finish with a 74–79 record, good for fifth place and well behind the runaway train that was the Chicago White Sox. Rice had immediately proven his value as an everyday player. He appeared in all the Senators' games, every one of them in right field, and his .302 batting average made him the only Washington player to top the .300 mark. He also stole thirty-five bases.[55]

"The case of Sam Rice is one of the most interesting of the baseball season," a newspaper writer noted. "Rice is a natural hitter and as he is still a youngster there seems no reason, if his baseball career is not interrupted, why he should not in another year rank with the consistent .300 batters. His is but another case of a pitcher who has become a good fielder."[56]

4

THE WAR IN EUROPE

Rice's military status would be a matter of much consternation, as well as speculation, during the ensuing offseason. Though the 1917 Senators were actually two games worse than the 1916 team, that was misleading. In 1916, the 117-loss Philadelphia Athletics had been so awful that their incompetence helped pad the records of the other American League teams. With Philadelphia improving by thirty-eight games in 1917, the Senators' seventy-four victories were well-earned, evidenced by the modest climb from seven place in the league to fifth place. With two Washington regulars, catcher Eddie Ainsmith and shortstop Howard Shanks, struggling around the .200 mark all season long, Rice's surprise performance at the plate helped keep the team afloat. The organization didn't exactly want to face a season without him manning right field.[1]

In December, it was reported that Rice had a physical exemption from military service.[2]

But another rumor swept through Washington D.C. soon afterward — that Rice had decided to enlist in the Navy while he was home for the winter. The organization waited anxiously to see if he'd show up at spring training.[3]

On March 2, Griffith got his wish. Rice arrived in Hot Springs, Arkansas. The enlistment reports had been nothing but rumors, a little piece of war hysteria so common in any trying time.

"The news that Rice will not quit the club until he is called for the Army pleased manager Griffith so much," the *Washington Post* reported, "that he started to play bridge yesterday afternoon with a pinochle deck."[4]

In late March, Rice left the team and returned home to Watseka, Illinois, to plead for an extension of his Army call-up in front of the local board.

"The Lieutenant Commander who listened to my story was one of those hard guys, all bristle and front teeth," Rice said. "He had been used to browbeating sailors all his life and he opened upon me a little too soon."

One can understand Rice's frustration. At age twenty-six, he had finally put the vagabond ways of his early twenties behind him and was settling in nicely in Washington. Life, thrown violently off track by the tornado back home six years before, was now going well. As a baseball player, traveling was still a part of his routine, but it was connected to the soothing predictability of the game's 154-game schedule. Rice had done his duty to his country, unasked and, in his opinion, under false pretenses. It was time to vent.

"I reflected that I had never had the opportunity to tell such a fellow as he was what I thought of him and might never have another opportunity, so I relieved my mind," Rice said. "I told him a few things in language that I thought he could understand."[5]

The answer would come soon enough. On April 3, four days after his contentious hearing, Rice's request for an extension was denied. He was headed back to the service. Clark Griffith, excited about his young team before the news, was understanding and tried to maintain optimism, but had trouble containing his disappointment.

"It is hard to be hit as we have," Griffith said. "But Uncle Sam needs Rice and his needs come before baseball. We are going to make a game race and we'll fight all the way for a first division berth. If Rice hadn't been called, we would have given the best club in the league a real fight. With Sam on the team I had the best combination that has represented Washington since I have been manager and I don't except the two years we were up there fighting for a pennant.

"As it is, every one of those boys is determined to fight the harder to make up for Rice's loss."[6]

Not that Griffith was insincere in his pledge of patriotism, but as the 1918 season unfolded, his team would take up the cause of the game against the United States military establishment. Though baseball, evidenced by Ban Johnson's military drill competition, had been well aware of the war effort since President Wilson declared war in April of 1917, external pressure was increasing on the game to display more than token support of the boys in Europe. Although Rice and other contemporaries, including Grover Cleveland Alexander, Joe Jackson, Red Faber and Rabbit Maranville, had already enlisted or been plucked out of one uniform for another, the American public and the men leading the war effort were longing to draft an even greater percentage of the nation's young men into service. And who was more able-bodied than professional athletes?

Early in 1918, Baker, the secretary of war, issued his famous work-or-fight order. The creed was intended to diminish the pool of draft-deferred men. Now, men employed in "non-productive work" were vulnerable to the draft, even if they had been able to secure some sort of deferment previously. Productive work was defined as anything that helped keep the country on its feet while the workforce was crippled by the war. The U.S. needed workers to fill factories, steel mills and farms, as well as war-specific jobs in munitions factories and shipyards. General Enoch Crowder, the provost marshal of the army, was placed in charge of the draft under work-or-fight, and he didn't take his job lightly.

For baseball, the battleground would be whether professional sports were considered essential or non-essential work. It partly pinned its hopes on a ruling that exempted actors, who were deemed essential in entertaining a potentially downtrodden population. Baseball hoped to earn the same blanket protection of its workers. Senators catcher Eddie Ainsmith would be its sacrificial lamb.

Baker had proclaimed that jobs playing baseball were considered non-productive. However, while Ainsmith's appeal worked its way through the system, he deferred to local draft boards, some of which saw things differently than the secretary.[7]

Ainsmith, twenty-eight years old, was entering his ninth season with the Senators. He wasn't much of a hitter, batting just .191 in 125 games in 1917, the most action he had received up to then. He struggled even more at the plate the season before, batting just .170. Though he would find his batting stroke in subsequent stops with the Detroit Tigers and St. Louis Cardinals, heading into 1918 Ainsmith had never batted better than .226 for a season.[8]

But that didn't mean that Washington wasn't willing to fight Uncle Sam to retain his services. Griffith liked Ainsmith, and had since he took over the club. Heading into the 1912 season, Griffith's first with Washington, one of his first moves was to deal incumbent catcher Gabby Street to the New York Yankees. That showed how confident he was in the duo of Ainsmith and fellow backstop John Henry, another weak hitter. Ainsmith was alternately described as "one of the nicest fellows in baseball, but also one of the game's toughest players." Despite catching Walter Johnson, he was known to stuff minimal padding into his glove. Though it barely registered in his home run totals—Ainsmith hit just two long balls in his first eight seasons—he was an early advocate of strength training for baseball players.

Walter Johnson once described Ainsmith's legendary toughness. "Eddie Ainsmith was a real sportsman," Johnson said. "Many's the time I've seen him actually bleeding from spike cuts. 'No,' he'd say, 'this doesn't amount to anything.' The trainer would say, 'Let me dress that wound, Eddie, let me bandage it up.' Ainsmith would reply, pushing him away good-humouredly, 'Say, what do you think I am? I'm not hurt. What's a little blood?'"

There was a drawback to Ainsmith's well-developed musculature — teams could monitor the twitch of his defined forearms when he signaled his pitcher and figure out from there what pitch might be on its way.[9]

Though Ainsmith was more than willing to spill a little of his blood for the noble cause of winning a baseball game, the idea of spilling blood on the battlegrounds of Europe made him squeamish. Enough so that he took his appeal all the way to the top. As everyone waited on Baker's decision on Ainsmith and, thus, every player, the season progressed into mid–July, minus a few stars like Rice but still strong and well-stocked with talent. Rising Boston star Babe Ruth provided a sideshow with his threat to join an industrial team, a popular choice for players hoping to avoid the draft but a threat made by Ruth simply as a maneuver in his grudge match with Red Sox management. But Ruth also provided a distraction from the seriousness of war news with his increasingly prodigious hitting, a new role for the left-handed starting pitcher.

Even Ruth's big play and even bigger personality weren't enough to temper the news that came down on July 19, news that would have an enormous effect on how the rest of the 1918 season played out. On that day, Newton Baker ruled against Ainsmith, ruling that his job as a Washington Senators catcher was not considered essential work. Ainsmith, and all other baseball players in his age bracket, could no longer appeal to what they hoped would be sympathetic local draft boards.

Since the decision wasn't completely unexpected, a lot of players had anticipated it by finding work in fields they knew would be considered productive, even as viewed through the prism of surging patriotism in the country. During the era, the baseball teams of various shipyards and steel mills could probably have given some major league baseball teams a run for their money. In fact, many industrial shops used their strong semipro baseball teams to actively recruit major leaguers into the temporary workforce.[10]

* * *

Upon leaving the Senators, Rice was assigned a spot in the Army's 68th artillery, something that wasn't easy to secure. "Only those men were taken who expressed a keen desire to go overseas," said J. Lindsay Hoyt, a captain in the regiment.

"Do you want to go across?" men were questioned.

Only a non-hesitant "Yes, sir" earned a solider a place in the company.

Though Rice had initially battled to stay out of the draft, he still remembered the empty feeling after he had enlisted in 1914 in an effort to see the world, only to find that the world for him extended only to a regrettable skirmish just south of the nation's border.[11]

Rice and the company were stationed at Fort Terry on a small island close to Long Island, New York, where they now simply waited for their voyage.[12]

Twice during the summer, Rice was granted a furlough from his service at Fort Terry. Both times, he used the occasion to play baseball.

Rice first re-joined his teammates in late May, showing up for a double header against the Boston Red Sox. It was relatively uneventful, with him going 1-for-5 in the two games.[13]

He was granted a longer leave in June, however, and it was then that he would really show what Washington fans were missing.

Rice caught up to the team in New York and Yankees fans, appreciative of Sam's service to the country, gave him a loud ovation when he made a tremendous catch to rob Yankee Del Pratt of what looked like a triple off the bat in the fifth inning.

The hometown press wasn't as impressed, however.

"Sam has been too busy with Army work to get much chance to practice baseball," said one story, "a fact that was evident today in his failure to hit the ball."[14]

Rice didn't look out of practice the next day against the Yankees, though. He doubled in a run in the seventh inning, but also made the game's key defensive play. In the eighth, the Yankees tried to mount a rally to challenge the Senators' 2–0 lead. New York third baseman Frank Baker lifted a fly to Rice in right. Rice not only caught it, but unleashed a throw to home to cut down Elmer Miller trying to tag up and score. Washington won 4–1.[15]

His furlough not due to end for a couple more days, Rice traveled back to Washington with his teammates. In front of the Washington home crowd, the soldier had three hits in four at-bats, and was robbed of another sure hit on a terrific catch in deep right field by Philadelphia's Charlie Jamieson.[16]

Before the following afternoon's game, Rice's teammates organized a modest ceremony to let him know how much he was missed — as well as how much his service to the country was appreciated. By presenting Rice with a watch, however, they tempted the baseball gods— there was no better way to jinx a man's performance, it was well known, than to present him with some kind of trinket of appreciation before a game.

The jinx met its match in Rice, however. In a game tied 0–0 between the Senators and Philadelphia, Rice singled in the seventh inning and then scored the go-ahead run. An inning later, after the Athletics had tied the score, Rice drove in what turned out to be the winning run.

Earlier in the game, he had thrown out a runner trying to score from second on a single, the second time during his short stay with the Senators that he had nailed a would-be run at the plate.

America's relatively short participation as a full-fledged entrant into the first World War was an odd time for the country. It was the first major conflict the United States had become involved with since the advent of spectator sports as a popular leisure-time activity for Americans. And born out of the time was a scourge on sports writing that pops up in newspaper copy to this day — sports-as-war metaphors.

When the sports pages of 1918 were forced to confront the reality of a war overseas, they often did so in cheerleading tones.

"If he can register as many hits with a big gun as he can with a bat," the *Post* said of Rice, for example, "he is going to be a big factor in putting the Hohenzollern league in the bush class."

But underlying the awkward bravado was the sobering knowledge that the players heading to Europe were not guaranteed a return any time soon. And they weren't guaranteed a return home in one piece, or even necessarily alive.

Other than the occasional flare-up like Rice's Veracruz incident, professional baseball had initially flourished during a period of extended peace in American history. But now that had been broken, and the country had no precedent for where the current situation was to lead.

His furlough over with, Rice would now be stepping away from baseball. That much was known. But an eventual return was scarcely even contemplated.

"Any way you look at it," an account of Rice's final 1918 appearance with the Senators reported, "Rice gave the fans plenty to talk about in saying his farewell to baseball."

The reference wasn't just to his last baseball of the season, but possibly the last appearance he'd ever make in the big leagues — Rice, it also said, had been "making what may be his last appearance in a major league uniform."[17]

The Senators clearly missed a bat of Rice's caliber in their lineup, and though his performance was a nice reminder of what fans had to look forward to when the war in Europe some day ended (maybe), it also was a reminder of how inadequate the Washington lineup was without him. Clyde Milan was batting .322 in his absence, but no other Senator was even at the .270 mark for the year.[18]

Soon after his return to the 68th, Rice and the men marched in a parade in New London, Connecticut, a parade that ended with several of them suffering from apparent heat stroke. But the men perked up at the news that they would sail out for Europe the next morning.

Armed with sandwiches, coffee and cigarettes from the Red Cross, the men boarded the British ship the *Leicestershire*. They were directed to the boat's hold.

"We thought we were going there to check out baggage and imagine our surprise when we were told that it was to be our home, sleeping quarters and mess hall combined," one soldier later wrote.

Rice and the rest of the men slept on hammocks hung from the ceiling at night. Many chose the less claustrophobic setting of the deck to sleep on, at least in clear water. Even reports of enemy submarine activity off the U.S. East Coast did little to discourage an adventuresome group.

"A perfect trip," Cpt. Hoyt wrote in his detailed memoirs of the 68th's time together, "had to include subs, storms, icebergs, whales and about everything else."

Rice's ship sailed from Boston to New York Harbor's Staten Island, a disappointment for many of them who thought they had boarded a direct ride to France, their ultimate destination. Finally, joined by several other ships, the *Leicestershire* set sail. Sam was off to see the world.

After fifteen days at sea, the men arrived in England. And they immediately were reminded that this wasn't a pleasure trip they had embarked on. After they had been docked for a short while, sirens began to wail — an air raid warning. The men rushed to the deck, watching as searchlight beams scoured the night sky. But it was a false alarm, and calm was soon restored.

The next day, Rice and the men marched through the English countryside through pouring late afternoon rain for about a mile to reach their rest camp. There they stayed for four long days, subsisting on rations of goldfish, bread, jam and tea while rain continued to pour down outside.

"There was little to do and worst of all, little to eat," Hoyt wrote.

Finally, Rice's ship sailed for France. During their holdover stay in England, the men had experienced one of the realities of war — boredom. And then upon arriving in France, they came face to face with some of its other more grim realities. A long American Red Cross train pulled in, and it was visibly packed with men sporting bandaged arms, hands and heads.

"The sight of it," Hoyt wrote, "brought the horrors of war closer to us."

After a long climb up a hill into the city of Le Havre, Rice and his company mates were greeted by a welcoming delegation from the city. A spokesman read a welcome address, then a band struck up the American national anthem while approximately fifty school children filed in carrying flags of all the allied countries.

Shortly thereafter, the men retired to their trenches, trenches where just a week before an officer had been seriously wounded in a German air raid.[19]

Back home, the baseball season had ended long before, prematurely due to a government order that all non-war industry cease on Labor Day.[20] Rice's Senators finished with a 72–56 record, their best winning percentage since Griffith's first two years as the team's manager, 1912–13.[21] The Boston Red Sox won the World Series, then disposed of the Cubs four games to two. With war on people's minds, attendance at the series was poor — just 15,238 watched the clinching game on September 11. But the 1918 World Series was historic, as young Boston pitcher Babe Ruth starred and extended his scoreless World Series streak to 29⅔ innings.²²

Back in France, a man named Johnny Evers, the director of the Knights of Columbus operations overseas, contemplated the formation of Army and Navy baseball teams to play exhibitions in France, teams that would include Rice and other professional ballplayers serving in the area. Nothing, however, seems to have come of the idea.²³ Meanwhile Rice and the soldiers of the 68th were housed in vacant stores, houses and other buildings. Rice's accommodations weren't exactly luxurious, but it beat some of the accommodations they had been given since leaving the United States. Then again, they weren't in France on vacation, a fact that was driven home once again as battle-specific preparations picked up in earnest.

By September 16, the 68th began to take serious steps to prepare for combat. Officers attended a heavy artillery course, a course that lasted until early November. It was eye-opening.

"It was a good course and made us realize how ill-equipped we really were for the method of artillery warfare that was then being conducted," Hoyt wrote.

Around that same time, the artillery arrived for the 68th, "six-inch seacoast guns mounted on massive carriage." Artillery drills packed the enlisted men's daily schedules.

After months of grueling travel, training and waiting, Rice and the rest of the men in his company were prepared for combat. But while waiting on the brink of their first action, Rice was spared of the second combat experience of his life.²⁴

On November 11, the peace treaty officially ending World War I, which would be known as the "Armistice," went into effect at 11 a.m. Germany had accepted U.S. President Wilson's "Fourteen Points," a list of conditions that included the resignation of German leader Kaiser Wilhelm the Second. The Treaty of Versailles, which formally drew out sanctions against Germany, wouldn't be signed until June of 1919. But as far as Rice and the rest of the soldiers were concerned, their work was done.²⁵

By early January, Clark Griffith began to push for the release of Rice and another Senators player, Mike Menosky, from duty in France.²⁶ Griffith was attempting to invoke a War Department order declaring that men who had entered the service after April 1, 1917, who submitted "good and sufficient reasons for requesting discharge," could receive that discharge immediately so long as they waived the military's promise to finance their sea travel allowance. American League president Ban Johnson met with War Department officials in Washington, D.C., regarding the matter, and exited optimistic.

"It is a foregone conclusion," the *Washington Post* reported, "that the release of players will be hastened and there is little doubt now but that Sam Rice,

Mike Menosky, Grover Cleveland Alexander and other big leaguers aboard will be back when the training season opens."[27]

If Griffith and Johnson had been aware of the delays Rice's 68th artillery was facing in France, they may not have been so optimistic. After rushing to put together a joyous Thanksgiving dinner in November after hearing their ship would be the next out, a long, unexplained wait began.

Finally, in January, Col. T.C. Barnes pushed the issue with a French official who acted mystified at Barnes' impatience, seeing since his men were "comfortably settled."

"Men have no beds, no stoves, not enough blankets, are living hand to mouth and are getting sick because of it," Barnes replied.

Barnes continued to be persistent and on February 3, Rice boarded the *S.S. Matsonia*.[28] Back home, those following Washington baseball rejoiced at the news that Rice was about to set sail back home, presumably to arrive in time for opening day.

"Sam Rice is on the Atlantic this morning bound for home and a .300 batting average in the American League this coming season," the *Post* reported. "The slugging outfielder cabled manager Griffith yesterday that he was sailing, and the closer he gets to these shores so much the better will the chances of the (Senators) to land in the first division this year appear."[29]

The journey home was rough — and had to have been difficult emotionally for Rice, in light of his tragic past. Storms ravaged the ship, which withstood eighty-five-mph gusts of wind for up to three days at a time. Men became sick, "so sick that they would rather have had the boat sink than prolong the agony," according to Hoyt.

Finally, on the 15th of February, the Matsonia arrived in New York.[30] At the same time, things were getting back to normal for the Washington Senators. Though the American League had granted permission for teams with returning soldiers to carry extra players on top of the standard 21-man roster, the frugal Griffith advocated an 18-man roster.[31] As Rice made his way across the country with the 68th, through the Midwest on his way to Illinois' Camp Grant for demobilization, Joe Judge battled with Griffith over his 1919 salary.[32] If he didn't receive what he wanted, Judge sent word, he'd just as soon remain in Baltimore building ships, his offseason occupation. Judge was one of several Senators who were slow to sign for the 1919 campaign.[33]

Rice, on the other hand, signed with little argument, so excited was he to get back into camp with his team.[34] After all, just a few months before the local papers had been writing his baseball epitaph.

"It seems longer than a year ago that I left here," Rice said. "I've done considerable traveling since then and I'm glad I have. It has been a long jump to France and back again and I'm mighty glad I'm back to where I started about a year ago this time. I feel so good about it all that I'd like to go out and get into uniform just to see how it feels. Baseball togs have been strangers to me for a long, long time."

Rice reported about twenty pounds heavier than he had been when he left, but the press marveled at how it was "solid flesh ... nothing flabby."[35]

***

Rice had been playing professional baseball since he was in his early twenties. But as the 1919 season dawned, he had still yet to string together two consecutive seasons with any kind of stability. His early minor-league career, of course, had been interrupted by the family tragedy in Illinois, then by the bullets of Veracruz, Mexico. Then, upon reaching the major leagues, he was shuttled between the pitcher's mound and outfield. By the time Rice finally settled into right field and established himself as a star in the making in 1917, the Selective Service Act loomed ominously over the season, and World War I robbed him of all of the 1918 campaign save for twenty-three at-bats.[36]

But when Rice reported to the Senators for the 1919 season, he looked to finally establish a permanent, annual place for himself in the team's lineup, barring anything unforeseen. And Griffith looked to begin stocking the club for long-term success, not just the nice respite from the second division he had delivered in the first years of his managerial tenure.

All of this was contingent, of course, on baseball not self-destructing, which would become a very real possibility by the time the season's World Series had been played.

As the 1919 season opened, Rice showed little rust from his summer away from the game. Batting cleanup and back in his customary right field spot to start the season, Rice had his first three-hit game just five games into the season, in a 4–2 victory over the Red Sox.[37] In late May, he made three spectacular catches in a row against the Yankees, in a game that saw him also smack three base hits.[38] By mid-summer, Sam had really found his groove, putting together a seventeen-game hitting streak in July.[39]

Rice was beginning to come into his own as a hitter and an outfielder, but he was doing so in an odd transition year for major league baseball.

Maybe the culture was ripe in 1919 for a scandal like the one that was to soon devastate the game. In the aftermath of the World War, some Americans were still attempting to sort through their feelings about fierce competition. In the post-victory glow, brotherhood among Americans seemed to be preferred over cutthroat competitiveness, even on the field of play. That was illustrated by the reaction to Rice's actions at the plate in a mid–August game against the Red Sox.

In the seventh inning of a tight game, Rice came to the plate. Senators base runners stood on first and second, and the customs of the game in those last throes of the "dead-ball era" dictated that he sacrifice both teammates up a base. Boston third baseman Joe "Moon" Harris, a future teammate of Rice's, accordingly crept up onto the grass.

Like Rice, Harris was a veteran of the war in Europe.[40] He had missed the entire 1918 campaign in service to the cause.[41]

"Did Rice bunt?" reported the *Washington Post*. "He did not. Instead, he crossed Harris by whistling a line drive past him at a rate of ten miles a minute."

Because both men were veterans of the same war, it was felt that Rice had a gentleman's obligation to take care of Harris in the situation. Instead, he had embarrassed the Boston third baseman by slamming the ball past him.

Or so the newspaper felt.

"Sam Rice ought to be ashamed of himself," the *Post* said, "to take advantage of a fellow overseas veteran like Joe Harris as he did in the seventh."[42]

Rice entered September batting right around .300, but a final push later in the month helped hoist him up to his final numbers.[43] In batting .321 with twenty-three doubles, it was clear that Rice had lost nothing off his batting stroke in his year in the Army. In fact, he had improved. Rice had increased his batting average nearly twenty points, and he had also cut back on his strikeouts, slicing his total from forty-one in his last full season to just twenty-six in 557 at-bats in 1919.[44]

Beyond the numbers, Rice's improvement was evident by the opposition's newfound respect for him — late in the season, teams began pitching around him in critical situations.

"Not until that is done," the *Post* noted, "has a batter really arrived."[45]

Unfortunately he did his hitting in the service of a team that was a disappointment, regressing to seventh place with a record of 56–84.[46]

Though the 1919 season was an unremarkable one for the Senators, with the club looking directionless in the wake of the war's end, Griffith used the otherwise lost summer to begin laying some important groundwork that would pay off exponentially for the franchise in the upcoming decade.

His first important move of the summer was to hire former Washington pitcher Joe Engel as a full-time scout.[47] Engel had not pitched for the Senators since Rice's rookie season. He had spent the early part of the 1919 campaign on Cleveland's roster, appearing in just one game.[48] Even as a young player, Engel had developed a reputation a man with a keen eye for minor-league talent. When the Senators traded Engel to the minor-league club in Indianapolis, they also gave him the first scouting assignment of his life. He was to observe his new teammates and pick out the players to be sent to Washington in exchange for himself. Engel had done a good job delivering players who helped the Senators, including catcher Pat Gharrity and pitcher George Dumont. Griffith hadn't forgotten Engel's bargaining ability in that case. So as the Senators struggled in 1919, and Griffith began to realize that his one-man scouting, managing and player personnel operation faced long odds against the increasingly sophisticated operations of franchises that were lapping his club in the American League pennant race, he called on Engel to help out.

Engel turned out to be both a successful judge of talent, but also a good people person who was skilled at ingratiating himself to prospects and, almost as importantly, their families.

"Naturally a fellow will do more for a friend than for a stranger," he once said. "And so I cultivate whole families and always remember to take the kiddies presents and in that way stand in with their dads."

Engel's first major move in his new career would be his most important one, and pay major dividends to the Senators in just a few years. During a trip to Binghampton, New York, to scout pitcher Pat Martin, Engel watched as the second baseman for the Buffalo team, a scrappy little player named Stanley Harris, engaged in a fight with a runner. That fierceness, Engel noticed as the game wore on, was reflected in Harris' play. But there was a problem — Griffith was aware of Harris. He had been a teammate of Joe Judge's on a Baltimore industrial league team, and Judge had been unimpressed by Harris' hitting ability. And he wasn't the only one — twice during the course of the summer of 1919, New York Giants manager John McGraw had an opportunity to sign Harris, first out of a tryout at the Polo Grounds and next as the completion of a trade with the Buffalo team. Both times he passed.

But Engel was persistent with Griffith, and he convinced his boss to travel to Buffalo and watch Harris play for himself. After a double header that saw "Bucky," a nickname he acquired while working in a Pennsylvania coal mine at the age of twelve, collect six base hits, Griffith went to the clubhouse to speak with his potential find. What he witnessed there clinched it — Harris was unwrapping tape from two fingers, having broken one of them a short time before.

"I never saw a competitive spirit the equal of his, not even Cobb's," Griffith would later say about Harris. "He was the gamest ballplayer I ever saw in fifty years of baseball. He was the smartest player I ever had."

Harris joined the Senators in late August. And Griffith made another key addition to the roster late in the summer when he signed twenty-three-year-old pitcher Tom Zachary.[49] Zachary went 1–5 in seventeen appearances, but showed some promise with a respectable 2.92 ERA. Like Harris, Zachary's value to the organization would surface down the road.[50]

While sending his new scout Engel on the road to find new talent, Griffith examined ways to make the most of some of the players he already had in the ballclub's fold.

"Rice is not only the outfield star of the Griffs," the *Washington Post* said, "but he is one of the best outfielders in the major leagues. He has come to the front with a rush in the last few years, but he has not yet reached his best. The next few years should see him climb to a place among the great outfielders of all time."[51]

***

While Griffith aggressively looked for ways to lift his seventh-place ballclub to the top of the American League, or at the very least back into the league's first division, eight members of the Chicago White Sox were busy consorting with gamblers who would convince them to do quite the opposite and lower their play. At one point in the summer of 1919, the *Washington Post* had felt that Sam Rice was obligated to essentially tank an at-bat in deference to a fellow war veteran. The "Black Sox," as history would come to know them, lowered their level of play for a far less noble reason—to get their hands on underworld king Arnold Rothstein's money. Rothstein, along with an elaborate web of shady associates, convinced the group, which included superstar "Shoeless" Joe Jackson, to throw the World Series against the underdog Cincinnati Reds.[52]

The Black Sox scandal took gambling scandals to new heights, and the stain would remain on the game and the organization for generations. Eighty-six years would pass before the White Sox won another World Series, and when the 2005 team made its way through the playoffs, national networks and print media concocted a "Curse of 'Shoeless' Joe Jackson" to familiarize viewers with the franchise's sordid past.

But the specter of gambling in baseball was by no means exclusively a recent development.

In 1867, as leisure activity returned to American life and baseball's popularity was beginning to boom in the immediate aftermath of the Civil War, an early incarnation of the Washington Senators organized a western tour unheard of at the time. The three thousand-mile, six-city trip took the Washington club, all amateurs financing the travels out-of-pocket, as far west as Missouri, and closed with a stop in Chicago to take on some of Illinois' best squads of the day.

The successful tour, which included convincing victories in cities like Columbus (Ohio), Louisville, Indianapolis and Cincinnati, took a dour turn in Chicago. The Forest City Club of Rockford, Illinois, behind the pitching of seventeen-year-old future Hall of Famer A.G Spalding, defeated those early Senators 29–23 on a late July afternoon. Chicago's papers celebrated the Rockford victory.

That jubilation quickly turned to skepticism, however. Next up for the Senators were the Chicago Excelsiors, widely considered even more formidable than the Rockford club, which it had beaten twice earlier in the month. Washington didn't just defeat the Excelsiors—they embarrassed them by a 49–4 final score.

Dumbfounded and trying to find an explanation, the *Chicago Tribune* publicly accused the Senators of tanking the earlier game against Rockford, in order to set up a huge back-channel payday against the suddenly heavily favored Chicago Excelsiors. Washington president Frank Jones and star player Arthur Pue Gorman, a future United States senator from Maryland, visited the *Tribune* office and demanded a retraction. Convinced, the paper complied.

Soon after the formation of the National League a few years later, four Louisville players were banned from the game for throwing games. At the time, Washington was without a professional franchise — and suddenly happy for it.

"It was not fast baseball," Shirley Povich later wrote of the amateur game that was popular in the District at the time, "but it was at least above suspicion."[53]

Once the Black Sox scandal broke publicly a few months later, it would be a long time before baseball was able to again operate "above suspicion." Luckily for the game, events would soon be put in motion to rescue the sport from the fallout of its darkest hour.

5

ROARING INTO THE 1920s

When and where did the "Roaring Twenties," the American decade notable for good-timing, free-spending, hard-partying ways, actually begin?

Of course, the perfect storm that gathers to give any particular era its distinct flavor always requires a wide range of factors, societal and otherwise, to coalesce. But looking back, it's hard not to see certain events thick with symbolism as evening fell on the year 1919.

Paul Johnson, a British historian, has pinpointed the "birth of the modern world," and hence the advent of the 1920s as we have come to know them, in the scientific realm. In spring of that year 1919, early afternoon May 29, to be precise, scientist Arthur Eddington tested and confirmed Albert Einstein's theory of relativity from an island near Africa. Because, as one author notes, on that day, "man's understanding of the universe was altered forever." Accordingly, Americans and people worldwide entered the decade to follow more world weary and secularized as they came to understand the world surrounding them on a different level.

As important as the professorly looking Eddington's discovery was, however, what the '20s truly required was a life of the party. No American has ever fit that description as well as one Babe Ruth.

Ruth offered many moments saturated with that sort of symbolism that summer. Because he had performed so well at the plate in limited duty in his first few seasons with the Red Sox, Boston manager Ed Barrow decided to convert his star pitcher into a full-time player. When he wasn't pitching, Ruth would play outfield for the Sox.

One might say the first tremors of a roar could be traced to May 20, when

No major league hitter has ever come closer to the three-thousand hit mark without actually reaching it than Sam Rice, who retired with 2,987 hits. (National Baseball Hall of Fame Library, Cooperstown, N.Y.)

after a slow start at the plate Ruth blasted a pitch onto Grand Avenue beyond the right-field wall at St. Louis' Sportsman Park. It was his first over-the-fence homer since the conversion to everyday player.

Then there was the shot he hit ten days later, just one day after Eddington's scientific work, in Philadelphia's Shibe Field. That long home run convinced Ruth to beg out of the Red Sox's starting pitching rotation. Barrow's acquiescence was a touchstone in itself—the retirement to pasture of Ruth the hurler and the birth of Ruth the slugger.

Finally there was the stretch from the middle of summer until its conclusion when Ruth held a baseball watching nation in thrall as he took aim at every single-season home run record that sports writers of the time could unearth. A 480-foot shot to center at Fenway Park to tie Sock Seybold's seventeen-year-old American League record. The one in August that incredibly cleared the right-field bleachers at Chicago's Comiskey Park. His twenty-ninth and final home run of the season in Washington, lauded as the longest ball ever hit at Griffith Stadium.

A decade as memorable as what was to come in the '20s needed a launch point. Ruth assembled them in bunches and strung them like a strand of holiday lights across the summer of 1919 (and all this after *The Sporting News* had urged the Babe not to try for home runs because it might put his batting average in jeopardy).

Ruth's season in the swan song year of the preceding decade was no fluke, but instead a sign of where baseball was headed in the decade to follow. In the 1920s, hitters would indeed roar.

With the exception of 1921, when Rogers Hornsby led baseball with a .397 average, at least one player batted .400 in each of the years from 1920 through 1925, including three in 1922 alone. In 1917, Rice's first full season as a big-league outfielder, major league pitchers sported an earned-run average of 2.68. In just eight years, that had soared to 1925's 4.33.

The Sporting News wasn't the only publication nervous about the direction of the game. Among the headlines in major magazines during the decade: "Baseball Shudders at the Home Run Menace" and "The Growing Problem of the Home Run." Baseball fans gasped at the spectacle of a 26–23 score in a 1922 game between the Chicago Cubs and the Philadelphia Phillies, a game the Cubs had led 26–9 after seven innings. They scratched their heads when St. Louis Brown Jack Tobin, a scrawny leadoff hitter, swatted thirteen home runs that same summer.

But while some shuddered at the outset of the '20s at the explosion in offense, fans stormed the gates in record numbers. In 1920, more than nine million fans attended major league games. The old record of 7.25 million had been set in 1909. Baseball writer and historian William Curran, who lovingly documented the decade in his book "Big Sticks," is on board with many when he describes the '20s as a baseball golden era:

> Pure Norman Rockwell? I'll let you in on a secret. I lived close enough to the period to say with some assurance that it was indeed that pleasant. Grass, sunshine, proximity to the players. No bat night, no helmet night, no night. No exploding score-

boards, no instant replay, no organ music, no roar of jet planes overhead. No sound except the chirp of vendors, the crack of the bat, and the cheering of the crowd.

Magazine headline writers aside, the country seemed ready. For example in New York, one of the flashpoints of the excess ahead, a ban on Sunday baseball was finally lifted in the spring of 1920 when Governor Al Smith signed his legislature's proposal into law. Ready to party, New Yorkers filled the Polo Grounds thirty-five thousand strong for the home team's first Sunday game.[1]

* * *

The Senators' two 1920 openers, their season opener and their home debut a week later, took on very differing hues. On April 15, Washington became the first team to visit Boston after Red Sox owner Harry Frazee's sale of Ruth to the Yankees over the winter. Though no one knew it at the time, this was the first day in what would turn out to be the eighty-five-year long mythical "Curse of the Bambino," with the Red Sox not winning another World Series until 2004 and the Yankees using the Ruth acquisition as a springboard to becoming the most successful franchise in the history of American professional sports.

Red Sox fans of 1920 hardly could have been concerned with, or aware of, the depths of anguish their children and grandchildren would deal with as a result of the offseason that had just passed. Certainly, however, they weren't pleased about the direction of the club at the present. The *Washington Post* wrote about the subdued atmosphere at Fenway Park throughout the 7–6 Sox victory:

> Boston fans gave Frazee their answer to the sale of star players today. In spite of fine weather, less than seven thousand turned out to see the Red Sox open the 1920 season. It was the smallest crowd, under similar weather conditions, that ever witnessed an American League opener. Fans threatened to stay away from Fenway Park after Ruth was sold last winter ... and they made good today.[2]

Washington fans, on the other hand, turned out in force to see the Senators' home opener a week later against the same Red Sox. In the spirit of home opener hyperbole that exists to the present day, the local press enthusiastically interpreted the Senators' 8–5 come-from-behind victory as representative of an imminent turnaround in the club's fortunes.

"The (Senators) didn't run true to their form of recent seasons," read the Post, "which pleased a crowd of approximately sixteen thousand, the biggest that ever saw an opening day game here, immensely. The Griffs showed a courageous, fighting spirit in the face of what looked like certain defeat. They were gluttons for punishment. They didn't know when they were beaten. That was where they didn't run true to ... their past form and how they were able to snatch the game out of the fire."[3]

If America was in the midst of a change in era as the new decade dawned, the Washington Senators franchise was in the process of a dramatic alteration, as well. Previously, Clark Griffith had owned nearly three thousand shares of the organization, about fifteen percent. Between the 1919 and 1920 seasons, Griffith and William Miller Richardson, a Philadelphia businessman who specialized in grain dealing and exporting, put up $400,000 for fourteen thousand more shares. Griffith and his partner were now the majority owners of the Senators. As the team president, Griffith now controlled both the on-field and the business-side operations of the franchise, with Richardson serving in the role of vice president.[4]

The Senators really did get off to a promising start that lasted into July — on the fifth of that month, they were seven games above .500 at 36–29 after winning three straight over the Yankees.[5] Rice struggled to start the season, with his batting average dropping to .239 during the first week of May. He began to put it together in late May, however, collecting three hits in a 17–8 bludgeoning of the St. Louis Browns then, three days later, going 4-for-4 in a loss against the White Sox that increased his average to a much more Rice-like .316.[6]

Rice helped key a seven-game winning streak in June that improved the team's record to 32–28 by month's end.[7] During a modest ten-game hitting streak, he batted .474 (18-for-38) and raised his season average to .343.[8] On the last day of the month, a double header at Boston, Rice enjoyed one of his finest offensive afternoons. In the course of the two-game split, he collected six hits in nine at-bats. He also stole four bases, including home.[9] Rice was on his way to a league-leading sixty-three steals, a marked improvement over the twenty-six he had swiped the season before.[10]

Though Rice had shown promise in his previous two full seasons, the 1920 campaign was a breakthrough for him. Rice turned 30 years old two months before the season began, but played like a man entering the physical prime of his mid-twenties. He had 211 hits, the first of six times he'd reach the magic two hundred–hit mark during his career. Not that Rice was any kind of free swinger before, but he was getting the bat on the ball even more in 1920, striking out just twenty-six times in 624 at-bats. And he was durable, leading the team with 153 games played. In all three of Rice's full seasons as an outfielder, in fact, he had led Washington in games played.

He also, once again, managed to finish among the top ten in the American League in hitting. Curiously, Rice's .338 final mark put him eighth in the league — in 1917, he had finished eighth, as well, but batted just .302. It seemed that Rice wasn't the only American Leaguer in 1920 who was improving his hitting, however. (Lagging a little behind, the National League saw Brooklyn's Ed Konetchy finished eighth in that league with a much more modest .308 mark.)[11] In a year and a league in which offense increased so dramatically, Rice managed to stay in the top five of the American League in batting average for most of the summer. Well into August, the newspaper listings of the American League top five in hitting read the same almost every day — Tris Speaker, followed by George Sisler, then Joe Jackson, Babe Ruth and Rice. The first four spent a lot of the season flirting with the .400 mark.[12] Rice couldn't seem to surpass his high-water mark of .370, a mark he actually reached as late as August 1 after a 4-for-5 game at Cleveland.[13]

August, however, would be kind neither to Rice nor the Senators.

After battling to stay in the race for a first-division finish for the season's first four months, Washington began to slide horribly during August. It started inconspicuously enough, with a 2–1 loss to the St. Louis Browns and the red-hot, soon-to-be batting champion Sisler on August 5. Rice went 0-for-3 in the game.[14] By the time the Senators won again, on the 15th against the Yankees, they had lost ten straight games and fallen to thirteen games below .500. Seven of the losses were by just one run, including four in a row to the White Sox.[15] From August 1 to the end of the ten-game slide, Rice's batting average plummeted twenty points. During the course of those two weeks, he had batted .119.[16]

It would have been impossible to see such a slump coming. Rice put together a twenty-nine-game hitting streak during June and July — it ended nobly when he elected to sacrifice Clyde Milan to second in the eighth inning of a tight game with the White Sox (the Senators lost anyway).[17] In the first game of a July 29 double header, in the eleventh inning of a tight pitcher's duel, Rice lined a rare home run into the right-field bleachers at Detroit that gave Washington a 2–1 victory.[18]

There were other memorable personal moments for Rice throughout the season. On June 26, Rice collected the 500th hit of his career. The fact was noted by the local press, curiously so since years later, fatefully, no one would seem to notice when he moved to the brink of 3,000 career hits.[19] And his fielding prowess in the outfield was beginning to draw some attention, as well. A newspaper account of the team's July 25 game against the Philadelphia Athletics, a 4–3 Washington victory, noted "another one of his brilliant catches."[20] In late August, he made a breath-taking one-handed catch in the deepest part of center field in Washington to rob Chicago's Eddie Collins of an extra-base hit.[21]

Indicative of what a humbling game baseball can be, the *Washington Post* described Rice's attempt two days later to haul in a ball hit by Ty Cobb: "Rice looked like a bush leaguer going after Cobb's smash…. The lightning Griff outfielder went into about four hysterics before he finally stumbled to his knees and let Cobb's drive go for a triple."[22]

As a team, the Senators finished 68–84 in 1920, in sixth place. It was a slight improvement over the shortened season before, but with Walter Johnson spending most of the summer battling an injury, the last couple of months of the 1920 season were an exercise in wondering what might have been after a solid beginning. The highlights of the season included Rice's long hitting streak, along with a Johnson no-hitter on July 1.[23] But Rice had been working on more than just a .338 batting average during the summer of 1920.[24] On October 23, he married Washingtonian Edith Owens in Alexandria, Virginia. To call it a small ceremony would be vastly overstating the nature of the event.

The nuptials occurred at 1:30 in the afternoon at the M.E. Church South, presided over by Rev. Dr. E.V. Regester, the congregation's pastor. There were exactly two people in attendance outside of Rice, his bride and their officiant. One was Kittie Biddle, presumably a close friend of relative of the bride, the other former Alexandria Mayor Thomas A. Fisher. Fisher had known about Rice's intentions for all of a week, and Rice made him promise to keep it a secret until after the wedding.[25]

Like the bestowing of his nickname of "Sam" at the beginning of his major league career, the marital status of Sam Rice is an aspect of his life that has strayed a few shades away from the truth over the decades since his death. In the most-read account of his life, a *Sports Illustrated* article from 1992, Rice's later marriage to the former Mary Kendall when he was thirty-nine years old was reported to be his first and only marriage since the one to Beulah Stam had ended in tragedy in Donovan, Illinois. That is the version that is typically repeated in subsequent tellings of the Rice story (including, admittedly, one that I wrote for *The Times of Northwest Indiana* in 2004, the story that led me to chasing down Rice's whole life story). It makes for a good tale, but it's simply untrue. It is also important to note here that we have no way of knowing what, if anything, Rice shared with Edith about his former life, though it's not a long logical leap to guess that she was aware of his past. Edith was an Indiana girl, and the pair would spend their first few winters back in the Indiana-Illinois area. Perhaps it would not have been impossible for Rice to keep that part of his past secret from his new bride, but it sure would have been unlikely. The fact that they were married with a such a minimalist ceremony, shrouded in tremendous secrecy, only adds to the certainty that Edith Owens would have known that her husband had been married previously.

"She traveled with him all those years, from what I heard," recalls Rice's old friend and broker Bill Birely. "A lot of ball players, like Babe Ruth, were out on the loose. A lot of them didn't take their wives. I won't say she went on all the trips, but she traveled with him a long time and was right with him when he was playing."[26]

* * *

In December of 1920, American League officials convened for their annual meetings in New York City, and on the seventeenth of the month rumors of a pending trade between the Philadelphia Athletics and the Senators grew to a boil. Griffith supposedly had offered Philadelphia manager and team president Connie Mack both Rice and Joe Judge in exchange for Athletics third baseman Joe Dugan, outfielder Tilly Walker and pitcher Scott Perry. It was, reportedly, a pure baseball trade, with no cash involved.[27]

The trade proposal would have been designed to help two second-division teams bolster glaring weaknesses. The 106-loss Athletics' .252 team batting average was by far the worst in the American League, and their 558 runs scored were nearly one hundred less than the second-worst offensive team, Detroit. Meanwhile the Senators had posted a .291 average as a team in 1920, good for fourth in the hard-hitting American League. So in offering Judge (.333) and Rice (.338), Griffith likely felt he was dealing from a position of strength.

Washington's pitching was in need of serious reinforcement, though. Johnson, for one of the first times in his career, was a question mark after a sore arm limited him to an 8–10 record and just $143\tfrac{2}{3}$ innings. His ERA of 3.13, though not bad considering the hitting renaissance going on in the American League that season, was gaudy when compared to his first thirteen seasons. In eleven of those, Johnson had posted a sub-2.00 ERA.

The Senators' other pitchers hadn't stepped up during Johnson's down year, and the result was a 4.17 team ERA that ranked dead last in the American League. That must have come as quite a shock to the system of a manager whose teams had posted the top ERA in the league three times under his direction, in 1912, 1915 and 1917, and ranked third just the year before with a 3.01 mark.

Losing Rice in the outfield would hurt, of course, but his potential replacement Tilly Walker had hit seventeen home runs in 1920. Dugan was an up-and-comer who would help the infield recover from the exit of Judge. Plus, second baseman Bucky Harris had just hit .300 as a rookie and the twenty-three-year-old looked like a budding star at the plate.[28]

For whatever reason, the trade was never completed. Upon returning to New York, Griffith swore it was never on the table at all. He did, however, say that New York Yankees manager Miller Huggins had made a run at Rice, offering cash for him and being turned down.[29] The offer would have made sense from the Yankees' standpoint. Huggins' team had won 95 games and finished three games out of first place after a remarkable three-way pennant race between the Yankees, Indians and White Sox, won by Cleveland.[30] The team's two outfielders besides Ruth, Ping Bodie and Duffy Lewis, were beginning to age a little bit, and didn't quite hit to the new 1920 standards set by the Cleveland pennant-winning outfield of player-manager Tris Speaker (.388 with a .483 on-base percentage), Elmer Smith (.316, 103 RBIs) and the combination of Charlie Jamieson (.319 in 108 games) and Joe Evans (.349 in fifty-six games). With hard-hitting youngster Bob Meusel scheduled to arrive in

New York in 1921, Rice would have been the final piece of a potentially dominant outfield.[31]

Whether Griffith fielded one, both or none of the trade propositions is, as it is with a lot of these kinds of offseason trade rumors, basically lost to history. But it's not too much of a stretch to imagine that he would have pitched the Rice-to-Philadelphia trade, which certainly did make sense for both languishing teams. Then when it both went public and fell through, he either fabricated the Huggins' inquiry all together, exaggerated its seriousness or, cognizant of the potentially bruised ego of one of his organization's star players, made a conscious effort to get the Huggins offer and subsequent rejection into the headlines as soon as possible.

As far as Griffith's workload goes, December 1920 was no aberration. For years, since he took over as Washington's manager in 1912, Griffith had been one of the busiest men in baseball. He now occupied the supreme seat in the organization's front office, made all decisions in molding his roster, and, of course, handled the grueling day-to-day duties as the Senators' field manager. After the 1920 season, after thirty-five overall seasons in a baseball uniform, including a total of twenty seasons as a manager and 1,491 victories, the only manager Rice had played for as a big leaguer decided to step away from that role and concentrate on his team president duties. Griffith would never return to the dugout, and the American League pennant he won with the 1901 White Sox, his first year of managing, remains the only league title he ever won.

When Griffith had taken over the Senators nine years earlier, he had injected the previously moribund franchise with instant life, remaking the roster and famously turning a sixth-place club into one that reached the ninety-victory mark two straight seasons.

But fighting history is a tough battle, and over Griffith's last several years in the dugout, the Senators slipped back into their former losing ways. They finished under .500 in four of his last five seasons, though Griffith was still able to retire from managing with a 693–646 (.518) mark with the franchise. Considering that he would make his biggest and most glorious impact while solely concentrating on player procurement, it was probably the right move, tough as it may have been for him.

As his replacement, Griffith handpicked his team captain of the last six seasons, shortstop George McBride.

Griffith had left the team in McBride's command several times over the previous seasons, mostly while Griffith himself was off somewhere to scout a prospect.

"McBride's the boss when I'm away," Griffith used to tell his team, "and I want you to know it. If he fines anybody, bear in mind I'll double it when I get back."

Scouting was becoming so vital, and so time-consuming, it would have probably been nearly impossible for Griffith to try to tinker his roster back to contending shape had he continued to try to occupy both roles.[32]

The manager was new, but Rice occupied the same number three slot in the Washington batting order when the 1921 season began. And he immediately showed he deserved it.

Unlike 1920, when Rice stumbled to a slow start at the plate before spending most of the middle of the summer in the comfort of a scorching hot streak, Rice started hitting on opening day in 1921 and carried it through most of the first month. He had three hits on opening day against the Red Sox, then a few days later contributed four hits to a 14–6 drubbing of the Athletics. Through six games, including four Washington victories, Rice was batting a torrid .520 (13-for-25). He wasn't done, either, as far as April went.[33]

"They call him 'Man o' War' at the Polo Grounds, and rate him second to their own Bambino Ruth," the *Post* gushed about Rice after one of the best performances of his young career at New York on April 26.

Rice collected four more hits in the game, including a two-run home run in the sixth inning that turned a 4–3 Washington deficit into a 5–4 lead that would stand as the final score. But it only stood as the final because two innings later, Rice raced deep into center field to rob New York's Wally Pipp of a potential game-turning extra-base hit. The home run was Rice's second in just over a week — however, any thoughts that he had found the power stroke that a lot of the rest of American League had discovered the summer before would have been premature.[34]

So would have been any thoughts that Washington, with a record of 9–3 after that fourth consecutive defeat of the Yankees, would challenge the New York club for the American League pennant that season. After those four, capped by Rice's tremendous day, the Yankees went 13–4 against the Senators the rest of the way. They swept six straight from Washington in late July and early August, most of them by extremely ugly margins, as Huggins' squad slugged its way to the first pennant in franchise history (it would win six over the next eight seasons).[35]

While the Yankees bludgeoned teams with an out-of-sight 134 home runs, the Senators, under their new manager McBride, continued to display the kind of hustle Griffith had instilled from the beginning of his involvement with the club.[36] Rice, in one notable manifestation of that desire, scored from second base on a Patsy Gharrity sacrifice fly in a June game against Cleveland. Tris Speaker gathered the ball in with his back facing the infield deep in center field at Washington. Thinking there were two outs in the eighth inning of a game the Senators had long since put to bed, Speaker didn't hurry at all to get the ball back in. Rice, noting this immediately, took off from second "like a shot" and scored the tenth run of a 10–3 Senators' blowout. Such a move today, showing up a fellow future Hall of Famer and the defending world champions, would probably earn a player a nice hard fastball to the rib cage in his next plate appearance against a team — or at the very least some hall of fame squawking between the two dugouts.[37]

Not only did the Indians not drill Rice the following afternoon, they let him go 5-for-5 with a pair of doubles and his third home run of the season, though the Senators lost the game 10–6.[38]

By mid–July, the Senators looked to be dangerously close to another tumble into the deep second division, a disappointing possibility to face after they had played good baseball for so long under McBride. A five-game losing streak dropped them to 47–48, the first time they found themselves on the wrong side of .500 in nearly two months.[39] Rice's second five-hit game of the season would help his team quickly get things moving in a favorable direction again, however.

Plenty of Washington batters hit well the afternoon of July 24, a 14–6 victory over Detroit that snapped the five-game skid (the Senators had scored two runs or less in four of those five defeats). But none better than Rice. His five-hit day included a triple, along with a pair of doubles and a pair of singles. The season before, the two-week freefall of Rice's batting average was a major contributing factor to the ten-game losing streak that secured the team's place near the bottom of the American League standings. In 1921, his big game against the Tigers seemed to get the Senators headed in the right direction again. Rice's performance, it seemed, acted as a pretty good indicator of how his team would fare. The turnaround was immediate.[40]

Washington won eleven in succession.[41] Even when Rice didn't hit, which wasn't very often, the morning paper was usually filled with raves about his glovework in the outfield. Almost every day he was either tracking down a ball in deep, deep center field, or he was connecting on relay throws to cut down important runs trying to score. In a 5–4 victory over the Tigers, number eight in a row, Rice drove in Milan with an eighth-inning single to snap a 4–4 tie.[42] And since it was his big day that helped pull his team out of the midseason doldrums nearly two weeks prior, it was only appropriate that Rice should come up big in the eleventh and final victory of the streak — he had two run-scoring doubles to go along with an RBI single in a 4–1 defeat of American League front-running Cleveland.

"Doff your hats to our own 'Man o' War,'" the *Post* reported the next morning. "He jumped out of his batting slump yesterday at (Clark) Griffith's ball orchard just in time to send Tris Speaker and his skidding Indians to their third defeat of the series."[43]

The *Post* must have had a pretty liberal definition of a batting slump —

Rice hit .382 (16-for-42) during the winning streak. The hot stretch firmly entrenched the Senators into third place in the American League and brought them within seven games of first place.[44]

Fun as it was, the stretch had a sad side note. Manager McBride was hitting infield practice before one of the games when he was nailed in the side of the head by a ball thrown by Washington outfielder Earl Smith. McBride never saw it coming. What appeared at first to be a minor concussion grew more serious as complications developed. Eventually McBride returned to manage the rest of the season, but the injury ultimately would force another shakeup in the Washington dugout, where leadership had previously been stable for so long under Griffith.[45]

Rice, so reliable the previous two seasons, had an injury to deal with in 1921, as well, though not comparable to the frightening situation his manager faced. When the Senators traveled to Richmond, Virginia, on August 12 for an exhibition game against that city's Virginia League team, Rice remained home nursing a sprained ankle he suffered in the preceding series against the Red Sox.[46] He returned in a pinch-hitter role on August 26, then returned to the lineup the following day in right field instead of his customary center field. He also took up the cleanup role in the lineup. Rice would soon return to right field, though the number four spot in the batting order belonged to him for the rest of the season.[47]

For the most part, the team had performed all right in Rice's absence, but lost ten games in a row upon his return to the active roster. Hopes of a third-place finish were dashed, but the up-and-down Senators ended the season on a high note — they won eleven of their last twelve games to finish with an 80–73 record.[48] That was good for fourth place, just one-half game behind third-place St. Louis.[49]

Rice didn't spend the summer of 1921 competing among some of the game's biggest names atop the American League batting leaders list like he did the year before, but by the time it was all said and done, his 1921 season was remarkably similar statistically to the season before. For example he scored eighty-three runs, identical to his 1920 total. And he drove in seventy-nine runs — just one less than he had the season before, despite missing eleven games battling the ankle sprain. Rice hit thirty-nine doubles and followed up his .338 average in 1920 with a .330 average in '21. After two straight years among the top ten hitters in the league, he slipped just out of the running — Chicago's Eddie Collins was tenth in the American League with a .337 mark.

Just three years earlier, a .296 average earned "Smokey" Joe Wood, a pitcher trying to make the conversion to everyday player, a spot in the top ten. Obviously things had changed quickly in the American League. If 1920 could be dismissed as a one-year aberration, 1921 brought the conspiracy theorists forward in full force.[50]

6

BUSH LEAGUE MANAGER

There is speculation to this day, and a hearty historical debate, over whether the baseballs of the 1920s, like the players of the 1990s, were indeed "juiced." The existence of a "rabbit ball," as it was often referred to at that time and in the many years since, would offer the simplest explanation for the tremendous shift in the balance of power to hitters starting almost precisely in 1920. It is an easy-to-grasp, tightly wound, horsehide covered and hand-stitched unified theory that would spare people the effort of examining the complexities of an array of factors.

And, if we are to believe a sound base of documentation, it's probably not true.

The *Post* decided to rule on the existence of a livelier baseball after a June 1921 thrashing of the home team at the hands of the Yankees—"The Manhattan tribe proved conclusively that the American League is using a 'rabbit ball,'" it reported that day (the same day of a 4-for-4 Rice "batting rampage").[1]

F.C. Lane, the famed writer for *Baseball Magazine*, directly asked National League president John Heydler whether the balls were intentionally livelier than they had been toward the tail end of the previous decade.

"At no time have the club owners ordered the manufacturer to make the ball livelier," Heydler answered.

And if that answer seemed like a pass-the-buck attempt on Heydler's part to shift the question to the manufacturers themselves, it is important to note that the suppliers of the baseballs used in big league games of the 1920s showed little to no resistance in inviting journalists and other curious investigators of the day to tour their facilities and witness quality control test after quality control test.

An earlier production alteration, the introduction of a cork center to replace the old India rubber cores, fueled an offensive uptick in 1911. In the years that followed, pitchers eventually caught up and the balance stabilized over the rest of the 1910s. During the period, Reach was the official manufacturer of balls for the National League while Spalding supplied the American League's balls. In actuality, while Spalding ran the business end of its sporting good operations, it actually outsourced its manufacturing to Reach, a secret Spalding subsidiary. That dirty little secret remained buried deep for many decades. In fact, to this day, some baseball historians will recite with authority the "fact" that American League balls became livelier one season before National League balls did. Both league's balls were produced in the same Philadelphia plant.

Early on in the speculation over a possible "rabbit ball," apparently mystified American League president Ban Johnson theorized that better materials were available, now that the war was over. Specifically, he mentioned Australian wool. Fans and writers saw this as a clumsy attempt at a cover-up, and "Australian wool" jokes began making their way into newspaper and magazine copy for years to come.

In its own 1922 annual baseball guide, the Reach company ran a full-page advertisement that read, "There has been no change in the construction of the cork center ball since we introduced it in 1910." Chicago-based reporter Edward Burns visited the Reach factory in 1929, witnessing resiliency tests that seemed to indicate no foul play. Balls were dropped from a certain height. To meet quality control standards, which were the same as they always were, they were required to bounce back precisely three feet, eight inches. Twelve baseballs did just that.

Among other entities that tested batches of 1920s baseballs were the magazines *Popular Mechanics* and *Scientific American*, as well as the U.S. Bureau of Standards, which concluded that a selection of 1920 Babe Ruth home run balls were to the same specifications as balls it had tested when seeking best buys in 1917 for soldiers' wartime recreation.

People inherently distrusted the men involved in any sort of scientific testing, viewing them as mere co-conspirators who could easily manipulate the data to serve their purposes—or out-and-out lie about it. One of Rice's teammates, however, a pitcher named Vean Gregg, helped throw cold water on the idea, as well. Gregg hadn't pitched since 1918 when he returned to baseball to pitch for the Senators in 1925. *Baseball Magazine's* G.H. Darcy saw Gregg as the perfect player to confirm whether the ball was livelier than when he had last thrown one. But Gregg said he noticed no difference.

So if there wasn't a "rabbit ball" helping out hitters, where was all the offense coming from?

For one thing, much like the chemically enhanced players of the '90s, though much more honorably, players during the '20s were increasing in physical size, yet another quality embodied by the barrell-torsoed Ruth.

The phasing out of the spitball was likely another huge factor in the offensive explosion, perhaps the biggest one of all. Before 1920, pitchers were permitted to sop whatever tickled their fancy onto the ball. The pitcher's mound became a virtual combination amateur physics and chemistry laboratory, with hurlers doctoring balls with everything from mud to saliva to tobacco to chewing gum. All with both leagues' blessings. Pitchers who were the best at loading up the baseball — Jack Chesbro went from twenty-one to forty-one victories in just one season after discovering its merits — could make the ball take paths to the plate that would challenge the most skilled modern-day NASCAR road course racers. But even beyond that, this was an age when one baseball was expected to make it through an entire contest. If there were "dead balls" during the so-called "Dead Ball Era," they probably got that way because they were too waterlogged by the late innings to lift out of the infield.

In 1920, baseball's powers that be issued a one-year, experimental ban on the spitter. Some specialists were grandfathered in. Then during the season, Cleveland shortstop Ray Chapman was killed by a pitched ball, a ball that was so darkened by New York spitballer Carl Mays that Chapman didn't attempt to move from its path until it crashed into his temple. Now it appeared that the spitball wasn't just a detriment to offense but could be dangerous and, aside from the grandfathered in pitchers, the ban on the technique was made permanent beginning the next season.[2]

* * *

Though Rice's 1921 season was another success at the plate, he did see a huge dropoff in one part of his game — stolen bases. After leading the American League with sixty-three steals in 1920, Rice stole just twenty-six bases the following season, fourth in the league. George Sisler actually led the American League with just thirty-five stolen bases — in 1917, Rice's first season as a full-time outfielder, six American Leaguers had stolen at least that many.

Juiced ball or not, the game was definitely changing.

Base-stealing had been losing popularity even before the live-ball era made it a graver risk for a manager to risk outs on the bases. In 1911, the New York Giants had stolen 347 bases as a team. By 1920, the Giants total was down to 131. The drastic drop was similarly realized by almost every team in both major leagues. Only the Pittsburgh Pirates ran more than they did at the beginning of the previous decade, an anomaly caused by the facts that the team was one of baseball's slowest in 1911 and the team had added Max Carey in the time since. By the late 1910s the Senators didn't run as often as they did before, either, but they still were running more than most teams. Clark Griffith was the reason.[3]

He was, of course, lucky enough to have Rice and Clyde Milan at his disposal. But Griffith wasn't about to let his two race horses take all of the credit for their own prowess on the base paths.

"The manager has greater control over base stealing than over any other department of the game," Griffith said. "He cannot make his men hit safely when he wants them to nor can he make them catch difficult groundballs. But he can, if he chooses, prevent their making any considerable showing as base stealers. And a good many managers do that very thing for they will and allow their men to steal half as often as they should."

Many decades later, the baseball thinker Bill James would more scientifically examine the relationship between the various components of offense and run-scoring. Base-stealing, an army of James disciples that call themselves "sabermetricians" accept as a general rule, only positively influences a lineup's ability to score runs when it is successful more than seventy percent of the time.

Of course, in the early 1920s Clark Griffith wasn't armed with the formulas and extrapolations that James would parlay into a career as a best-selling author beginning nearly sixty years later. But he believed he'd seen enough baseball to grasp when was a good time to run and when it might get a team into trouble.

Griffith was wary of generalizations. He had heard ad nauseum that trying to steal third was a risk not worth the reward, especially with the runner already in scoring position. But he felt that the element of surprise could make a steal of third a less risky gamble than an attempted steal of second.

Not that he was all for running all the time. Particularly, Griffith didn't want a greedy base thief to break up a hit parade by giving away an out on the base paths.

"I have a standing rule on my club that the base runner who tries to steal in such a case does so at his own risk," Griffith said. "If he gets away with it, well and good. But if he tries to steal and is thrown out, he can expect everything short of manslaughter to happen to him when he comes back to the bench."[4]

Baseball writers lamented the decline of base stealing, feeling that suddenly conservative managers were extracting much of the color and excitement out of the game. *Baseball Magazine's* F.C. Lane, for example, wrote: "The decline of the stolen base cannot fail to cause regret in anyone who has known baseball in former years. A certain system of play gradually develops, becomes crystallized and is accepted as the best possible system of play. If you seek for a snappier, brighter, more varied game of baseball, you will not find it in pitching nor infielding nor even in batting. The only hope for such a game is the stolen base."

Incredibly, Lane likened his nostalgia for the stolen base to others romanticizing about Native Americans, whose "vanishing before a superior race contributed greatly to the world's prosperity, and yet many romances have been written about the tragic life of the North American Indian."[5]

Rice blamed his fall-off in stolen bases to the trend of "freak deliveries" by pitchers. With the dead-ball era having just passed, pitchers of the early '20s were attempting to try whatever they could to regain their former competitive edge over the hitters in the game. Deception was a popular option, not just in the flight of the ball after it left the pitchers hand, but in his various machinations of his wind-up.

Rice had never been keen on "freak deliveries." He claimed that the Virginia League had been full of pitchers corkscrewing their bodies before the pitch, and said the gimmick wind-ups were the main reason that his batting performance in his two seasons in Petersburg wasn't noticeably better than the marks he had put up upon arriving in the American League with its superior pitching talent.

"They have no place in baseball," said Rice, not a surprising stance from a hitter.

But he wasn't the only one that felt that way. The leagues clamped down on the unorthodox wind-ups, as well.

According to Rice, the deliveries themselves weren't so much responsible for the stolen base drought as their impact on the pitcher's repertoire of pitches. As they are today, curveballs were the easiest pitch to steal on, because the ball took a split second longer to get to home plate. Plus, the catcher, busy concentrating on the ball's path to home, wasn't as able to catch the ball and throw it in a smooth motion to second or third base as he would be on a fastball. Those split seconds were valuable. But in 1921, said Rice, pitchers were throwing far less curveballs, relying more on their delivery deception to throw hitters off rhythm.

It's ironic that Rice was so put off by unorthodox pitchers, since he himself had an unorthodox style of stealing bases. Unlike most speedsters, who explode out of a crouch, Rice always found it easier to gain full speed from an upright position.

"That peculiarity," he said, "is an advantage in getting a quick start stealing bases."

It would be, with opponents less able to read his body language to discern Rice's intentions.[6]

Ultimately, most purists accepted the demise of the stolen base as a primary offensive weapon.

"Under conditions such as they are at present, where pitching is indifferent and almost every batter is a potential slugger, the home run is always a possibility," one such purist wrote. "And before this imminent prospect the manager is prone to throw into the discard such relatively feeble efforts as the stolen base.... Why should this base-runner risk getting caught at second when the next man up may knock out a two-bagger or a homer?"[7]

The home run's growing prominence in baseball mirrored the instant gratification and newfound bombast of the times. At the beginning of the decade, one household in three owned a car. By 1929, four out of five families owned a vehicle, with twenty-seven million of them on the road in the United States all told. Information was beginning to travel faster, as well. In fact, it would soon be instantaneous— in November of 1920, the month after the World Series concluded, Americans tuned into the nation's first commercial radio broadcast.[8]

With times changing like this, who had the patience to play for one run at a time?

* * *

After the 1921 season, the Rice-to-the-Yankees rumors began yet again. This time, writers had Rice heading to New York not for cash but for Yankees captain Roger Peckinpaugh. Supposedly, the plan was for Peckinpaugh to not only play shortstop for the Senators, but to take on the role of player-manager.

"There is absolutely nothing to it," Griffith said, calling the report "all bunk.... And I cannot figure where this absurd rumor started. I have not the slightest idea of letting Sam go, nor has Peckinpaugh's name even been thought of as a possible successor to McBride."[9]

A couple weeks later, another Senators-Yankees trade rumor broke out— this one had Stanley Harris going to the Yankees in exchange for J. Franklin Baker and Mike McNally. The rumor came with the standard Griffith vehement denial, and the *Post*, in print, accused its counterparts in the New York media for making up trade rumors "with the sole object of getting players disgruntled." The paper reminded readers that "the same practices were indulged in early last season in regard to Sam Rice," and claimed no one in the Yankees hierarchy entertained any realistic hope of prying Rice for the Senators.[10] Of course, that was a bit of revisionist history, since it had been Griffith himself who had floated the post–1921 Rice-to-New York rumor, presumably to reingratiate himself to the star after his unsuccessful efforts to trade him to Philadelphia went public.

It soon turned out that the Peckinpaugh rumors must not have been so silly after all— the day after the *Post* ranted about the rumor-mongering New York sports writers, it carried a story that a trade for the shortstop had essentially been agreed upon. Between the time of the first Peckingpaugh trade rumor in mid–December and the actual acquisition of him now right before New

Year's, Peckinpaugh had been traded from the Yankees to Boston. With Frank O'Rourke batting just .234 as the Senators' shortstop in the 1921 season, Griffith needed to acquire a shortstop who could hit in the new offense-minded American League. Peckinpaugh fit the mold, and Boston owner Frazee had him on the trading block. But Frazee had faced so much heat for recent sales of players that he was gun shy about doing so again, even with a player the Red Sox had had under contract for only about two weeks. Griffith had nothing Frazee was willing to give up for Peckinpaugh, but was able to engineer a three-team trade, bringing Philadelphia into the fold, as well. So he had his shortstop.[11]

The constant rumors about a possible Rice trade — yet another one had him headed to Boston[12] — must have worried Washington fans, especially since fellow fan favorites Joe Judge and Bucky Harris also frequently turned up in the news as possible Griffith trade bait. The *Post* pointed out that Judge and Rice had purchased homes in the D.C. area, so any trade would presumably be against their wishes. In the same article, a not-so-subtle plea was sent Griffith's way to hold onto a core of players that the city had grown attached to.

Said the paper, "If ever five ball players have ingratiated themselves any more into the hearts of Washington fans — the most fickle and exacting collection in any part of the universe — than Johnson, Milan, Judge, Rice and Harris, then memory fails to recall them."[13]

Also, sadly in the aftermath of the 1920 season, manager George McBride's head injury proved to be too much for him to continue in that demanding role. Initially, the blow had bedridden McBride for nine days as he battled both a concussion and partial paralysis of the left side of his face, and his return to the dugout occurred against the wishes of both his doctors and those close to him. McBride suffered dizzy spells as the season went on, and lost a noticeable amount of weight. He stubbornly stuck it out, though. At the time of the announcement, early December of 1921, Griffith called McBride's resignation temporary.[14] But he would neither manage nor play in another major league game. One must figure that decision was for the best — McBride died in 1973, a few months short of his ninety-third birthday.[15]

* * *

After stringing together three standout seasons, Rice was looking to be rewarded prior to the 1922 campaign. With a new home and a new bride, he was itching to cash in on his skills and consistency and earn some financial stability. Rice visited Griffith the morning of January 23, and left after a "word battle lasing more than an hour" without signing a deal for the coming season. Judge wanted more in his paycheck, as well — Griffith met with him about the same subject the following morning.[16]

The president worked quick to reach a deal with his star outfielder — Rice signed two days later.[17]

Even early on, there were signs that Rice might not be in shape to put up the kind of season Washington fans had grown accustomed to. After spending much of the winter back home hunting in Indiana, he was a few pounds overweight when he showed up to negotiate his contract. By the time he returned again in March for spring training, Rice was still carrying a few extra pounds (to his credit, he did arrive a week before he was required).[18]

Rice had encountered difficulty picking up ground balls to the outfield in the past, but new Washington manager Clyde Milan thought his star was a little bit too nonchalant for his taste when a ball rolled through his legs during a late March relay throw drill, singling the star out in the newspapers.[19]

Rice wasn't the only Washington star who sent up red flags about the upcoming season. Right around Christmas, Walter Johnson's two-year-old daughter Elinor died of influenza.[20]

As opening day approached, though, any such signs were widely disregarded and the arrival of the 1922 season was greeted with tremendous excitement in Washington.

"Never in the history of the game in Washington has the club been so highly touted as having a chance at capturing the flag," the *Post* reported.[21]

The dramatic improvement of the team from 1920 to '21, along with the way the Senators closed the previous season, had fans abuzz about the possibilities in 1922. And they had good reasons to like the roster Griffith had assembled for the '22 season. Personal tragedy aside, after his injury-riddled 1920 campaign, Johnson had turned in a healthy 1921 season, making thirty-two starts and leading the American League in strikeouts as he had done in eight straight seasons before the disaster the season before. Beyond that, Leon "Goose" Goslin, who Griffith had signed from the South Atlantic League the season before, had been a spring training sensation, Roger Peckinpaugh was now in the fold and Johnson had a reliable sidekick in the rotation — George Mogridge had emerged from obscurity in New York to become an eighteen-game winner in 1921, his first season in Washington.[22]

There was no reason to believe, at least as far as the Washington public went, that the Senators weren't primed to join the American League's elite teams in 1922.

Baseball being baseball, they of course fell flat on their faces.

Glad to finally see him in uniform after the second straight winter of trade rumors, Washington fans greeted Rice with a loud ovation when he came to the plate on opening day against the Yankees. In hindsight, they may have wished to hold that applause.

Rice's fielding difficulties may have been good for a little laugh during spring training, but when the bad habit of not getting down on base hits to the outfield cost the Senators runs in the regular season, it wasn't so funny any more. Rice made a key error on such a chance in an early-season loss to the Yankees, Washington's fifth consecutive defeat and their eighth in nine games on the young season. The *Post*, begging for Griffith to retain Rice just months before, blasted him for the gaffe.

"It was none other than Sammy Rice, the outfielding star of the troupe," Senators beat writer John A. Dugan reported, "who pulled what is becoming an almost daily stunt with him of allowing a ball to roll through his legs."[23]

After his rough winter, Johnson wasn't ready to begin the season at full strength, and he didn't join the rotation full-time until May 10. By that time, Washington was already buried in the American League standings with an 8–16 record.[24]

The '22 season was a struggle. Even when things went well, they were overshadowed. During a May series against the Yankees, Rice reached base in eight consecutive plate appearances, including two home runs (one inside-the-park). But even the hometown *Washington Post* gave top billing in the next morning's paper to Babe Ruth's temper tantrum in the game that drew a threat of suspension from the league. With the Yankees coming to town the next afternoon, the Post argued vehemently that suspensions should be outlawed in baseball because they hurt fans who take great pains to attend ballgames (the suspension was lifted after just one game in favor of a $200 fine).[25]

By objective standards, Rice didn't have a terrible season at the plate in 1922, but it was certainly a step backward for him. His thirty-seven doubles and thirteen triples put him among the league leaders in both categories. And a year after being forced out of the lineup for a couple weeks with a nagging ankle sprain, Rice was back to playing in all 154 games—plus, in a league-leading 633 at-bats, he struck out just thirteen times. Among American League regulars, only Cleveland veteran Stuffy McGinnis, with a remarkable five strikeouts in 537 at-bats, whiffed less frequently. McGinnis, a man who would finish his career with three World Series rings, 2,405 hits and a career batting average of .307, wasn't horrible company to keep. But just two years earlier, Rice had spent the summer putting his name alongside guys like Ruth, Sisler and Jackson as one of the American League's top hitters.

Rice's .295 mark wasn't bad, especially since it was a steady .295, with few prolonged slumps or hot streaks throughout the course of the 1922 season. But it wasn't close to the pace he had set the previous two years. And he was playing in a league in which Ty Cobb batted .401, yet still failed to win his thirteenth batting title. That honor went to Sisler, who hit .420.[26]

In August, Milan shuffled his batting lineup, moving Rice from the third spot to the leadoff spot because he wasn't getting the job done with men on base.[27] Not that anybody else on the team was, either—the Senators finished second-to-last in the American League in both batting average (.268) and runs scored. After a promising 1921 campaign that had Washington fans dreaming of a pennant, the 1922 team plummeted to a 69–85 mark and sixth-place finish, twenty-five games behind the Yankees, who battled it out with the Browns for the American League crown.[28]

Late in the lost season, Griffith voiced public support for his manager, trying to put down rumors that he was pursuing former Boston Braves manager George Stallings who had won the 1914 World Series with a team that finished in fifth place just the season before.[29]

"I'm not contemplating any changes in the management of the club for next season," Griffith said in September, when the buzzards began circling in full force. "Washington fandom may think that Milan has made mistakes, but I am satisfied with his work. He was working under strenuous conditions this season.... Milan will pilot our club next season."[30]

As modern fans are well aware, such a show of public support is often the kiss of death for a manager. Milan certainly was working under strenuous conditions— too strenuous for his own good. The stress of managing an underachieving club triggered a worsening of stomach problems that had beset Milan for years.[31] In January, he announced that he was leaving the organization to take a minor-league managing job in Minnesota.[32]

In actuality, Griffith had made the move himself behind the scenes, then waited for Milan to secure another position somewhere before making it public that he was searching for a new manager. Griffith wanted someone more aggressive to lead the 1923 team.[33]

"He was too good a fellow to manage a ballclub," Walter Johnson said. "The fellows took advantage of his good nature and that hurt."[34]

* * *

The Senators, stable for so many years with Griffith in charge, were again seeking a manager. Griffith replaced Milan by promoting back-up shortstop Donnie Bush, a hell-raiser on the base paths in his days with the Detroit Tigers.[35] Bush fit the profile of a more aggressive manager that Griffith was looking for— Bush had nine times finished in the top ten in the American League in stolen bases, swiping a career-high fifty-three in 1919 as a brash twenty-one-year-old. That was Bush's first year in the big leagues, and he apparently was rearing to let the league know he had arrived. He would remain a vital part of the Detroit lineup until 1921, when Griffith acquired him toward the end of the year.[36] Dealing with blurred vision that were causing his baseball skills to rapidly deteriorate, Bush's best days a player were behind him. But Griffith thought his fighting, competitive spirit would serve the team well.[37]

Like Rice, Bush was an Indiana native, from Indianapolis. And Indianapolis is where he received his professional start, starring on a farm team there at a very young age before being snapped up by Detroit.

When he was hired as Washington's manager, an acquaintance from Bush's early days in the pro game, former Boston and New York pitcher Marty McHale, assured Washington fans they were getting a fine man to lead the team to the next level.

"Donie Bush has been a fixture in the American League because he combines the majority of essentials that are necessary to complete a star's equipment," he said. "He has brains, ability, speed, a sense of appreciation and cooperation and above all else he is game."[38]

Brains? Check. Ability? Absolutely. Speed? At least in his younger days. A sense of appreciation and cooperation? That last bit of praise would be severely put to the test during what would turn out to be Bush's very brief tenure with the Senators.

"When I make up my mind that a certain course is best for the team, I expect to have my orders carried out," Bush once said, "and my wishes respected. I am not going to be dictatorial, but I am going to be the boss—and there aren't going to be any others.

"I am interested only in the production of a winning ball team, and I want the perfect cooperation of every man on it."[39]

At the plate, Rice had a tremendous year in 1923. He batted .316, rebounding from the off year in 1922. He led the American League with eighteen triples and he stole twenty bases, the sixth consecutive season he had reached that mark (not counting the war-shortened 1918 campaign). Rice scored 117 runs, the first time he had scored more than one hundred in a season.[40]

But things were not exactly as they appeared. The Senators struggled on the field again, though they did show some improvement from the year before under Milan. Even that was misleading, however. Because the season was effectively over for the Senators by the end of July, as disastrous a stretch as a team or player, in this case Rice, can have.

A July 2 loss to the Yankees by a 13–1 score set the tone for the rest of the month. By the time the Cleveland Indians nipped Washington 3–2 on July 19, the team was 5–14 for the month and had fallen to 34–49 on the year.[41] Once again, a manager couldn't seem to guide an obviously talented collection of players to even the outer edges of a pennant race. The Senators won some games at the end of the month, but that was window dressing—under Bush, the groundwork for a disastrous campaign was being laid daily.[42]

Though it didn't keep him out very long, Rice had a frightening run-in with the right-field fence in St. Louis on July 11. He raced back on a long fly ball by Browns first baseman Dutch Schliebner. While the ball sailed over the fence, however, Rice collided with it. A nail in the fence dug a gash in his scalp and knocked him out cold. Obviously, a player who would sacrifice himself like that in a game that was already out of reach — the Browns won 10–4 — would likely gain the respect of his manager for his effort. Bush, however, didn't really see it that way.

In early September, Rice was suspended for insubordination. The trouble began when he and second baseman Bucky Harris argued over several short fly balls, which had been dropping between them at an unacceptable rate. Each blamed the other.[43]

But Bush screamed at Rice in front of the entire team, and Rice, usually a picture of calm, "lost all restraint and fired both verbal barrels back at his manager," as one Senators historian put it.[44]

Bush benched him. Griffith, for his part, was staying out of it, at least publicly. He said, "Bush is the manager of the (Senators) and the whole case rests in his hands. I do not believe, however, that Donie will keep Sam on the bench long. These little arguments are bound to come up in baseball from time to time and the chances are that the two will straighten things out between them when the team comes back here for its long home stay, which opens with the New York Yankees Saturday."[45]

The suspension lasted five days before Rice was finally reinstated by Bush. Though he backed his manager in the newspapers, behind closed doors there was no doubt whose side he was on in the dispute — Rice's. Rice returned for a game against the Yankees on September 8. The fans, holding no grudge against him, gave him a "rousing welcome."[46]

The stubborn dispute with Rice, along with the team's under whelming performance, sealed Bush's fate. After one season, he was fired.[47] The Senators went 75–78. They finished in fourth place, though that was misleading because they had spent most of the summer anchored in the American League's second division before winning some meaningless contests near the end of the season to move a half-game past St. Louis.[48] Bush hadn't inspired the club with his fierce competitiveness, as Griffith had hoped after installing him to replace the easy-going Milan. Instead, he had alienated many of them.

Bush had established a pattern for his managerial career. He had milked a few more wins out of the team, but at the price of harmony. A few years later, he would manage the Pittsburgh Pirates to the 1927 National League pennant. But the joyous occasion was marred by a public battle of wills with star outfielder Kiki Cuyler. Bush benched Cuyler for the entire World Series, which the Yankees swept. Before owner Barney Dreyfuss finally pulled the plug on Bush's act, he was forced to trade away Cuyler and shortstop Glenn Wright for less than market value because Bush undermined Pittsburgh's leverage with his petty feuds. The year after the 1927 Pittsburgh pennant was a disaster with the non-"dictatorial" Bush in charge.[49]

"There have been tales that some of them have had differences with me," he said during the course of a tense summer in the Steel City. "There have been no differences between me and my players."

The Sporting News begged to differ, reporting that though the Pirates hadn't staged an open "insurrection," there certainly was disagreement and frustration fomenting among the players about Bush's various questionable baseball maneuvers.[50]

Griffith didn't let it get to that point with Bush, sending him out of town before his abrasive personality could cause permanent damage to the Senators franchise. So once again, he began the offseason searching for a manager. As his first target, Griffith zeroed in on Chicago White Sox second baseman Eddie Collins, who had aspirations to be a manager but wasn't done playing, either.

The Washington Post called Collins the "fading king of the second basemen," which was somewhat of a misnomer. It was true that Collins would turn thirty-seven early in the season, but there wasn't any indication that his skills were diminishing. He batted .360 in 1923, his best mark since he batted .365 in 1911 with Philadelphia. He still had one of the sharpest batting eyes in the league. He stole forty-eight bases. Collins, who had led the league in games played six times, played in 145 of the White Sox's 154 games in 1923.

On November 1, the Senators and White Sox were reportedly close to a deal. Chicago wanted Rice and Bucky Harris. Griffith felt the price was too steep. Even though Collins wasn't showing signs of slowing down just yet, Griffith felt the drop-off was coming. Rice and Harris were both still in their twenties, and he expected long careers out of them.[51] The Washington owner countered Sox owner Charles Comiskey's terms with an offer of Harris and cash for Collins. He was willing to part with Harris, whom Collins would replace at second base anyway in a short-term upgrade, but wanted to hang onto Rice.

The talks cooled off for a few weeks, during which time Comiskey hired Frank Chance as his new manager. On December 11, Griffith met with Chance to resume the effort to bring Collins to Washington. Griffith offered Harris and Goose Goslin. Again, the White Sox demanded that Rice be part of the package, the conversations taking place at baseball's winter meetings at Chicago's Congress Hotel.[52] The meetings by nature have always stimulated trade talk and, in later years when they would become part of the game's landscape, free agent wheelings and dealings. It's an enticing atmosphere in which to pull the trigger on trades, to feel like you're improving your ballclub to keep up with the rest of the league. No one wants to appear stagnant while other organizations are boldly moving forward. Trades are never so tempting as they are at a table (or bar stool) at the winter meetings, not then and not now.

Nevertheless, yet again when it came to Rice, Griffith held his ground. A deal was never struck, and though Collins was openly on the market, the White

Sox simply demanded too much for him from every suitor. He would play three more years with Chicago, and wouldn't have to wait long to earn the managerial position he desired. He replaced Chance during the 1924 season, and also batted .349 and played in 152 games. It was the last time Collins would play that much, appearing in 118 games in 1925, 108 in '26 and then ninety-five in 1927, the year he left the White Sox for Connie Mack's Philadelphia Athletics, the place where he'd first made his name as a player. Though he would be used sparingly over the next three seasons, earning a combined forty-two at-bats, Collins days as a player were pretty much over (he never stopped hitting, however, batting .336 as a semi-regular for the '27 Athletics).

Collins managed just three seasons for the White Sox, never finishing better than fifth place.[53]

Unable to acquire his first choice to manage the ballclub, Griffith turned to Plan B: Stanley "Bucky" Harris.

7

STREAKING TO A PENNANT

After the tension he had dealt with playing for Bush in 1923, Rice seemed eager for an incident-free winter when he signed his contract without any degree of haggling for the following season. [1]

But yet again, Rice found himself in the middle of a mini-controversy, and this time he wasn't alone.

Golf had become a very popular recreational activity for Americans in the 1920s, particularly among ballplayers. Rice was certainly among those smitten by the game, a love affair that would long outlast his baseball career. And he was actually a very skilled player, perhaps the top golfer among all major leaguers, as a matter of fact.

By this time eschewing Illinois/Indiana and their rough winters, nevermind the constant reminders of his buried past, Rice had spent most of the winter of 1923 in Florida, taking advantage of the warm southern weather to work on his golf game during his down time. Reportedly, Rice was a good enough player to shoot even par.

"Rice, with a little luck, could enter the open golf championship and hold his own," the *Post* reported.

In reaching the level he had, Rice had battled a stigma that existed at the time that left-handed golfers were at a disadvantage and could never really reach top levels. Problematically for left-handed swingers like Rice, that idea had been endorsed by many teaching professionals, who had a difficult time applying their right-handed swing mechanics to lefties. Rice, who hadn't played the game in his youth but took it up after he reached the majors with the Senators, was fortunate enough to find a teacher in the D.C. area who held no prej-

Rice was off trying out for a low-level minor-league baseball team in Galesburg, Illinois, when six members of his family were killed in a horrendous storm. His father Charles would later also die from injuries suffered in the storm. (National Baseball Hall of Fame Library, Cooperstown, N.Y.)

udice toward left-handers. A Mr. Thorne, of the Town and Country golf club, shaped Rice into the golfer he had become as spring training 1924 dawned.[2]

But suddenly, it began to look like Rice wouldn't have much of a chance to apply the lessons he had absorbed, at least for the next few months.

A few baseball old-schoolers, led by Griffith and John McGraw, were opposed to players participating in the hobby during the baseball season. McGraw didn't even want his players to speak of golf once the baseball season began.

"On the diamond the players are prone to fight over their battles on the links," McGraw reportedly believed. "Too much thought and talk about golf are bad, and the only way to cut them out is to cut golf out."

McGraw was interested in writing a no-golf clause into his players' contracts.

"Golf is a great game and I'm for it," he explained. "But like everything good, it can be overdone. In fact, golf is too good, for it sometimes grips a ball player so tightly that he gives more attention to perfecting his mid-iron shots than he does to polishing off his batting style.

"The first-class baseball player must think, talk and eat baseball in addition to playing it, and I don't want any of my players sitting around and talking nothing but golf in the heat of a pennant race."

Some members of the press picked up the chorus, as well.

"There is a good deal of exertion involved in golf, let scoffers say what they wish," said one writer. "The average man at the conclusion of eighteen holes has had enough. He would have no desire to take part in a nine-inning ball game as a chaser."

Following the lead of Griffith and McGraw, Yankees manager Miller Huggins instituted a golf ban of his own a few weeks before the beginning of spring training.[4] Detroit manager Ty Cobb actually went as far as to confiscate the clubs of his golf-playing Tigers.[5] The reasoning given by the developing unified front was that golf, particularly when played on the morning before a baseball game, was an energy drain to players.

"In the long run," wrote one columnist, "he very possibly would be passing up some of the chances that he would otherwise go after and find that getting down to second was not as easy as it seemed on other days."[6]

This was the company line, at least, filtered nicely through the press by baseball's powers-that-be.

There seemed to be an ulterior motive, however, by these men who fancied themselves as the knights of the round table of their sport — protecting their grand old game from what they perceived as a gathering threat.

Tension between the two sports wasn't simply limited to baseball clubs' fears that star players would be affected in the field by too much time on the course. In fact, it's very probable that the stances of Griffith, Huggins and others was probably, at least in part, a sort of pre-emptive strike against a game that many in baseball feared was beginning to steal a piece of the national pastime's popularity.

For years, the arrival of baseball in the southern and western states in late winter and early spring had been a financial boon for small towns in those regions. But lately, promoters for professional golf tournaments had been approaching many of the same locales to pitch the idea of events in the out-of-the-way towns. This was enticing to the towns. They realized that hosting a baseball team in spring training gave locals entertainment for a few weeks, as well as the economic boost of hosting a franchise and its employees, along with their money, for that time. But while exhibition baseball might earn a town a mention in the newspapers of the team's home city, a high-profile professional golf tournament would likely earn publicity in almost every major newspaper in the country.[7] Golf and baseball had been competing for the sports fan's summer dollar for a while. Now they were becoming combatants for the February and March discretionary income of customers, as well. Without a doubt, baseball saw golf as a potential threat. Players like Rice, pawns in this little ongoing power play, were paying the price. There was no way that men like Griffith, Huggins and McGraw wanted their star players populating America's golf courses all summer long, cast in the role of extremely effective endorsers for a sport that was eating into baseball's popularity as a spectator sport.

As early as 1918, Philadelphia manager Connie Mack, in a conversation with golfer Jim Barnes, expressed concern that golf was threatening baseball's future popularity. What was developing, it appeared, was a battle for the hearts and minds of America's youth. What particularly concerned baseball was the lure of caddying. While summer days on baseball's sandlots provided boys with hours of entertainment, exercise and some memories to bore their own children with in years to come, working as a golf course caddy put real money in their pockets. Two of the nation's top golfers, Walter Hagen and Gene Sarazen, had been introduced to the game through caddying, and now were among the nation's most successful and well-paid sportsman.

One estimate placed the number of working caddies at the United States' approximately three thousand golf courses at about 150,000.[8]

Sports writers all over the country crunched various numbers, trying to quantify the popularity levels of the two sports.

"The world is in the grip of golf," wrote one big-city columnist. "It is obvious that it has become our national game; it is played by more individuals than any other game."

Reading this, National League secretary Cullen Cain scoffed — no golf match he was aware of could draw forty thousand to fifty thousand fans on a single afternoon.

"I don't believe any game which requires so much time and money on the part of those interested ever will become the national sport," he countered.

But golf was beginning to shed its reputation as a game exclusively for the wealthy. The opening of affordable public courses, even in rural areas, was opening the game to more people.[9]

For talented young athletes, there was certainly a lot that was attractive about golf as a future endeavor, compared to baseball. The national pastime's top stars — Ruth, Cobb, Speaker — still pulled in salaries that far outpaced even the most famous and successful golfers of the time. However, even middling golf professionals, including teaching pros, were able to make living wages comparable to that made by the majority of baseball's estimated 350 major leaguers and 450 players competing in the three most prestigious minor leagues of the period.[10]

Plus, the boys "swinging golf-sticks at imaginary objects" during breaks in their caddying duties probably realized that the life of a healthy golf salary was far longer than a job playing professional baseball. Golfers continued to make a living far after baseball players of the same age were relegated to spectator status.

"The time may not be far distant when the game of our own making will give way to the game of our adoption," one magazine writer concluded.[11]

A break in the thaw between the two sports came on March 3, when Cobb agreed to except his pitchers from his own no-golf rule. Cobb said he thought that golf adversely affected "the batting eye," but since most pitchers were poor hitters to begin with, he didn't see the harm. The ban remained in place for his position players, however.[12]

By late July, Griffith, who actually did enjoy playing the game himself, apparently had relaxed his team's golf ban. Goslin and Rice were involved in a foursome at Washington Golf and Country Club, with onlookers marveling at Goslin's unorthodox left-handed swing — more like a baseball swing — which, while at the same time admiring Rice's less awe-inspiring yet more steady game.[13]

* * *

Since building his youth movement around Rice and Judge in 1915, Griffith had steadily acquired a lineup of talented players, though with the unrest in the managerial position the previous few seasons, the results of his deft scouting hadn't really manifested themselves on the field as 1924 dawned. Griffith had picked up Leon "Goose" Goslin, a hard-hitting outfielder, in 1921, infielder

Ossie Bluege and pitcher George Mogridge the same year, shortstop Peckinpaugh in 1922, and catcher Muddy Ruel in 1923. Perhaps his most important acquisition, or so it would turn out, came back in 1919, when Griffith, on the urgent advice of new full-time scout Joe Engel, had agreed to sign second baseman Bucky Harris.

As calendar year 1923 ended and 1924 began, the Senators remained the only team in baseball without a manager in place.[14] After failing to complete a trade for Chicago's Collins, Griffith decided to make an unconventional hire. Harris was in Florida in January, getting in some golf while he still could, when, according to legend, he received a telegram from Griffith.

"If you want the job it is yours," he said. "But I must know quickly."

Griffith had also discussed the job with former White Sox manager Kid Gleason, who had endured the "Black Sox" scandal and the franchise's subsequent nosedive.

Harris scurried to a telephone. "Hello, Mr. Griffith," he said. "I want that job."

But the phone connection was poor, and Griffith couldn't hear Harris. So the young manager-to-be sent a telegram instead, according to the myth, which read, "I'll take that job and win Washington's first American League pennant."

Just a few weeks before, Harris was in danger of being supplanted at second base by Collins. Also around that time, he had gotten onto the bad side of his boss by secretly playing professional basketball in Pennsylvania for some extra offseason money. Now he would be in charge of the whole on-field operation.

Understanding that his youth could be an issue with some of the team's veterans, and watching what had happened to the previous season's team after Bush and Rice sparred, one of Harris's first tasks was to court the team's elder statesmen. He sought out Johnson and Judge and asked them for their support in front of the rest of the team.

Then he rounded up the entire team in spring training.

"I didn't know I was going to be the manager of this club a month ago," he told them. "Far be it for me to tell you fellows how to play ball—but what I'm asking is that you go out there and make me a good manager."[15]

As March closed, three of the key members of the Senators' lineup were beginning to hit their batting stride. Late spring hot streaks had boosted Harris, Judge and Peckinpaugh all over .300. Goose Goslin, benched earlier in the spring for failing to run out a play at first, was red hot the entire spring—as April dawned, he led Washington with a .522 spring training batting average.

"The left fielder's appearance at bat is becoming one of the treats of the exhibition games," one writer said, noting that Goslin sometimes took such a hard cut that he ended his swings on the seat of his pants.

With his teammates all swinging hot bats, Rice was able to work out some spring difficulties in the batter's box with relatively little scrutiny. After starting out hot, Rice went through a 1-for-13 slump to drop to the .250 mark, "several degrees below," one confident columnist offered, "what he should, and undoubtedly will, hit in the regular season."[16]

As the season drew nearer, Rice began to hit like his usual self.

"He has recovered from his batting slump with a vengeance in the last few games," the same columnist who noted his difficulties the day before gleefully reported, "and is murdering the ball on virtually every trip to the plate."[17]

An opening day crowd of twenty-six thousand showed up at Griffith Stadium to cheer the Senators to a 4–0 victory over the Philadelphia Athletics behind Walter Johnson's 101st career shutout. Harris, baseball's youngest manager, had defeated Philadelphia's Connie Mack, at age sixty-one the game's oldest manager.[18] On May 2, Rice hit a two-run home run in the top of the ninth in New York, breaking a 4–4 tie to give the Senators an exciting victory over the defending world champion Yankees.[19] But overall the victories would prove difficult to come by in the early-going, and it looked like, yet again, a talented roster that should have just been entering its prime would fall far short of its potential. Harris had been tinkering with his lineup a great deal, trying to do whatever he could to coax victories out of the roster. But it wasn't quite enough to overcome some of the team's deficiencies. No matter which of the revolving cast he used as a third outfielder, no one seemed to be able to seize the job alongside Rice, splitting his time now between right field, his home in his first couple of seasons and in the previous season, and center, where he had spent all of his time between 1920 and 1923. Goslin had not carried his spring training hitting into the season, while Peckinpaugh was batting just .154 after thirteen games. The relief pitchers were proving almost universally unreliable.[20]

The season reached its low point on Memorial Day, when the Senators fell to a season-worst four games under .500, at 15–19, after a 9–4 loss in the first game of a double header in Boston.[21] Rice, apparently healthy now, had three hits in the loss, then added four in the second game, a 10–5 Washington victory.[22]

The Senators, behind Rice's still-hot bat, showed still more life the next afternoon, the last day of May. They bludgeoned the Red Sox 12–0, knocking Boston out of first place. The Senators were showing some signs of life, with Rice leading the way. After his seven-hit holiday, he had four more hits in five trips to the plate in the one-sided victory, giving him eleven hits in fifteen at-bats in the three games in Boston.[23]

June began and, before anyone could really understand what had happened, the Senators vaulted from the second division into first place in the American League. It was a stunning turn of events, with the team playing at a blistering 21–9 pace during June. They won ten in a row at one point, including a four-game sweep of the Yankees in New York, to surge into first place.[24] The Senators were already rolling as they headed to New York, with Rice hitting a bases loaded triple the day before in a 5–4 victory over the Philadelphia Athletics.[25]

As the summer wore on, Washington continued to battle near the top of the American League standings, passing around the lead at various times with both the Yankees and the Detroit Tigers. Down the stretch, Griffith and Harris collaborated on two key roster moves. Even though outfielder Wid Matthews had batted nearly .350 in June and was batting over .300 for the season, the pair felt the team still needed to upgrade in the outfield.[26] The Senators traded Matthews to Sacramento of the Pacific Coast League, along with $35,000 and three more players, for Earl McNeely. Right away, the trade looked like a terrible mistake, with McNeely admitting he was nursing a dislocated shoulder.

Yet with Griffith battling to have the trade nullified by commissioner Kennesaw Mountain Landis, McNeely batted .330 in his forty-three games with the Senators.

The other player Washington traded for late in the season, pitcher Curly Ogden, also wasn't in the best of health. After every game he threw, Ogden would pace the floor of his hotel, wondering if he would ever be able to pitch again. Yet somehow, he coaxed nine victories out of that sore arm after he joined the Senators.[27]

On August 23, in a 2–1 victory over the White Sox, Rice drove in a run with a single. It is notable, because it would be a long time before he would go through a game again without at least one base hit — thirty-one of them, to be precise. Meanwhile, the Senators moved to 68–52 on the season, two games behind New York in the loss column at the end of the day.[28]

While Rice began to put together a modest hitting streak, in their next series, the Senators split four games with St. Louis, failing to pick up any momentum with an enormous series against the Yankees beginning the next afternoon in New York. With a 71–54 record, Washington trailed the first-place New Yorkers by just a half-game in the standings.[29]

"Right now the (Senators) feel convinced that beating New York in its own back yard is an easy thing to do," the *Washington Post* reported, noting the club's success against New York throughout the 1924 season.[30]

Yet while the Senators were stumbling against the Browns, the Yankees had been busy taking two of three from Cleveland, and their play continued into the August 28 series opener against Washington. Ruth's forty-first and forty-second home runs of the year staked the Yankees to a 6–3 lead, which they held into the eighth inning.

It was the eighth inning, as it turned out, that more than any other single turn of events all summer that helped propel the Senators in the direction of a world championship. They chased New York starting pitcher Herb Pennock very early in the inning, and by the time the bloodshed had ended, the Senators had sent thirteen men to the plate, scored eight runs, and sent New York manager Miller Huggins through three more pitchers. The Senators had taken an 11–6 lead, which stood as the final score and set a tone for the rest of the series—and the season, now entering its critical period.

"The (Senators) have staged many rallies in their young lives," sports writer Frank Young wrote. "But that of today was the daddy of 'em all."

Rice had five hits in the game, including two doubles. Goslin, meanwhile, hit for the cycle in the spot ahead of him in the lineup.

"Watch us from now on," Harris, brimming with confidence, said after the game. "The Yankees will have Walter Johnson to beat tomorrow, and I don't think there is a team in the world that can beat him in the form he is in now."

Unbeknownst to anyone present that day, amid the excitement surrounding Rice's five-hit day, Goslin's cycle and the Washington eighth-inning heroics, was that the Yankees, with a phone call, had effectively signed the death warrant on the Senators' burgeoning American League dynasty. Stepping away from the carnage long enough to make a phone call, Huggins phoned Hartford and sent for the Yankees' top prospect, who had hit well in a very brief stint the year before. Twenty-one-year-old Lou Gehrig, "home run king of the Eastern League," would have no impact on the pennant race developing in 1924, though he would impose his will on many others before his career and life were tragically cut short.[31]

Harris had been right about one thing—Johnson was on his game the following day, beating the Yankees 5–1. He was working on the 108th shutout of his career when a line drive clipped him in the hand, a frightening moment for the Senators that had a happy ending—nothing was broken. Rice hit another double, while Goslin homered yet again, one of three hits. Ruth and Gehrig would soon team up to be the most fearsome lineup duo the game has ever seen. But for the time being, the Washington three-four punch was doing all right for itself.[32]

The Yankees managed to win one the next day, 2–1, though Rice earned an appreciative and hearty cheer from forty thousand New Yorkers by making a catch in deep center field off the bat of Bob Meusel while falling backward. Rice's body was "half turned away from the plate," his mitt twisted awkwardly as he grabbed the ball over his left shoulder, then tumbled onto the ground. He also scored the Senators' only run in the game, which pulled the Yankees back within a half-game of first.[33]

Rice would come up even bigger the next afternoon, setting the Senators' season back on the path the team had set with the eight-run, eighth-inning rally in the series' first contest. The game was tied 2–2 heading into extra innings, but Rice came to bat in the tenth inning with the bases loaded. He lifted a long fly ball to deep left-center off Yankees pitcher Joe Bush. Meusel attempted to haul it in, but couldn't hang onto it against the wall, and Rice's double brought two runs home — a third was cut down trying to score — and after Marberry set the Yankees down in the bottom of the inning, the Senators had escaped New York having won three out of four, and building a 1½-games lead in the American League as the season's final month dawned.[34]

The teams raced down the September stretch neck-and-neck, and on September 22, the Senators won a 8–3 game over the Chicago White Sox to maintain a slim margin. Johnson was victorious in the contest — his thirteenth consecutive victory. And Rice extended his hitting streak to twenty-nine games.[35]

The Senators won the next two games in Chicago, as well, with Rice hitting safely in both of them to extend his hitting streak to thirty-one games, and move the team to thirty games over .500 at 90–60. Since their low point early in the season, the Senators had gone 75–41. Yet they still hadn't totally shaken the Yankees, who trailed by just two games with four to play.[36]

Off the following day, the Senators returned to action on September 26, but lost a heart-breaker to the Boston Red Sox, 2–1. Johnson's winning streak ended, and Rice was held to no hits in four at-bats. The lead over the Yankees was down to a precious single game.[37]

The Senators were, admittedly, nervous about the prospect of trying to secure a World Series berth.

"You know," said Earl McNeely, "it was the first time I realized just what our pennant chances really are. Before the game today I began thinking about the World Series and how wonderful it would be. And the whole thing scared me."

"Everybody," Walter Johnson would say later, "from Clark Griffith on down, was in a pretty nervous state of mind, to say the least."

The next day, the choke appeared at first to be grabbing hold, as the Red Sox torched George Mogridge for four first-inning runs. Even Boston's fans, Yankee haters even back then, were pulling for the Senators at this point. When pitcher Howard Ehmke struck out Peckinpaugh in a key situation, they booed him.

But the Senators would right their ship, winning the game 7–5 to retain their two-game lead with two to play. In the game, little-used Wade Lefler smacked a pinch-hit double to lift the Senators past Boston. Before joining the Senators late in the year, Lefler had just one career major league at-bat, it coming earlier in the same season with the Boston Braves. And the twenty-eight year old Duke University graduate would never play another game in the majors.

Rice's family tragedy was a secret until several years after his death, when Newton County, Indiana, historian and freelance journalist John Yost uncovered the events in a scan of old newspaper articles. (National Baseball Hall of Fame Library, Coopertown N.Y.)

But on this afternoon, he was a hero, along with everyone else who donned a Senators uniform.[38]

Assured of at least a tie for first place in the American League, the Senators went out two days later and beat Boston 4–2 to bring the pennant to Washington. Rice set the tone in the game, singling in the first inning, stealing second, then sprinting all the way home when the catcher's attempt to throw him out skipped into center field.[39] Fans, both Senators fans who made the journey and surely Red Sox fans happy to see Harris's squad put away the Yankees for good, rushed the field by the hundreds. They attempted to lure the final out ball away from Joe Judge, but he managed to hand it to Johnson, a relay man on the way to getting the ball into the hands of Clark Griffith.

"I wouldn't take a million for it," said Griffith, who then spent time bowing to fans on all sides of him.

Washington partied well into the night, a party that included the players, excused from clean living for this night at least.

"This town was not big enough to hold the Washington players tonight," the *Washington Post* said the following morning. "For this one night there is no such thing as training rules in the Harris camp."[40]

This party, however would pale in comparison to the one just over the horizon. Rice had batted .334 in 1924, just shy of his career-high .338 he had posted in his breakout season of 1920. He had collected what was to that point a career-high with 216 base hits. But his work, nor any of the Senators' work, was still not finished. The Senators had vanquished the Yankees. Another New York team, the National League champion Giants, was next.[41]

8

TO THE BRINK

Though the Giants had to win just one of three remaining games against the lowly Philadelphia Phillies to secure the National League pennant, they were surely tense because of the late charge of the Brooklyn Dodgers. The Dodgers had played great down the stretch, slicing a formerly large New York lead in the National League standings to just 1½ games. Probably panicked, Giants rookie outfielder Jimmy O'Connell approached Philadelphia shortstop Heinie Sands before the Series, offering him a bribe of $500 to throw the first game so that the Giants could breathe a little easier.[1]

Though some theorized that O'Connell made the offer in jest, or was set up by veteran teammates in a prank gone too far, Sands reported the approach to his manager Art Fletcher. The specter of Buck Weaver, who was banned along with the seven guilty Black Sox just for having knowledge of his teammates' impropriety, still hovered menacingly over the game. So Fletcher, the Phillies manager, reported the incident to commissioner Judge Kennesaw Mountain Landis.

O'Connell was called in front of Landis, where he confessed to his bribery attempt and also implicated New York assistant coach Cozy Dolan. Landis, not surprisingly, immediately banned both from the game for life.

O'Connell's action wasn't nearly as heinous as that of the Chicago seven. While Eddie Cicotte and company lost games on purpose to collect from gamblers, O'Connell was trying to secure victory of his team. Landis, the hardliner, didn't see the distinction. In the wake of 1919, the public's faith in baseball had to be unwavering. "Professional baseball is one of the cleanest institutions in the whole range of human activity," F.C. Lane wrote in a *Baseball Magazine* article about the scandal.[2]

Landis didn't want to set a precedent by splitting hairs. Either the competition on the field was one hundred percent pure or it was not. Anything less was an unacceptable slippery slope.

One of the strongest reactions came from American League president Ban Johnson. Johnson wasn't content with Landis's cut-and-dry investigation followed by the quick closing of the case after he was done dealing with O'Connell and Dolan. In Johnson's opinion, the scandal touched every New York Giant, and Landis should have treated it accordingly. He requested that the Giants be banned from the World Series, and the second-place team in the National League be sent to represent them. At the height of his ranting, Johnson even suggested that the National League not be allowed to send a team to the World Series, and Washington automatically be declared baseball's champion. As nice as it would be to secure the city's first world title, Johnson's old pal Clark Griffith wasn't so hot on that idea, not with capacity crowds ready to line his pockets.[3]

Of course, baseball was sensitive to gambling scandals at the time, only a few years after the Black Sox scandal. So there was probably a note of sincerity in Johnson's wild protests. But he wasn't above playing politics, either, and some of it has to be taken as good old-fashioned posturing. First of all, Johnson and Giants manager McGraw had a mutual dislike that dated back to Johnson's formation of the American League. He also was a constant thorn in Landis's side, and would not have let the opportunity to embarrass the commissioner pass. In fact Johnson might have voiced a dissenting view no matter how Landis had handled the Giants scandal. Finally, Johnson surely thought this was a nice opportunity to smear the National League with some of the egg left on the American League's face after the shame of the Black Sox scandal.

National League president John Heydler, on the other hand, expressed tremendous sympathy for O'Connell. He felt that O'Connell had made a large but forgivable mistake, and that in any other walk of life would never have met with such a swift and severe penalty.

"Here's a young fellow ruined, degraded," Heydler said. "It would have been better for him had he been in jail and served his term. Then people would be inclined to give him another chance. You read of episodes in government, of satchels containing $100,000, of Cabinet officers close to the President bribed, and nothing is done about it. They're still enjoying the fruits of their misdoings so far as anybody knows. But in baseball it's like being struck by lightning. One bolt and it's all over."[4]

That Heydler was soft on gambling should have come as no surprise at all to the limited few who were aware of his past actions in dealing with the issue. In 1917, when gambling was becoming an ignored but growing cloud over the game, Cincinnati first baseman Hal Chase was probably about the most active game thrower in baseball. Chase associated with gamblers and was adept at flubbing games for the Reds without detection. He even tried to get teammates involved, and they either didn't take him seriously, tried to ignore the problem or, we must surmise considering the times, went along. There was one notable exception. Chase visited relief pitcher Jimmy Ring and told him there would be something in it for him if he would just blow a lead he was brought in to save. Ring blew the game, but not on purpose. Chase mistakenly thought Ring had come through for him, and slipped him $50 the next morning, which the pitcher promptly reported to manager Christy Mathewson, who took it up the chain of command to Heydler. The president let Chase off the hook, however, claiming there wasn't enough evidence to punish him.[5]

Such naivete could be forgiven in the pre–Black Sox days. But in 1924, it seemed everyone except Heydler was aware of the threat that gambling posed to the shaky reputation of major league baseball.

Well, everyone except Heydler and his mouthpiece, *Baseball Magazine*. Lane's article in which he praised baseball as one of humankind's cleanest institutions contained several other pseudo-eloquent ramblings on the purity of the game.[6] It was just the magazine's latest embarrassing attempt to cover up for baseball's inability — or unwillingness — to police its own associations with the gambling underworld. In the wake of the Black Sox scandal, the publication had reserved all of its disgust for Chicago journalist Hugh Fullerton for uncovering the conspiracy, ignoring the players sins: "Fullerton had picked up an ugly story that was kicking around in the gutter — a story that decent writers would refuse to handle — and blew it up into a muckraking tirade against organized baseball. There are two kinds of people in the world: one builds up, the other tears down. Hugh Fullerton, of course, belongs to the latter."[7]

Landis was the kind of anti-romantic that baseball needed in the post–Black Sox era. Because of his swift action, the 1924 World Series could proceed without suspicion.

* * *

The 1924 World Series began on a perfect Saturday afternoon, October 4, and anybody who was anybody in the District found a way to score entrance into Griffith Stadium.

"You couldn't have thrown a ball," said Walter Johnson's wife, Hazel, "without hitting an ambassador or senator or a cabinet officer or famous writer or an actor or prize fighter or some other distinguished individual."

Johnson and Rice were introduced to the cramped confines before the game. The pair tried to play a game of catch on the field before the game, but there were simply too many camera men crowding around to do so.

It was, in fact, nearly impossible for Johnson to take a step in advance of

Game One of the World Series without someone or another wanting to wish him well, chat for a few moments, or even shower him with an unexpected gift.

Before the biggest game of his life, Johnson was presented with an $8,000, seven-passenger Lincoln car, the most expensive car produced in the country at the time. The start of the World Series had turned into a celebration of Walter Johnson's excellence and longevity, while all he wanted to do was get himself into the right mind frame to pitch effectively.

"I knew what he was thinking," his mound opponent Art Nehf would later recall. "He was thinking he mustn't let down the fans all over the country who were rooting, even praying, for him."

After setting down the Giants in order in the first inning, Johnson gave up a solo home run to George Kelly in the second and another to Bill Terry in the fourth. The Giants led 2–0. Rice's slow roller to second in the sixth inning drove in McNeely with the Senators' first run to cut the deficit to 2–1. A double play in the seventh inning staved off a New York threat and set up the game's thrilling final innings.

The Senators, still trying to chip away at the Giants one-run lead, had no margin for error in the top of the ninth. A single New York run, though it wouldn't necessarily bury the Senators, would certainly take a lot of the steam out of any comeback hopes. The Senators, after all, weren't a high-scoring team to begin with. They weren't a team built for the big inning, although they had shown time and again their ability to scratch out a late run when need be.

Certainly the Giants had this on their mind coming into the inning. Hack Wilson opened the ninth for the Giants with a single, and with the idea of adding that one important run to the lead, McGraw had his next hitter sacrifice him to second base.

With two outs, Wilson remained on second when Nehf roped a single into centerfield. It was time for Rice's first shining World Series moment. He picked the ball up on a hop and, well aware of the stakes, launched the ball toward home plate. Here's where the arm that had brought him into the major leagues as a pitcher nine years before came in handy. Though the ball was slightly off-line — Ruel corralled it about five feet up the third-base line — it reached the catcher quickly enough that he had time to apply a hard tag to Wilson's neck as the stocky Giant came rushing by.

It was, as stated, Rice's first great defensive play on baseball's grandest stage. It wouldn't be his last. For the time being, it kept the Senators within striking distance, as they trailed 2–1 heading into the bottom of the ninth. And it finally gave Washington the all-important momentum.

The fans at Griffith Stadium, awaiting a reason to erupt, finally got it in the bottom of the ninth. Perhaps feeding off Rice's play in the top of the inning, the Senators quickly tied the game. Judge struck out to lead off the inning, but an infield single by Bluege followed immediately by Peckinpaugh's double tied the score.

"The crashing artillery of thirty-eight thousand voices," Grantland Rice described the scene, "in one of the wildest vocal frenzies anyone ever heard."

Fans littered the field with hats and cushions, delaying the game while the playing surface was cleared.

With one out and a runner on in the tenth, Rice singled to put two men on with just one out. But he was left there, and the game continued on.

In the top of the twelfth, two Earl McNeely blunders on one play put the Giants in position to take the lead. He misjudged a fly ball by Nehf, and it popped out of his glove as he tumbled to try and catch it. Then, compounding the play, McNeely hurled the ball wildly into the infield. It bounded toward the Giants dugout, and by the time a Washington player could track it down, New York had runners on second and third.

McGraw looked for a pinch-hitter for his rookie third baseman Freddy Lindstrom, and rustled Jack Bentley from the bench.

Bentley, a former Senators pitcher and future Rice neighbor, could also hold his own with the bat. In fact, when his pitching ability seemed to be fading, Bentley joined the minor-league Baltimore Orioles and began fashioning a comeback as an outfielder. The time off did his arm wonders, though, and he became a sixteen-game winner for the '24 Giants, as well as one of the team's top pinch-hitters. Knowing this, Harris ordered Bentley intentionally walked, loading the bases. Ross Youngs lofted a soft liner to centerfield, and for the second time in the inning, Nehf would benefit from McNeely's inexperience in center. The ball dropped in and Nehf, who had reached base to start the rally on a McNeely miscue, trotted home with the go-ahead run.

The Senators, who showed so much resilience coming back to tie the game in the ninth, again staged an uprising in the bottom of the twelfth. Harris' RBI single tightened the Giants lead to 4–3, and Rice came to the plate with a chance to fuel the rally, and perhaps even drive in the tying run with just one out.

He connected, smacking the ball into center field. Harris raced around to third, but instead of throwing there, Giants center fielder Billy Southworth threw into second. Rice, trying to put the potential winning run into scoring position, was tagged out.

With Harris standing ninety feet away representing the potential tying run, Goslin grounded out to end the game, and the Giants led the series 1–0.[8]

As disheartening as the loss was, the Senators could draw comfort from the fact that they had battled the Giants to the bitter end, and still had a chance to split the two home games by winning in Game Two the next day, Sunday. Washington had played well in New York throughout the 1924 season, going

9–2 against the Yankees. They swept a Series there in June, and captured three of four as the pennant race heated up in August.

Still, an 0–2 deficit after two home games would put the team in an extremely difficult position.

The twelve-inning Giants victory in the opener had established a pattern the rest of the series would follow—close games that would be in doubt until the final out was secured.

* * *

With the Senators needing to get off to a good start in Game Two and put the extra-inning disappointment of Game One behind them, starter Tom Zachary found himself in trouble immediately in the first inning, as the Giants loaded the bases with only one out.

However, Zachary made the pitch he needed. Muesel grounded to Bluege at third, and he started a 5-4-3 double play as Zachary somehow exited the opening inning unscathed. It would be the first of three double plays that Washington would turn in the game, and sufficiently calmed Zachary down. He began to sail through the Giants lineup after the first. And he would do so while sitting on a 2–0 lead, which Sam Rice was at the heart of delivering.

In postseason series in any sport, the details of early games can be forgotten in light of the compelling drama that takes place as the outcome reaches its final conclusion. Remarkable deciding games are the ones that history remembers, and the 1924 World Series, which would include what still stands up as one of the most dramatic Game Sevens ever played, would be no different. But if Washington hadn't seized the momentum it had given away the day before early on in Game Two, the World Series of that year may have unfolded much differently. It is certainly not a reach to imagine the favored Giants, boosted by the Senators' offensive woes, gaining even more confidence than they already carried and rolling toward a World Series rout.

Earl McNeely, who had doubled in Washington's first run in the sixth inning of Game One, again was Harris's choice to leadoff. He grounded out, as did Harris.

It was up to Rice to keep the inning going. He did that, singling to center field. With only twenty-two home runs all season, the Senators couldn't expect to score a runner from first base with two outs without a little help, and Rice stole second base to get into scoring position for Goslin. Goose, just beginning to feel his October power stroke, promptly homered to right field to give Washington a 2–0 advantage.[9] Ironically, McGraw had started Bentley in Game Two as a means of trying to shut down the left-handed heart of the order, Rice, Goslin and Judge. In front of the hometown folks, however, the Maryland native had set down the two right-handed hitters to begin the inning with ease, maybe letting down his guard a bit when he reached the lefties.[10]

The Senators added to their lead in the fifth inning. Harris, who hit just one home run in 544 at-bats all season, slammed a shot over the left-field wall, making up for his first-inning error. Again, the damage was done with two outs. Washington led 3–0. With Zachary now mowing the prolific Giants lineup down with relative ease, things were looking good. Too good to be true, it would turn out.

The Giants put a run on the board in the seventh. George Kelly scored on Hack Wilson's double play grounder. Still, at that point, the Senators were more than content to trade the outs for a run. They still led 3–1, and Zachary had escaped his first real danger since the first.

He took the mound in the ninth, only three outs away from evening the series headed to the Polo Grounds. But things began to unravel. Frisch walked to lead off.[11] Two batters later, Kelly sent Rice chasing a base hit to right field. Even though the Giants trailed by two runs, Frisch decided to challenge Rice's arm. The curious decision paid off, though. Unlike in Game One, when Rice's strike home cut down Hack Wilson, he bobbled the ball momentarily in right and his throw home was, thus, a split-second too late to gun down Frisch. With two outs, Wilson drove in Kelly with the game's tying run. Fred Marberry came in for the spent Zachary at that point, preventing further disaster by striking out Travis Jackson to end the inning. However, unless Washington could scratch across a run in the bottom of the ninth, the World Series would be going to extra innings for the second day in a row.

Joe Judge worked Bentley for a walk to begin the bottom of the ninth on a positive note for Washington. Not intoxicated by the sudden power surge of his ballclub, Harris stuck with what had gotten the Senators to this point of the season, ordering Bluege to sacrifice Judge into scoring position. Peckinpaugh was next, and with Judge in second, he lined a rocket past Lindstrom at third base to drive in Judge with the winning run. The World Series was tied, one game apiece.

Peckinpaugh's game-winner had implications that would cost Washington for the rest of the series, however. He somehow injured his leg rounding first base, and by the next morning his thigh was black and blue.[12] It probably didn't help at all that he had to battle through celebrating Washington fans to get back to the dugout. Fans surrounded the dugout, gleefully demanding a curtain call after the entertaining two-day introduction to postseason baseball. "Anybody who thinks these two games have not been worth fifty dollars is a goat," shouted one fan leaving the stadium, his investment to a ticket scalper paying off.[13]

For the players, there was barely time to celebrate the tying of the series at a game apiece, nor to contemplate the excitement of the past two days. They boarded a train and headed north to New York, a most familiar trip that, toward the end, veered away from the Bronx and into the Harlem section of Manhattan, where sat the famous Polo Grounds.

A crowd of more than forty-seven thousand crammed into the Giants' park for Game Three. Many were Washington fans, still buzzing after the drama of the first two contests.[14] The Polo Grounds was the most unusually configured ballpark in the majors. The fence down the right-field line stood only 257 feet from home plate, while it didn't take much more of a poke to reach the seats in left field, where the fence was just 279 feet away.

It would be up to Marberry to try to keep the power hitting Giants in the ballpark. After he had been so impressive the day before retiring Travis Jackson to end the ninth-inning New York threat, Harris decided to try to bottle Marberry's magic and bring it north with the team. The move backfired, though, as Marberry fell behind 3–0 and exited after just three innings. In fact, not much of anything went right for the Senators in Game Three. Most disconcerting was the precarious status of Roger Peckinpaugh.

After injuring his leg after smacking the winning hit the day before in Washington, Peck decided to try to make a go of it in Game Three. For one thing, he was well aware that the Senators could ill afford to lose him at shortstop, where they were thinner than anywhere else on the field. One option Harris liked was to shift the veteran Bluege from third base to shortstop, sending Tommy Taylor to play third.[15] But Taylor was unable to go because of a broken hand, mysteriously injured after the pennant-clinching victory in Boston (Taylor may have been feeling a little too feisty, with speculation circulating that he had injured the hand over the head of an unfortunate Boston bar patron).[16] Though Bluege had played only six games at shortstop in his major league career, Harris had no choice but to plant the veteran at the important position. At third, he would use Ralph Miller. Miller hadn't played in the majors since 1921 before Washington picked him up late in the year. Even then, he made it onto the field for just three appearances, all at second base.[17] Not surprisingly, Miller let a sixth-inning groundball scoot right through his legs.[18]

Both teams could have used a modern travel date to get healthy. Giant Frankie Frisch was now playing with two injured hands, which didn't stop him from twice robbing Goose Goslin of base hits on flares to center.

"The right-field stands is just my dish," Goslin told reporters before the game. "They must have built it for me."[19]

Goslin would get his before the Series was over, but it wouldn't be on this day.

The Giants won the game 6–4, a run-of-the mill contest that didn't measure up to the thrillers of the previous two days. It did allow a couple of lesser-known players to collect on their fifteen minutes of fame. While Ralph Miller botched his good fortune, Giant pitcher Rosy Ryan cranked a home run into the upper deck in right field, the first home run of his major league career. Mule Watson shut the Senators down in order in the top of the ninth inning for the save. It would be the last major league game he would ever pitch in.[20]

The Giants led the series two games to one.

Rice would struggle the next afternoon in Game Four, going hitless in five at-bats.[21] Fortunately for his team, the men batting around him in the Senators lineup would more than make up for his off day.

Goose Goslin, robbed of base hits twice the day before, made sure that no such thing would happen when he batted in the third. With Washington down 1–0, he came to bat against New York's Virgil Barnes with two outs and a pair of runners on base. He lined Barnes' first pitch into the right-field bleachers to give the Senators a 3–1 lead. Before the game, Goslin had received on-field counsel from Babe Ruth on how to hit in the Polo Grounds. "I sure do owe a lot to the Babe," Goslin said. "(But) I'll be giving that lad lessons next year."[22] Goslin collected four hits in Game Four, a 7–4 Washington victory that tied the World Series at two games apiece, including three singles. He drove in four runs and scored twice.[23]

George Mogridge started for Harris, pitching into the eighth inning before tiring. Even though he had pitched the last two days, including his brief, unsuccessful stint in Game Three, Marberry got the nod from his manager to come in and try to nail down a late 7–2 lead. In classic closer fashion, he utilized his margin for error, allowing a couple more runs to cross the plate as Washington sloppily tried to close out the game and reduce the World Series to a two-of-three skirmish for the title. Rice contributed to that late-inning ragged play, trying to throw behind Hank Gowdy, who had just singled, at first. His peg was wild, bouncing off the bag and bounding far enough away to allow Gowdy to cruise into third. Eventually Gowdy would score, and Kelly came to the plate with two outs representing the tying run. Like he had done two days prior, however, Marberry ended the drama by blowing three straight fastballs by the Giants hitter.

Optimism among the Washington players and faithful was riding high, particularly since going to the mound for Game Five would be a rested Walter Johnson. And there was no way he would lose two games in the same World Series, could he?

Not in his mind.

"Give me a few runs tomorrow," Johnson said on the eve of his second World Series start. "That's all I want."[24]

But Johnson knew that the Senators, no high-powered outfit even when fully armed, were playing at a serious disadvantage with Peckinpaugh still walking on a tender leg. Johnson pleaded with him to play, for the sake of both the lineup and the defense behind him, but Peckinpaugh couldn't go.[25]

Though Johnson started the game with a steady two innings of scoreless baseball, the first sign that it wasn't going to be his day came when he batted in the top of the third. Always a decent hitter, Johnson lined Jack Bentley's offering against the left-field wall. New York outfielder Hack Wilson was well-trained, however, in playing the Polo Grounds angles this far into the season and postseason. Johnson made the wide turn for second, but realized that he had no chance to reach second safely. He tried to scurry back, but it was too late, and he was cut down returning to first.

The Giants scored first, pushing across a run in the bottom of the third. Fueled by two fielding gaffes by replacement Ralph Miller, the inning could have been even worse. However, Rice caught a Ross Youngs liner for the second out of the inning, then nailed New York pitcher Bentley, who was tagging at third, at home plate to end the bases-loaded threat.[26]

(Future Hall of Famer Youngs, who hit the liner to Rice that started the key double play, would sadly eventually join Rice on the list of baseball's tragic figures. But while Rice's days of despair were already twelve years in the past by the 1924 World Series, Youngs' remained ahead of him. Two years later, when he was just twenty-nine years old, Youngs was diagnosed with a kidney ailment, specifically the very serious affliction Bright's disease. It would be fatal in his case — he died a year later. He was just thirty.[27])

After seven innings, the Senators trailed 3–2. However, Johnson's endurance, once one of the hallmarks of his dominance, wasn't what it used to be. The eighth inning would prove fatal. The Giants strung together a series of singles, with a walk and a Johnson error tossed in to help keep things going. By the time the inning was over, New York led 6–2. Goose Goslin hit a home run in the game, tying Babe Ruth's record for home runs in a single World Series, but it was of little consolation.

Giants pitcher Bentley also homered in the game, and if the Giants hadn't rallied off Johnson in the eighth, the game's outcome might have felt even more depressing, if that was possible. Bentley hooked a fly inside the right-field foul pole, just 225 feet from home plate. The two-run home run would have provided the New York margin of victory, a cruel way to succumb, had the Giants not knocked Johnson around later.

Glum writers of the time, who had looked at the World Series as a chance for Johnson to put the final feather in his Hall of Fame career's cap, waxed in the tone of a eulogy the next morning.

"What took place yesterday at the Polo Grounds was a tragedy, one of the real tragedies of baseball," Fred Lieb wrote. "Walter Johnson's great moment came, and it will leave a lifetime of tragic recollections."[28]

Harris would endure much scrutiny for possibly leaving Johnson in too long while the Giants tallied thirteen base hits against him.

"Trying to fulfill the hopes of the nation," the *Washington Star* reported, "Johnson over pitched himself."[29]

Harris's loyalty caused at least one near-riot in the stands. Umpire Billy Evans, who had the utmost respect for Johnson, attacked a fan who was yelling, "Take him out! Take him out!"

"The youth was gone," wrote Damon Runyon. "By some tragic quirk of the imagination there stood in his place an old fellow with stooping shoulders, as if they felt the great weight of years. That was Johnson, once called the great; that seemingly old, old man!"[30]

If Johnson's pre-game bravado was a touch out of character, so too was his post-game defeatism.

"I couldn't hold them," Johnson said. "I'll finish up my career in the big leagues with two World Series defeats."[31]

"Nothing could rouse him from his depression," Muddy Ruel would recall.

Clark Griffith was much more optimistic.

"Go home and get to bed early," he told the downcast Johnson as they rode back to Washington, D.C. "We may need you."[32]

9

Party Town

The site for a potential Game Seven had been determined by a coin flip, with the Senators securing home-field advantage in that unscientific manner.[1] Of course, they'd have to get there first, which meant somehow winning Game Six. They would do so, and Rice's fingerprints would be all over the dramatic victory.

It wouldn't be easy, with New York's Game One victor, Art Nehf, taking the ball for the potential clinching contest. But Washington liked its guy, too. Tom Zachary was coming off a gem of his own in Game Two. Not only would the left-hander send Senator-killer Bill Terry to the bench, but New York's distinct offensive advantage would be further neutralized by the return of Roger Peckinpaugh.

"I'll get into that game if I break the leg," Peckinpaugh said beforehand.[2]

It was eerily close to the truth. But before he'd have to leave the 1924 World Series field for the final time, Peckinpaugh would make another huge contribution to the Washington cause, as he had done with timely hits in Games One and Two. With Washington trailing 1–0 in the fifth, Peckinpaugh singled and eventually came home, followed by trailer Earl McNeely, when Bucky Harris singled to give the Senators a 2–1 lead. It was nice redemption for Harris, who had been roundly criticized for leaving in Johnson the day before. Then, in the first inning of the current game, he had been picked off of base to kill a developing Washington rally.

Harris wasn't the lone hero, however. McNeely, who had walked, had gotten himself into scoring position with a daring two-out steal. He barely beat the throw by New York catcher Hank Gowdy, setting up his manager for his big moment.

A writer from *Baseball Magazine* saw the steal as nothing less than the turning point in the entire World Series:

The Senators, thanks to Walter Johnson's Game Seven heroics, won the 1924 World Series in seven games over the New York Giants, setting off one of Washington, D.C.'s, most raucous parties. (National Baseball Hall of Fame Library, Coopertown, N.Y.)

A flash of time: a fraction of a second: a single step, or the slowness of that step — such things have uncrowned kings, wrecked empires, won pennants, sealed the championship of the world. When Earl McNeely stole second base in the fifth inning, the fate of that ball game hung in mid-air as the ball swept down and the plunging runner slid. The tiniest space of time; the slightest hesitation, meant the third out, and meant that the Giants were champions of the world.

By the time Harris gave his team the lead in the fifth, Zachary was cruising through the Giants lineup. Keeping the momentum squarely in the Senators court, he retired New York on just three pitches in the top of the sixth. In what would be a ninety-seven-pitch gem, Zachary never went to a three-ball count on a Giants hitter.³

McNeely's steal of second, Harris' two-run single and Zachary's pinpoint control were certainly key components of the Washington victory. But the continuing defensive wizardry of Rice helped keep Washington alive for one last winner-take-all battle on Friday.

In the first inning, with one Giants run already in and the team looking for more to perhaps put Washington away early, Rice ran down Irish Meusel's wicked drive right against the right-field bleachers.

"Rice's work in the outfield was wonderful," Harris said. "And he covered an awful lot of territory. That drive of Meusel's in the first inning would have been a sure home run if Sam hadn't made a leaping catch. A home run then would have beaten us, too, for Kelly was on first base at the time. I guess Rice deserves as much credit for winning that game as anyone else."

Rice made what was noted as "another fine catch to rob Nehf of a hit" in the fifth inning. In the seventh, Rice missed another sensational catch by mere inches, this time off the bat of Wilson.

"(Zachary's) fine pitching, Harris's timely hit, Rice's great fielding and our misfortune in letting McNeely steal (of) second at just that time were the main factors in our defeat and Washington's victory," said John McGraw.[4]

Scribes covering the game echoed the sentiments of the two managers.

"Sam Rice showed Freddie Lindstrom what a veteran can do in the field," one writer said.

"Of the many great features of the Washington team's work, Rice's great fielding was conspicuous," wrote Ted Sullivan.

In a story that credited "Rice's amazing feats in the field," the *Washington Post* set the scene for the all-important Game Seven.

> The supreme test comes today. The teams are at a razor's edge of fitness. The weather is propitious. The presidential campaign and all other business stands holding its breath, awaiting the all-important bulletin from Griffith Stadium. The nation waits impatiently to hail the world's champions and cheer the losers for their plucky fight. Above all things just now we yearn to flash the glad tidings—Washington wins![5]

* * *

With precious little time to regroup his thoughts after the tightly contested sixth game, Bucky Harris racked his brain for a way to gain a strategic edge from the game's outset, perhaps even a psychological one. After some thought, Harris thought he had discovered one—New York first baseman Terry, though one of the top hitters on the team, struggled against left-handers. He struggled to the point that McGraw often didn't bother to play him when a left-hander was throwing for the other team.

But Harris, decades younger than McGraw, would pull a trick on the old master. He started right-hander Curly Ogden, in order to induce McGraw to put Terry in the lineup. Meanwhile lefty Mogridge, who Terry surely would struggle against, warmed up out of sight. The plan was to let Ogden pitch to one hitter, then bring in Mogridge. Harris doubted that McGraw would pull Terry after he had committed to him and, even if he did, the Senators would be at an advantage knowing that Terry wouldn't be available as a late innings pinch-hitter should Harris go to a right-hander at some point.

Harris left Ogden in until he gave up a base runner, walking number two hitter Frisch, then made the switch.[6]

The manager's second great contribution to the game came on the field. With the teams battling to a scoreless tie in the early innings, Harris came to bat in the fourth. Giants pitcher Virgil Barnes delivered the 3–2 pitch down the middle of the plate.

"There came a loud crack of wood meeting leather," the *Washington Post* reported, "followed by a roar from the stands which was heard in China."

Hack Wilson chased the ball all the way to the wall, falling over the fence into the stands in an effort to track it down. But it was no use, as the ball sailed into the stands to give the Senators a 1–0 lead. Wilson made up for it on the next batter, as he robbed Rice of a hit on a diving catch, but the damage had been done.[7]

Mogridge sailed until the sixth, when the Giants finally began to come to life. Mogridge walked Ross Youngs to begin the inning, then George Kelly singled to put two men on with nobody out. McGraw recognized the opportunity, and decided to send in a pinch-hitter for Terry, Irish Meusel. Terry had grounded out and struck out in two at-bats against the lefty, and McGraw decided that with opportunities limited in what had been a pitcher's duel to that point, he had to give in. Harris countered by bringing in Marberry in relief of the left-hander Mogridge.[8]

Marberry had been Harris' security blanket out of the bullpen all season, and was sort of a pioneer in the reliever's role, carving out a niche on a pennant-winning club in an era in which pitchers still were expected to finish what they started. Marberry saved seven of Walter Johnson's 1924 victories, and that kind of performance didn't go unnoticed.

"I believe he was responsible for their winning the pennant," St. Louis Browns star George Sisler said of Marberry.

Experts recognized Marberry's value, as well.

"The pinch-hitter who wins a game by his timely (base hit) has many to sing his praise," wrote F.C. Lane. "In fact, he is a familiar figure in baseball, and his importance in the scheme of things is never underrated.

"The pinch-pitcher is just as important, perhaps more so. For it is usually his role to save a game that is trembling in the balance, that would in all probability be lost were it not for his fresh vigor, control and speed."[9]

But for all Marberry had done throughout the season to help the Senators raise the American League pennant, inning six of Game Seven of the World

Series was not to be his moment, though he could hardly be blamed. The Washington defense was about to let him down in a big way.

Things began quietly as Meusel flew to Rice, scoring Youngs from third to tie the game. But then Travis Jackson hit a ground ball to first that Judge misplayed badly. Hank Gowdy was next, and Marberry induced him to ground to shortstop. But Bluege, unaccustomed to the position, began thinking double play before he had the ball secured, and it rolled through his legs into left field.[10] Things could have been even worse, but a play by Rice helped keep things from spiraling completely out of control. With Jackson standing ninety feet from home plate, Virgil Barnes lifted a fly ball to Sam in right field. Rice caught the ball for the second out, and positioned himself to make a bullet throw to home plate. Jackson was forced to hold, and Marberry struck out the next batter to end the inning. By the time the inning's damage was complete, however, the Giants led 3–1.

Rice would make his own contribution to the ongoing nightmare, though, hitting into a double play in the bottom of the seventh just when the hopes of Washington's fans had begun to rise again.

The Senators weren't done yet, though. All that the errors had done was set up a climax to this World Series that today, more than eighty years after it was played, still keeps it ranked among the greatest baseball games ever played.

After going down quietly in the sixth and seventh, the Senators finally rallied in the bottom of the eighth, loading the bases for Harris. Fate, in the form of a pebble or something like it, was set to intervene. Harris hit a hard, but catchable, ground ball to Lindstrom at third. But the eighteen-year-old could only watch the ball bound over his head after it struck whatever the obstruction was, then rocketed up over his head. Two runs scored and the game was tied, the sudden turn of events "making howling dervishes of thousands of usually quiet and respectable citizens."[11] Some fans jumped onto the field, with police rushing to send them back to their seats. While U.S. President Calvin "Silent Cal" Coolidge "clapped his hands in his precise manner," his wife Grace was among the most excited fans in the ballpark. She jumped up and down, screamed and waved both arms.

With a chance to put the Senators ahead, Rice grounded out to finally end the threat. One could forgive him, though. Instead of getting to face the imploding Barnes like his rallying teammates, Rice faced new New York pitcher Art Nehf, who was making his fourth consecutive appearance in the final game of a World Series. He had won two of the previous three deciding contests.[12]

There would be more howling forthcoming from the Washington fans. Marberry had been pinch-hit for during the Senators' eighth-inning rally, and Harris, who had told Johnson he may need him before the series was over, made good on the promise. Having sent him out to warm up in the bullpen earlier, he called on Johnson to pitch the ninth.[13] The crowd, still in a frenzy after Harris' routine ground ball turned into a game-tying single, reacted to the sight of Johnson.

"As the Giants came to bat in the ninth, with the score knotted at 3 and 3, there came once more the old familiar figure, slouching across the infield sod to his ancient home in the box," wrote Grantland Rice. "Here once more was the mighty moment, and as thirty-eight thousand stood and cheered, roared and raved, Johnson began to set the old-time fast one singing on its way."[14]

Clark Griffith, who had superstitiously stayed in the same spot near the Washington dugout where he had been standing during the eighth-inning rally, later recalled the scene.

"Utter strangers were hugging each other in the stands because Walter was getting one more chance in the series," he said. "It was his ball game now."

Meanwhile on the pitcher's mound, Harris patted Johnson on the back.

"You're the best we've got, Walter," said the man who had alerted Johnson just a couple days before that he might be calling on him again before this was all over with. "We've got to win or lose with you."

Johnson unleashed his fastball during five warm-ups, pounding Muddy Ruel's mitt with "the crack of a rifle shot." But with one out, Frankie Frisch timed Johnson's fastball, ripping a triple deep into right-center where neither Rice nor McNeely could catch up to it. Harris called for an intentional walk of the next batter, left-handed swinging Ross Youngs, to bring up George Kelly. It was a courageous move, considering Kelly was the National League's RBI leader in 1924, and had hit a home run off of Johnson earlier in the series.

Rather than trying to finesse his way around Kelly, Johnson decided to go after him with his best. He blew three straight fastballs by him for the second out. The next batter was Irish Meusel, still batting in Terry's original lineup spot. He slapped a ground ball to third, and the crowd held its breath as the throw to first from Ralph Miller died in the air. But Judge, making up for the error that fueled New York's seventh-inning rally, stretched his body as far as it would go to make the play and end the inning with the game still tied.

After the Senators went down in the ninth, Johnson induced a double-play ball to get out of some more danger in the tenth. Then in the bottom of the inning, the pitcher, batting for himself, received a standing ovation as he came to the plate. Johnson connected with a Nehf offering, and for a second, the crowd began to roar as the ball headed for deep left-center field. But it ran out of steam on its way, landing harmlessly into Hack Wilson's glove a few feet short of the wall.[15]

And onward the game went through the eleventh inning and the top of the twelfth, with both teams seeing runners reach base, but neither able to get anyone home. A sign that it was Johnson's day? In a key situation of the eleventh inning, he struck out Frankie Frisch on a sweeping curveball. Frisch had struck out three times in 101 previous World Series at-bats, including none in his last seventy-one at-bats spanning the last three series. As the bottom of the twelfth began, the game remained tied 3–3, as it had since the eighth.[16]

The Senators could not have sent two poorer option to the plate to begin the bottom of the twelfth than Roger Miller, who was just 2-for-10 in the series, and Muddy Ruel. Miller grounded out to begin the inning, bringing up Ruel, who was struggling even worse over the seven games. The catcher had just one hit in twenty at-bats in the World Series to this point. But he had also guided Johnson through all kinds of danger unscathed from the ninth inning onward. As it seemed Harris was planning to stick with Johnson until the game's conclusion, no matter what, it only went to figure that he would also stick with the man calling the pitches. There would be no pinch-hitter.

Ruel swung at the first pitch, quite often the sign of a struggling hitter, and he lifted a high pop foul behind the plate. Reliable fielding Giants catcher Hank Gowdy circled under it. But just as Gowdy seemed to have camped under the pop-up, his foot became caught in his own mask. Gowdy tumbled to one knee, trying to maintain his balance and secure the out at the same time. He couldn't do it, and the ball popped out of his mitt to give Ruel new life.

He took advantage of it, driving a one-out double down the left-field line.

Everything that had happened in the game seemed to develop in excruciating slow motion, but the events that followed Ruel's double came in a rush.

The pitching hero Johnson batted for himself and was swinging away, hitting a ground ball to shortstop that Jackson bobbled.[17] It was the seventh error of the game for the two teams, and the continuation of a nightmare afternoon for the Giants shortstop, who had also nearly handed the Senators victory with a costly error in the bottom of the ninth.

To the plate strode Earl McNeely, hitless in five Game Seven at-bats to that point.[18]

McNeely fouled Bentley's first pitch straight back. The second one he sent bounding toward Lindstrom at third base. To Ruel, it looked like a possible double-play ball, and he began digging hard for first base. Lindstrom waited back for the ball, then found himself hopping up — as it had in the eighth, the ball hit something and took a bad hop, bouncing over Lindstrom's head into left field.[19]

"What caused these bounds?" writer Damon Runyon conjectured. "A bit of hard ground near third base, perhaps. It may have been no larger than a twenty-five-cent piece. No ball struck there during the season or the Washington groundkeeper would have meticulously removed it.

"Do you believe that fate, seeking a way of giving Washington the victory, twice directed the ball to that bit of hard ground?"[20]

Ruel was the slowest runner on the team, but third-base coach Al Schacht had already decided to send him on anything close. Ruel rounded third and headed home with the possible winning run of the World Series, his teammates agonizing at his lack of speed.

Caught off guard that the ball had reached the outfield, Giants left fielder Meusel picked up the ball when he finally got to it, and held onto it. Ruel still hadn't scored when the Giants left fielder conceded the run, trotting into the infield rather than even attempting a desperation heave. Ruel crossed the plate, and Griffith Stadium erupted. Improbably, the Senators had won the game, and were finally world champions.

Within moments, the field was swarmed by celebrating Senators fans, pouring onto the field from all sections of the Griffith Stadium seats. The lucky among the players hustled to the dugout and disappeared. McNeely wasn't among them. The fans tore his jersey apart, popping the buttons clear off, before D.C. police cleared a path for him.

President Coolidge, led by a secret service brigade, headed for the same dugout exit through which the Senators players had disappeared. He needn't have worried, and reached the dugout unmolested and relatively unnoticed.

"The immense crowd did not care to bother with a mere President," one writer joked.[21]

There were less people in the Senators dressing room than on the field, but the scene was no less celebratory. Bucky Harris was perhaps the most disheveled of all. Harris managed to steady his emotions long enough to shower, but was so joyous afterward that he forgot to get dressed, and paced the clubhouse naked, slapping his players on the back in congratulations.

Outside, the crowd continued to celebrate. One fan climbed onto the roof of the Washington dugout, taking his shirt off and whipping it around above his head "like a madman." Somehow, Giants catcher Gowdy made his way through the pandemonium to the Washington dressing quarters. Still in uniform, he shook Harris' hand.

"I am proud to have played against such a splendid club," he said.

Then Gowdy found Johnson.

"Walter, now that we have lost, I am glad it was you that pitched us out," Gowdy told him. "I'll never regret losing to you."

Frisch also tried to make his way into the Senators clubhouse, but by that time the team was counting its World Series money, and police officers were not letting anyone into the room. Johnson saw Frisch wandering, however, and rushed to the door to acknowledge him.

"Your work was great, Walter," Frisch said. "Tell Harris for me he has one of the gamest clubs I have ever played against. I hope we meet in another series next year."[22]

9. Party Town

A column in the *Washington Post* tried to capture the emotion of the overall scene:

> The cup of joys spills its intoxicating bubbles over the Monument, the Capitol, the White House, the Griffith Stadium, and all over the town. Washington has found something that is more heady than wine, more exhilarating than strong drink. It is victory! Triumph!

The story went on to congratulate all of the key players by name and primary contribution, including "Rice of the magic mitt."[23]

Eventually, the celebration moved from inside of Griffith Stadium to the streets of Washington. That night, the District of Columbia was host to a celebration to shame any it had experienced since at least 1918, "when another world championship was settled overseas." Washington parties, commonly of the political variety, have always been known for their elegance and, at least behaviorally, reserved tone. Not so this one.

"All the years of cultivated dignity that the city had stored up exploded with a bang," one accounted explained.

Up and down Pennsylvania Avenue, fire trucks arriving from the nearby suburb of Cherrydale, Virginia, screamed up and down the street. The men aboard carried banners reading, "Let Cherrydale burn!"

At F Street and Thirteenth, young men had tossed aside orthodox fashions, donning women's hats and rolling their pants above their knees. Gleefully, they "directed" traffic. People roaming the streets popped open their umbrellas, not to protect against the rain, for there was none. Instead, they needed the accessory to keep falling confetti out of their hair and clothing.

Players Ruel, Ogden and Goslin sought sanctuary at the city's Wardman Park Hotel, but were mobbed there just as they were mobbed on the field at the game's conclusion.[24]

On a balcony overlooking the celebration, Kennesaw Mountain Landis stood with sports writer Fred Lieb.

"Freddie," Landis said. "What are we looking at now—could this be the highest point of what we affectionately call our national sport?"

"Greece had its sports and its Olympics. There must have been a year at which they were at their peak. I repeat, Freddie, are we looking at the zenith of baseball?"[25]

10

Another Pennant Run

The World Series championship seemed to loosen up some of the powers-that-be within the Washington organization, including Griffith himself. That was good for Rice as it concerned his primary offseason passion, golf. A year after the ban "cow-pasture pool," as Griffith derisively termed it, appeared to be back on the table for good, at least for Rice.

"Griffith gives golf credit for having made a new man out of outfielder Rice," said the *Washington Post*. "Three or four years ago, Sam was pretty well run down, showed signs of slowing up on the diamond and caused the (Senator) president no little worry."

But, Griffith said, after a winter of golf Rice had reported the following spring having packed twenty healthy pounds onto his frame. And he hadn't stopped hitting since. Griffith figured that the golf swing had no deterrent effect on players with certain types of batting swings, including Rice and Goslin on the Senators, as well as Babe Ruth.

The credibility of the ban also suffered when Harris, one of its primary proponents, saw his batting average actually drop during his summer away from the golf course.[1]

But Rice's winter golf tour of Florida was delayed after the 1924 season, as he had more baseball to play — and some sightseeing to do. Back in 1913, Rice had joined the Navy in an effort to see the world. During World War I, he camped in France under duress. Now he'd really get his chance. Just a few days

Opposite: Rice enjoyed another strong season in 1925, leading the Senators with a .350 average and 227 hits. (National Hall of Fame Library, Cooperstown, N.Y.)

after the World Series ended Rice, along with Muddy Ruel, traveled to Montreal to join up with players from the White Sox and Giants, who had planned a winter tour to try to spread the game to Europe.[2]

The players traveled across the Pacific on the Canadian ocean liner the Mont Royal, playing catch to stay in shape on the ship's decks and dancing with their wives in the cabins at night. A logistical mess upon arrival was an omen for how the trip, as a whole, would go in its effort to spread baseball globally. Giants pitcher Walter Huntsinger, who had gotten married between the end of the season and the trip to Europe, had in all the excitement forgotten to pack his passport. After some negotiation between American and European officials, he was permitted to enter England.

The first game of the tour was played on October 23 at Liverpool's Everton Field, and the tiny field led to a 16–11 slugfest won by Rice, Ruel and the White Sox. The confused British fans had to be told to leave after nine innings, so unfamiliar were they with the rules of the sport. The next day in London the Giants won a more orthodox game 8–2.[3]

Many of the stops drew nothing but a few curiosity seekers, including one game played in front of an estimated forty people.

"Just why the trip has been undertaken is a deep mystery," the *Sporting News* cynically wondered.

There was some speculation that European fans were turned off by the latest baseball gambling scandal involving the Giants. Whatever the reason, the paper reported that the tour had been met with "cold indifference" by many of the British.

"With the exception of Australia, Japan, Cuba and France," the story continued, "baseball has never amounted to a row of ash cans in foreign countries."[4]

The tour broke up in mid–November after its final stop in Paris, with the players all going their separate ways. While many stayed for a few days longer to enjoy the sights in the French City, Rice, Ruel, Jennings and Nehf took off for Rome, where someone had arranged for them an audience with the Pope himself.[5]

Back in the United States, reports continued to circulate that the games were a "scenic success but a financial flop." Rice did not necessarily agree with these reports.

"Really good crowds turned out for the games," he said.

But he did concede that the tour wasn't a smashing success at all of its stops. Dublin, Ireland, in particular, was a disaster, though an entertaining one. Political factions within the town aligned against each other over the intrusion of the American national pastime on their winter. The local newspapers, fiercely protective of the Irish national sport of "hurling," which resembled soccer, were against the baseball tour stop. Meanwhile the local government was desirous that baseball made a successful stop through town, seeing it as a way to bolster political relations with the United States.

On the other hand in London and Liverpool, England, huge crowds showed up, perhaps as drawn to the presence of King George and the Prince of Wales as they were the demonstration by the American baseball players. The people watched the games in confusion, however, as they were too used to the rules of cricket to understand what was going on in the baseball games.

"Long hits are what bring the applause over there," Rice said. "It made no difference whether the clouts are homers, foul balls or were caught, as long as they traveled far and high."[6]

World Series championship nonwithstanding, Griffith felt there was work to accomplish in the offseason if the Senators planned to contend for a repeat performance. So he identified weak spots on Harris's roster, then set about shoring them up. In December, he bolstered the pitching staff with a pair of deals, adding Stan Covelski, a thirty-five-year-old with Cleveland who had won more than twenty games for four consecutive seasons, and Walter "Dutch" Ruether, a thirty-one-year-old left-hander who had been one of the heroes for the Cincinnati Red in the 1919 World Series.

Not one to pass up on the opportunity, Griffith had added approximately thirty-five hundred seats to the ballpark by constructing a second deck in right field.

It was a smart move, because on the heels of the World Series championship, the Senators were the hottest ticket not only in the District of Columbia, but internationally. After going 4–2 during a six-game season-opening road trip, the Senators returned home on April 22 to a packed house coursing with excitement. It was also a gathering that was unmistakably Washingtonian. Rice had two hits and scored three runs in an impressive 10–1 Senators victory, but any deeds by individual players was far eclipsed by the festive atmosphere.

"The crowd was one of those intelligent looking, well-grooming, orderly, but enthusiastic and demonstrative throngs that Griffith and his associates are so proud to entertain," said one report of the game. "It included prominent people of nearby cities and of most of the principal foreign nations."

President Calvin Coolidge threw out the ceremonial first pitch. He was surrounded by members of his cabinet. The Spanish ambassador to America also was in attendance. Perhaps reinforcing some of the present dignitaries' thoughts about themselves, wintery conditions just two days prior to the opener made way for a summery ninety-three degrees by the game, the highest temperature recorded in the United States that afternoon.[7]

With the pomp and circumstance of opening day in Washington in the rearview mirror, Rice embarked on his greatest season. The summer of 1925 would be the only time he'd bat .350 in his long career, and his 227 hits would be also be a career-high. Rice drove in eighty-seven runs, a career-best, and also scored 111 runs.

Best of all, it all came in support of a second straight American League pennant for the once hapless Senators.

* * *

We have extolled the virtues of Rice's thirty-one-game hitting streak, rising as it did unsuspectingly out of the summer of 1924 to help carry the Senators to their first American League pennant and, ultimately, a World Series championship. During the 1925 season, a streak even more majestic, in terms of its place in baseball history, began. And its beginning, as the beginnings of these things so often are, was as humble as can be.

On June 1, the Senators were in the very early stages of defending their pennant when they traveled to New York for four games against the Yankees. The arrival of the champs in town for the first time since the season's opening series was overshadowed, however, by the biggest event in baseball up to that point in the season — the return of Babe Ruth to the Yankees lineup.

A few days before the season began, Ruth had come down with excruciating pains in his stomach. America held its breath over what was initially diagnosed as an intestinal abscess. The Babe's life wasn't in jeopardy, as some people fretted, but he would be laid up in a New York hospital for several weeks. Ruth didn't join the team until May 26, and he didn't play in a game until that afternoon against the Senators.

Ruth's long journey back to the Yankees lineup ended in an 0-for-3 day. Even less notable at the time, but immensely historic in hindsight, was the late-inning pinch-hitting appearance by young Lou Gehrig. The game remained tight into the latter innings, and looking for a spark for the lineup, Yankees manager Huggins sent Gehrig in to bat for shortstop Peewee Wanniger. A few weeks before, Wanniger had replaced Everett Scott in the New York lineup, ending his record-breaking consecutive games streak at 1,307.[8] It took less than a month for someone to begin the streak that would topple that "unapproachable record," as one story termed it.[9] Gehrig did not get a hit, but he would collect plenty of them before health finally forced him back to the bench. The Senators won the June 1 game 5–3. They lost the next day 8–5, a game in which Gehrig was started as an emergency replacement for first baseman Wally Pipp, beaned in batting practice by Yankees batting practice pitcher Charlie Caldwell. From those two days forward, Gehrig would go on to appear in 2,130 consecutive games, one of baseball's most famous records (though since broken).[10]

After Gehrig had been in the lineup a few days, *The Sporting News* described him as "the youngster who is making a strong bid for permanent employment." More prophetic words have scarcely ever been written.[11]

Momentous as Gehrig's feat was, and headline-worthy as Ruth's illness became, the Yankees were a nonfactor in the 1925 American League pennant race. Without Ruth, they bowed out of the race early on.

Meanwhile, the Senators and Athletics were positioning themselves as the American League front-runners for the season. By the end of May, Philadelphia, all the way back seemingly from its talent purge of the Federal League era, led the Senators by 3½ games. Writers urged fans to remain patient — it was a long summer.

"There is one thing that every superior team is entitled to which the A's haven't had yet and that is a slump," wrote one reporter.[12]

The Senators stormed back into the race, with Rice playing a huge role in some key games during June. On June 14, he went 4-for-4 and scored twice in a 9–8 victory over St. Louis, pulling Washington within a half-game of the Athletics. A few days later, Rice's "brilliant" catch prevented a Cleveland run from scoring in the bottom of the eleventh in a tie game. The next inning, Rice reached base for Goslin, whose third home run of the game gave the Senators a thrilling 7–5 victory. Rice had provided a surge just as the Senators had needed one, and by mid–June he was batting .364.[13] Rice's average soared to the .370 range at the end of July, though he slumped a bit in August, hitting around .250 for the month. But at the same time, the Senators began to finally take charge of the race for the American League flag.[14] After chasing the Athletics for about a month straight, Washington won its sixth out of seven in dramatic fashion on August 20, beating Cleveland 1-0 in twelve innings while the Athletics lost their game to St. Louis by blowing a ninth-inning lead.[15]

An A's collapse, which included a twelve-game losing streak at one point, ensured that the Senators would not lose their grip on first place for the rest of the season.[16] At the same time, Rice rediscovered his hitting stroke. In a remarkable stretch on September 17–19, he had a string of nine consecutive base hits, sandwiching the stretch around a walk for ten consecutive plate appearances in which Rice reached base. The nine straight hits challenged Tris Speaker's five-year-old record of eleven in succession, and the streak included two consecutive 4-for-4 performances.[17]

In a decade that saw the Yankees slug their way to prominence, with Philadelphia also taking that tract, as well, the 1925 Senators continued to be a throwback to baseball's past, when runs were scratched out one at a time. Though Goslin's eighteen home runs and 113 RBIs gave them just enough power in the lineup, they led the American League in stolen bases.[18] So enamored of the Senators' style of baseball was the Washington public that manager Harris actually came under some criticism for not calling for the sacrifice enough.[19] (Harris himself actually led baseball with forty-one sacrifices. Rice had nineteen).[20]

Pitching continued to be a strength for the Senators, with the late-season acquisition of Alec Ferguson giving them five victories down the stretch.[21] Griffith's roster tinkering had worked wonders in '25. Another in-season trade had brought Joe "Moon" Harris over, giving them an extra bat on the bench that would really pay off come World Series time.

The Senators had become the darling franchise of baseball, the organization with a long history of ineptitude that could suddenly do no wrong. Griffith was a master dealer. Harris, meanwhile, was tagged with a label that, to this day, gets quickly attached to any manager or coach who tastes early success.

"Washington has a manager," a story in *The Sporting News* said, "who is a genius in whom the recognized authorities on the game have never been able to find a fault."[22]

As it remains today, though, the bestowing of that label is subject to immediate withdrawal. The Senators' World Series opponent was to be the Pittsburgh Pirates and, before another thrilling fall classic had ran its course, Harris would come under harsh criticism for some of his strategic decisions.

For Rice, the beginning of the 1925 World Series marked the dawning of his finest hour in baseball, both at the plate and in the field.

* * *

The Pirates were owned by Barney Dreyfuss, a German immigrant who first entered the baseball business when he purchased the Louisville Colonels of the old American Association in 1889. Louisville joined the National League soon afterward. When the league looked to contract the Louisville franchise, Dreyfuss sold star players like Honus Wagner and Fred Clarke to Pittsburgh, using the money he made that way to then buy them back as the new owner of the Pittsburgh Pirates. Dreyfuss built the dominant national league franchise of the early twentieth century, winning pennants in 1901, 1902 and 1903 (after which his team played in the first N.L.-A.L. World Series against Boston). The Pirates won their first and only World Series in 1909, and without a doubt Dreyfuss was ready to add another one by 1925.

Dreyfuss irritated Pittsburgh fans before the 1925 season was under way by pulling off an unpopular trade with the Chicago Cubs. For the last couple of years, Dreyfuss had been trying to shuttle middle infielder Rabbit Maranville. Though Maranville was a defensive wizard at either shortstop or second base, and an adequate offensive player with better-than-average ability at the plate as well as speed on the bases, Dreyfuss had grown tired of worrying about

Maranville's off-the-field behavior. He was well-known as a hard drinker, and in fact once engaged in a flask-passing during a pitcher's mound conference. For a long time, Maranville's drinking didn't affect his on-field performance — he broke a major league record with 672 at-bats in 1922, hardly the telltale sign of an unreliable slave to the bottle.

But Maranville and the Pirates organization took a public relations hit in the next year when Maranville was convicted for drunk driving.

Baseball and booze were longtime bedfellows.[23] As far back as 1896, for example, the *Washington Post* reported that a few players' late-night activities were dragging down the team: "Certain members are indulging in the flowing bowl. In justice to the fans, the *Post* appeals to the management to take certain measures to correct this fault." Washington owner Earl Wagner took the paper's advice, shipping his star player elsewhere.[24] After Maranville's arrest, Dreyfuss would look to follow the same path.

Though it would take a while to carry out the action, from that day on Dreyfuss really tired of Maranville's actions and wanted him gone. Dreyfuss made the trade just in time — Maranville was released to the minor leagues during the 1925 season. He would eventually sober up, however, and return for several triumphant seasons to cap a Hall of Fame career. "The national consumption of alcoholic beverages took a sharp downturn after May 24, 1927," Maranville is to have said. "That's the day I quit drinking."

It wasn't just the trade of Maranville that had fans upset. They could have dealt with that if they felt that the Pirates had gotten equal value in return. But Dreyfuss carried out a blockbuster trade with the Chicago Cubs. Pittsburgh sent the Cubs Maranville, fellow partier and .288 hitter Charlie Grimm and twenty-game winner Wilbur Cooper, the workhorse of the pitching staff who had sopped up 268$^{2}/_{3}$ innings the season before, in exchange for Chicago's right-handed curveball Vic Aldridge, poor-fielding, good-hitting shortstop George "Boots" Grantham (yes, the nickname was in honor of his penchant for errors), and an unknown first-base prospect, Al Niehaus.

It seemed like a drastic retooling to fans who had watched the Pirates win at least eighty-five games a season for the last four years. The 1924 team won ninety games, finishing just three games behind the Giants in the final National League standings. But like Clark Griffith a few years before, the Pittsburgh tandem of owner Dreyfuss and manager Bill McKechnie must not have felt like the current group of players were capable of taking the team over the top. It was time, they felt, for an attitude infusion. However, the trade looked especially bad in the early-going, when new pitcher Aldridge held out over a contract dispute until right before the season, then reported in horrible shape. Then Niehaus was traded to Cincinnati for a relief pitcher, Tom Sheehan, who had an 8.07 ERA through ten appearances. The Pirates began the season 6–14, sinking into last place on May 10.

However, the lineup was too talented to stay down long. The Pirates, led by Kiki Cuyler and Max Carey, began to hit. In consecutive June games, they scored twenty-one runs against Brooklyn and then twenty-four against the Cardinals. Carey hit for the cycle in the romp against the Dodgers. Not to be outdone, Cuyler hit two home runs, a triple and a single.

McKechnie's guys also showed some fire for being the youngest team in the league. After Giants pitcher Jack Scott hit Grantham with a pitch, Grantham hurled his bat at Scott. Later in the season, Carey got into a fight with Brooklyn's Burleigh Grimes in a rundown between first and second. The Pirates were coming of age, thanks in no small part to the important additions of Fred Clarke, a star player and manager of Pittsburgh's past, as McKechnie's right-hand man on the bench, and Stuffy McInnis, a seventeen-year veteran with a well-earned reputation as a winner. McInnis had appeared in four World Series.

By the time the season was over, the Pirates had left their slow start far, far in their dust. They finished with ninety-five victories, 8½ games in front of the rest of the National League. The Pittsburgh victory total was the most for the franchise since the legendary 1909 team won 110 games on the way to a World Series victory over Detroit. The '25 Bucs even carried a sentimental link that that Honus Wagner-led club — pitcher Babe Adams was 6–5 with a 5.42 ERA for the 1925 team, a far cry from his 1.11 mastery in '09.

With the lineup they would bring to play the Senators, the Pirates could afford to carry an aging, ineffective pitcher or two. The youngest lineup in baseball was quite simply also the most dominant. In 1924, only one Pirate, Glenn Wright, drove in more than one hundred runs. In 1925, four Pittsburgh batters reached the milestone. Only one regular position player failed to hit .300. It was leadoff hitter and second baseman Eddie Moore, who fell just short at .298.

The Pirates clean-up hitter was Clyde Barnhart, who played left field. Barnhart wasn't a particularly adept fielder, and was always under pressure to produce at the plate in order to keep a place in the lineup. He came up as a third baseman in 1920, but lost his starting job there to Pie Traynor two years later. In 1924 he struggled at the plate as an outfielder, and only made his way back into the lineup in 1925 because of Carson Bigbee's recurring sinus problems. Barnhart responded with a .325 batting average, knocking in 114 runs despite only hitting four home runs.

Batting behind him, in the fifth spot, was Traynor, the man who had supplanted Barnhart at third base three years earlier. Traynor was somewhat of a late bloomer. New York Giants scout Art Devlin actually took a pass on him at one point when Traynor was in the minor leagues, an oversight that eventually cost him his job. But it would have been easy to overlook the young Traynor, who batted just .212 in his first stint in the big leagues and once made sixty-

10. Another Pennant Run

four errors in a minor-league season. By 1925, however, Traynor was well on his way to becoming the player who would long be recognized as the greatest third baseman in the history of the game. He hit .320 with 106 RBIs, 114 runs scored and fourteen triples.

Wright played shortstop and batted in the sixth spot. Again he led the team in RBIs with 121. He hit eighteen home runs, matching Cuyler for the team lead and franchise record. Incredibly, Wright was only in his second year as a major leaguer. Sadly, injuries would eventually derail what looked like a sure-fire Hall of Fame career. But in 1925, Wright was one of the most feared hitters in baseball.

At catcher, the Pirates started hard-hitting, fast-talking Earl "Oil" Smith. Before the series ended, he and Rice would be forever linked.[25]

* * *

Before the first game began, the Pirates gave a nod to the last World Series played in town, in 1909. Honus Wagner, the great Pirate, and Ty Cobb, his foil that fall with the Detroit Tigers, appeared at home plate as 41,723 rabid fans boomed applause.

Aside from a relatively meaningless Pie Traynor solo home run, there would not be many more opportunities for Pittsburgh fans to empty their lungs the rest of the afternoon.[26]

The Senators struck first. After Lee Meadows began the game by inducing four straight groundballs, Joe "Moon" Harris hit a home run to stake Washington to a 1–0 lead.[27] Washington had picked up the right fielder early in the season from Boston, who shuttled him for a couple of reserves despite three productive seasons. Harris, like his manager with the same surname, was a former coalminer. He'd lived a rough-and-tumble life outside of baseball, seeing combat in France in World War I and suffering severe facial scarring after his transport overturned.[28] He gave Washington a shot of power in 1925, hitting twelve home runs during the season.[29] Now he had launched another in his first World Series at-bat.

But a one-run lead, even with Walter Johnson on the mound, against these Pittsburgh Pirates was not the least bit comfortable. Rice helped Washington breathe a little easier, however, in the fifth inning. With the Senators still clinging to that 1–0 advantage, Joe Harris, Bluege and Peckinpaugh singled in succession off Meadows to begin the inning. But then the Pittsburgh pitcher struck out the next two batters, Ruel and Johnson, leaving Rice to try to bring the men home. A huge momentum swing, the first of many in this World Series, hung in the balance as he stepped in.

Rice didn't disappoint, slashing a single that brought in Harris and Bluege.

The score was 3–0. It wasn't insurmountable, but with the way Johnson was throwing, the Pirates would have their work cut out for them.[30] In the last month of the season, a Pittsburgh scout reported back to McKechnie that age had robbed Johnson of a few miles per hour off his fastball. He either saw the "Big Train" on an off day, or grossly miscalculated in this era before radar guns. Johnson was on top of his game, causing the Pirates to flail a this breaking ball in the early innings, then dialing up the fastball as the shadows crept in. The Pirates were capable of producing runs in various fashions. With Johnson cruising they tried to get aggressive, but Ruel nailed Carey stealing second and picked Cuyler off first.

Johnson struck out ten and allowed only five hits, as the Senators won 4–1. The pitcher called it the highlight of his Washington career.[31] Rice went 2-for-4, adding an earlier single to his two-run hit.[32]

* * *

Players from both teams wore black armbands for Game Two the next day. It was in recognition of great pitcher Christy Mathewson, who had died the evening before in his home in New York state.

The Senators received a scare when Aldridge beaned Ossie Bluege in the sixth inning. In the post–Ray Chapman era, such incidents took on an added layer of fright. Bluge was taken to a hospital, where X-ray revealed no skull fracture. Regardless, he was kept under observation for two days and wouldn't reappear in the World Series again until Game Five.[33]

Rice had two more hits in the game, two more singles, but unfortunately for the Senators, the rest of the lineup didn't rise to the occasion with him. Joe Judge homered to lead off the second, the second straight day Washington had taken an early lead on a solo home run. Glenn Wright answered him in the fourth, though, for Pittsburgh. From there, Vic Aldridge and Stan Coveleski settled into a classic pitcher's duel. Coveleski, however, blinked first. The Pittsburgh lineup, in hibernation for the Series' first sixteen innings with the exception of a pair of isolated solo homers, came alive in the eighth. Eddie Moore reached on an error by Roger Peckinpaugh, an omen for the rest of the World Series. Kiki Cuyler followed two batters later with a home run into the right-field bleachers.

Washington wasn't through yet, though. The first three batters in the ninth reached base, two on walks as Aldridge appeared to be tiring after battling through danger spots all afternoon. Bobby Veach, a pinch-hitter, brought one of the runs across with a sacrifice fly. Then, with two outs and men on first and second, Rice grounded out to second to end the game, which Pittsburgh won 3–2. Though he had two more singles, it was a frustrating game for Rice. In the eighth, he had led off with a single, advancing to third with two outs for Judge. Representing the go-ahead run at the time, Rice could only trot back to the dugout when Judge popped out to Moore at second base.[34]

Aldridge and Coveleski had both turned in outstanding performances as the Series took on a pitching tone. Though they had lost the second game, these were the kind of games that Washington wanted to engage the Pirates in if it had hopes of repeating as World Series champions.

The Series was moving to Washington for Game Three. If Rice felt frustrated by the late innings of Game Two, he'd be right in the thick of the excitement when the Series resumed.

His finest moment as a big leaguer was about to arrive.

11

THE CATCH

A rainstorm backed up Game Three for one day. As day turned into night, temperatures dropped and the latest weather annoyance wasn't rain, but a bone-chilling cold that made it feel more like winter in Washington than early autumn.[1]

Deciding whom to throw against the Pirates in Game Three, Harris went with strategy over loyalty. With left-handers Dutch Ruether and Tom Zachary available, he instead picked right-hander Alex Ferguson.[2] Purchased from Brooklyn in the offseason, Ruether had won eighteen games for the Senators.[3] He even had a post-season win on his resume, though how much a victory in the tainted 1919 classic really meant was debatable.[4] Zachary had an off year in '25, going 12–15.[5] However, in light of his clutch performance against the New York Giants in the 1924 Series, as well as a tenure with Washington that dated back to 1919, it was a gutsy snub for Harris to make. But Harris knew how important Game Three could be. Coming home tied 1–1 wasn't such a bad thing, but now it was important for the Senators to seize momentum on their own turf. The manager felt like sending Ruether or Zachary to the mound against the booming right-handed bats of the Pittsburgh lineup would be like throwing them into a den of wolves. Except for Cuyler's home run late in Game Two, Johnson and Coveleski had done a great job keeping the Pittsburgh lineup in check so far. The odds of keeping the Pirates floundering favored Ferguson over either of the two lefties, in Harris's opinion.[6]

Opposite: Rice was a fine outfielder, and his catch in the 1925 World Series ranks among the greatest in fall classic history — although he didn't reveal wheather he actually caught the ball until a letter opened after his death. (National Hall of Fame Library, Cooperstown, N.Y.)

Washington was Ferguson's third team in the 1925 season. He struggled with Boston and then the New York Yankees, but then somehow found his stride with the Senators, going 5–1 with three complete games in six starts. He'd never come near that kind of success in the major leagues again, but for now, Harris felt like Ferguson was his best option.[7]

He was shaky early, walking Moore to lead off the game then hitting Carey, the second batter, with a pitch. But the danger was erased by a double play.[8]

Taking the mound in the bottom of the first for the Pirates was Ray Kremer, a thirty-two-year-old left-hander who McKechnie had rescued from a career in the minor leagues the year before. Kremer, who could be described as a crafty right-hander, responded with a combined thirty-five victories in his first two seasons.[9] Behind the plate catching him would be Earl Smith.

Like Kremer, Smith had arrived the year before, acquired from the Boston Braves. Throughout his career, he had rubbed plenty of people the wrong way, including one very notable baseball luminary. But at the plate, Smith had done nothing but produce in all three of his big league stops. Personality-wise, he was Sam Rice's polar opposite.

Smith was known around the league as a pest behind the plate, chattering in his opponent's ears in an attempt to get into their heads. His language could be salty at times. In fact, he had practically elevated vulgarity to an art form. "Smith's command of the English language and its more emphatic derivatives is extraordinary," one writer said. "He calls a batter's attention to his erudites of stance at the plate and general batting form quite as an art critic might do. And such chance remarks as he may introduce from time to time about the batters mental deficiencies, physical peculiarities and general ancestry are added merely for good measure."

If Smith had mastered the heckler's dictionary, it may have been because he had learned under the master of the well-chosen curse. Smith first came up with the New York Giants, spending parts of five seasons playing for John McGraw.

"I didn't pay as much respect as he wanted me to some of his little rules," said Smith, a humorous way of putting it.

Though Smith produced for McGraw, batting .336 in 1921, their personalities would clash too much and too often for the marriage to survive long-term. They were too much alike, and one John McGraw was quite enough personality for one big league clubhouse, particularly when he was the one in charge.

"I spent five years with McGraw and there's no denying they were hard years," Smith said. "McGraw has a system that is designed to win. But it's certainly not designed to make great ballplayers.

"Naturally over the course of five years I had a number of little arguments with McGraw."

McGraw didn't trust Smith, and would employ spies to camp out near his catcher's hotel room to report back on his comings and goings. But McGraw wasn't the only person rankled by Smith's idiosyncrasies. Opponents often left home plate for first, vowing to make their way around the bases if for no other reason to get the opportunity to make the Pittsburgh catcher pay for his stream of insults during the at-bat. It backfired in a World Series game against the New York Yankees. Smith, then of the Giants, had to concede home plate to Bob Meusel when the Yankee came barreling into home, spikes high. He managed to summon more courage when Gus Felix employed the same revenge tactic. Felix spiked Smith hard in the shoulder, and Smith retaliated. While the pair duked it out over home plate, the umpire, perhaps hoping for a Felix knockout of the chatterbox catcher, conveniently turned his back and let them scrap.

"The catcher ought to get the batters mind upset, if he can," Smith said. "A fellow isn't likely to hit so well if he's thinking about something else. That's why I talk to some batters so much. Often, they're foolish enough to let my remarks get their goat."[10]

If there were two differing dispositions in the game, they were the loquacious, pesky Smith and the reserved Rice. Before the game was over, however, in one of those cosmic occurrences of chance that baseball seems to confer from time to time, a moment would link them forever. Rice's connection to Smith would survive the series, retirement — even death.

It didn't start off so exciting, though, with Rice grounding out to begin Washington's half of the first for the third consecutive game. He would fare better his next time up, in the third inning. Rice singled for the fifth time in three games. He came around to score on Judge's double later in the inning. The score was 1–1. Pittsburgh led 3–1 against Ferguson at one point, but Goslin's sixth-inning home run, followed by two runs the next inning against Kremer gave the Senators a 4–3 lead heading to the eighth.

In the meantime, Rice had added his sixth single of the series in the fifth. He was doubled off shortly thereafter. However, even though he was continuing to pile up base hits at a record pace, Rice would make his biggest mark upon Game Three in the outfield.

Harris made a couple of defensive changes to start the eighth. With Ferguson having been pinch-hit for in the bottom of the seventh, Bucky Harris sent his ace reliever Marberry to the mound. He also moved Rice from center field to right, the position he had played for most of the past three years (and for the rest of his career), to start the inning. The move was necessitated by McNeely's entry into the game as a pinch runner in the bottom of the seventh. Harris kept McNeely in the game, batting in Ferguson's original ninth spot, and placed him in center.

It would be a fateful move.

Marberry dispensed of Glenn Wright and George Grantham easily to begin the inning, striking both men out. Grantham was now 0-for-11 in the three games of the series, and McKechnie's patience was beginning to wear thin.[11]

Smith, the brash Pirates catcher, came to the plate with two outs and the Senators still clinging to that 4–3 lead they had just seized. Smith had put together a decent series to that point, reaching base once in each of the first two games, and twice already against Ferguson in Game Three. But the damage he had been able to cause was minimized by the fact that he was batting between the slumping Grantham and the pitcher's spot.

The *New York Times* described Smith's seeming arrogance as he looked toward Marberry: "He looked over Marberry's pitching with an arrogant sneer. Crouched at the plate, Earl is not an easy batsman to pitch to. He worried Marberry. Then Smith caught hold of one of his pitches. His left-handed swing was deadly and true, and the ball went soaring far and straight into right field."[12]

Rice spotted Smith's drive off the bat and turned to sprint toward the right-field wall. He beat the ball to the wall, stopping and turning around to gauge his leap as the ball seemed destined for the bleachers and a tying home run. Rice leaped. Everyone in the ballpark could see him snag the ball, at least initially. But hardly anyone could see what happened next, and in fact it wouldn't be resolved for another fifty years.

The momentum of his leap and the ball's trajectory carried Rice over the wall and tumbling into the right-field bleachers. Running out to try to make a call on what had happened was second base umpire Charley "Cy" Rigler.[13] Rigler was a large man, a 6-foot-2, 270-pound Ohio native who had played semipro football before setting out on his umpiring career. Rigler was an intimidating presence because of his size, though he managed to avoid many ugly confrontations. He avoided profanity, and rarely threw players or managers out of games.

"It will be the fault of the player or spectator if I am called upon to exercise physical authority," Rigler once calmly explained.

Rigler had a reputation as a man of great restraint when it came to on-field disagreements.[14] It would serve him well on this afternoon.

As Rice worked his way out of the bleachers, Rigler could only judge based on what he had seen. Rigler saw Rice snare the ball in his glove when he left his feet. And when Rice re-emerged from a fans lap, he still had the ball secured. What happened in between was anyone's guess, but Rigler raised his right hand to call Smith out. The Pirates half of the eighth was over, and the Senators still clung to their 4–3 lead.[15]

"In all the future years that World's Series will be played, in all the games that have been played under high nervous tension in the past, one will never see a more thrilling catch than that grand grabby Sam Rice," Harry Cross wrote in the *New York Times*. "All Washington, and, in fact, American League fans from the Atlantic to the Pacific, who followed this afternoon's battle before the scoreboard or on the radio, raise their hats to Samuel Rice tonight."[16]

The Pirates, on the other hand, weren't in much of a saluting mood. They refused to believe Rice had made the catch, and demonstrated that belief loudly.

Rice, meanwhile, in a rare quote attributed to him during his playing career, said in the immediate furor after the play that he had held on.

"I caught the ball all right, don't worry about that," Rice said. "I got it in my gloved hand as I was running and never dropped it. When I hit the bleacher baseboard, I juggled the ball from left hand to my right, but it never left my clutch. Not once did it hit the floor in the bleachers."[17]

Commissioner Kennesaw Mountain Landis, usually not one to shy away from controversy, called for Rice after the game. The "czar," the unofficial title conferred upon Landis often by the press in the days since his landmark Black Sox ruling, had witnessed the hysteria surrounding Rice's tumble into the bleachers. While others scrambled to assemble eyewitnesses to the play, Landis was eager to take the primary participant's account.

"Sam," the commissioner asked him, "did you catch that ball?"[18]

Landis was no one to mess with. Though most famous for tossing eight members of the infamous 1919 White Sox out of the game for the World Series-fixing scandal, that wasn't Landis's only decisive moment in his role. Before the 1922 season, he was so infuriated with Babe Ruth that he suspended the game's greatest player, along with slugging Yankee teammate Bob "Irish" Meusel, for a quarter of the season. The pair's offense had been participating in a barnstorming tour during the offseason, a practice banned for World Series participants. A few months later, Landis had become irritated when umpires called a tied World Series game due to darkness in the tenth inning. He ruled that all profits from that day be given to charity to avoid baseball any embarrassment.

Rice carefully answered Landis' inquiry.

"Judge, the umpire called Smitty out," came Rice's non-answer answer.

"That's exactly what I wanted you to say," replied Landis. "and that's the way I want you to answer anybody else asking you that question."[19]

Landis almost always meant business and so, for nearly fifty years afterward, that's what Sam Rice did. Of course, with the images of a storm-ravaged farm in Iroquois County, Illinois, still buried deep, deep in the dark corners of his memory, Rice had about thirteen ½ years of practice keeping a secret. If he could hold onto that one, and if he could hold onto—perhaps—the drive from Smith's bat, surely he could keep this one tucked away.

The meeting between Landis and Rice has become the accepted version of Rice's public statement regarding the play. The play-by-play of the face-to-face became further larded with juicy details as the years passed. In a later version,

Landis "glared" at Rice, then poked a finger in his face. In this version, Rice leans back and gives his answer. Landis, then, "immediately relaxed."[20] Whether the details are apocryphal or not, the spirit of the meeting between the men must be represented fairly accurately, because Rice seemed to take playful pleasure in keeping the details to himself in the years to follow.

For example, in a 1965 television interview for a Washington-area production called "The Last Out," host Jim Simpson quizzes Rice about the play during a conversation that takes place near the home plate area at Griffith Stadium, by this point overgrown with weeds:

SIMPSON: Sam Rice either caught it or he didn't. Was that it? What kind of catch was it, Sam?
RICE: Well, I had paced off the distance to the stand. I had measured it off.
SIMPSON: May I interrupt you? You mean from where you were playing, you knew how many steps it was to the stands?
RICE: Practically. The ball was on my right-hand side a little bit, and turned and went back as far as I could go. I jumped up in the air, and there it was.
SIMPSON: Now, there are those, Sam Rice, who say you didn't catch the ball.
RICE: Well, the umpire said I did.
SIMPSON: All right, this is—what?—thirty-nine years later. Did you catch the ball?
RICE: I'll have to take the Fifth Amendment.[21]

And so ends that portion of their conversation.

It was a response Rice had been using for decades. In 1930, legendary baseball writer Fred Lieb wrote about how he tried to pry the secret from Rice during a friendly game of bridge.

"Well, Cy Rigler said I caught it," Rice told him. "It's not up to me to question an umpire."[22]

In 1963, when Rice was inducted into the Hall of Fame, he was approached by a waiter at a dinner party in Cooperstown. The waiter served Rice, then asked him a question.

"Mr. Rice," he began, "did you catch that ball?"

"The umpire said I did," Rice replied.[23]

Why would Landis have instituted a gag order on the one man seemingly able to corroborate Rigler's decision? It would go to figure that Landis didn't really want major umpiring decisions, particularly those made on the game's grandest stage, tried in the court of public opinion. At the least, he didn't want participants themselves testifying in this sort of trial. In a case such as this one, an umpire's judgment call was final on the field. And surely Landis saw no reason to perpetuate scrutiny of the umpire's decision in the aftermath. In these days before instant replay and multiple angles, and even people's short-term memories can be strangely subject to personal biases, as well as the power of suggestion. As far as Landis was concerned, assumedly, the decision had been handed down by the field authority. Rice's version of the play was irrelevant.

11. The Catch

And that was the case whether he endorsed the ruling or not — as soon as his fist punched the air, the result belonged to Rigler, not Rice.

Landis's feelings were of little consequence to the Pittsburgh fans and press, unified in their quest to get to the bottom of what happened while Rice was sprawled out over that right-field railing.

Pittsburgh manager McKechnie, having withdrawn his initial protest after Landis told him an umpire's judgment call wasn't subject to an official protest, was offered signed affidavits by two Pirates fans who claimed to have witnessed a small boy hand Rice the ball after it rolled into the seating area, R.I. Ashman of Altoona, Pennsylvania, and Army Sgt. Ralph Lewis, a Pittsburgh native who was stationed in Washington.

"Rice did not catch the ball at all," Ashman told McKechnie. "Instead, a boy picked it up and gave it to him. Naturally, the Washington fans would say nothing about it, but it was all done not six feet from where I sat and I watched every move that was made."

A Pittsburgh paper quoted an anonymous "newspaperman"— the writer himself perhaps?— who "distinctly saw some person hand the ball to Rice." *Pittsburgh Gazette Times* sports editor Chester L. Smith felt Rigler should have waited to make the call until he surveyed the fans sitting in the right-field bleachers. Even though the section would have been heavily weighted with Senators fans, Smith said he believed they would have answered honestly.[24] One account had Rice catching the ball, having it taken out of his glove by a fan who then, realizing the possible ramifications of his impulsive move, placed the ball back into Rice's glove.

According to another tale, friends of several Pittsburgh players — anonymous, of course, in the printed report — happened to have a hotel room adjoining that being stayed in by some Washington players (why any Senators would need to stay in a hotel in their home city is, of course, not addressed). They claimed to overhear Washington players talking about how their teammate Rice had gotten away with one.[25]

The sequence of events was analyzed like the Zapruder film would be four decades later. Rice, some pointed out, didn't hurry out of the bleachers after diving in there. Surely, had he actually caught the baseball, he would have been in a rush to display the ball caught in the webbing of his glove. Since he stayed sprawled over the railing for several seconds, some conjectured, the only possible conclusion was that he was fumbling with the ball during that time.[26]

The Pittsburgh press didn't believe that Rigler was scurrilous, simply incompetent. One conjectured that the National League umpire was caught overcompensating to make up for any potential doubts about his ability to fairly umpire the World Series games.

Gazette Times columnist Chilly Doyle, meanwhile, said it was par for the course for Rigler.

"Rigler's amazingly incompetent decision is lamented by all those who want the classic to be dominated by sportsmanship," Doyle wrote. "Rigler's honesty is unquestioned. The hard-working official has shown many a time in the National League season that he is not the arbiter to preside over the important games. Cy has a strong tendency to 'guess' decisions instead of making the rulings in a decisive manner.'"

Pirates owner Dreyfuss claimed that Rigler had erred the summer before on a would-be home run by a Pittsburgh batter.[27]

And on and on and on.

While Pittsburgh fans and participants continued to fume, Rice's teammates and supporters simply marveled at his catch, even more so than the year before when he had spent a memorable afternoon picking sure hits out of the pockets of the New York Giants.

"Old baseball men, players and writers searched their memories for a catch that could rival Rice's," but found none, the *Washington Star* wrote. "Clark Griffith, who played baseball when the game was in short trousers, declared he had never seen any catch approach it.

"'It was a catch you are lucky to witness in a lifetime,' he observed."

Senators coach Nick Altrock was rendered speechless. All he could do in the clubhouse after the game was to murmur, "How did he do it?"[28]

The Senators won the game, but not before one last fright in the top of the ninth. With one out, Marberry loaded the Pittsburgh bases on a pair of singles by Moore and Carey, followed by a hit-by-pitch of Cuyler. A base hit by either of the next two hitters, and Rice's supposed catch would be rendered meaningless beyond the great theater it had provided. In classic relief pitcher style, however, Marberry induced Barnhart and then the future Hall of Famer Traynor to harmlessly pop out to end the game and give Washington the 2–1 Series edge.[29] He certainly was a pitcher decades ahead of his time.[30]

* * *

Almost everything said and written in the aftermath of Game Three represented someone's stab at revisionism — with so many versions of the truth floating around, all amazingly supporting the source's agenda, it is clear that the definitive truth about whether Rice did or did not hold onto the baseball was impossible to come by. The attacks on umpire Cy Rigler represented some of the most ludicrous revisionism to come out of the game, however.

Rigler wasn't indecisive. In fact, he was known as an expert, for example, at judging balls and strikes. Rigler underwent frequent eye examinations to make sure his judgment was never impaired.

"His voice was unhesitant, clear and boomed like a foghorn," wrote one of Rigler's biographers. "Despite his massive size, he was quick to move into position to make a call."

So the facts about Rigler undermine almost every argument the Pittsburgh press tried to present in order to undermine him. His vision was fine. He excelled at getting into position to make the correct calls. And he never hesitated over a call.

Rigler's reputation around baseball was spotless. For one thing, he was a pioneer in his profession. While umpiring in the minors, during a game in Evansville, Indiana, Rigler began raising his right arm to signal strikes, the first time hand signals had ever been used in the minor leagues (they were being introduced into the majors at precisely the same time by Bill Klem). In all, Rigler umpired more than six thousand games. Those included ten World Series, at a time when World Series umpires were selected on merit, as well as the first All-Star Game in 1933 at Chicago's Comiskey Park.

Of course, all of this doesn't mean that Rigler couldn't have gotten a call wrong. Even the best occasionally did. But his record sure stands up strong against much of the unfounded criticism being leveled against him in the wake of his out call on Smith's would-be homer.[31]

Baseball Magazine decided to have a little fun with Rice's catch. The publication published a play surrounding the controversy. Though it is a fictional account of a meeting between most of the major players in the did-he-or-didn't-he drama, there's no doubt that the magazine piece captures the spirit of the controversy, if not the verbatim dialogue.

It is set in the baseball quarters of commissioner Kennesaw Mountain Landis, in the evening after Washington's Game Three victory. The piece captures Smith's ebullience to a "T." At the outset, Pirates manager McKechnie begins the dialogue by attempting to lodge a formal protest before a fired-up Smith cuts in.

"Any guy who'd call that a catch is a cross-eyed porch-climber and if Sam caught that home run bust o' mine then Napoleon copped the battle o' Waterloo and Jesse James is got wings now."

As the character of Smith rages, various other players involved in the controversy chime in, with McKechnie attempting to lodge a professional protest while Rigler, the umpire, rebuffs him in "dignified tones."

Rigler justifies his decision by explaining that Rice was in possession of the ball when he left his sight, and was in possession of it again when he re-entered the umpire's line of vision.

"And in the five minutes between them times, Mr. Commish," Smith responds, "the Washington fans was playing ping-pong with it before they slipped it back to Sam to show to the ump again. Didn't they, Sam? Now, on the level, didn't they, Sam?"

The play even lampoons Rice's coy avoidance of Landis's real-life inquiry, noting that he is "grinning cheerfully as he faces his accuser."

"No, I don't think it'll rain tomorrow, Oil," Rice says, "the paper says fair or maybe hail."[32]

* * *

Smith would be a part of one more World Series controversy that involved a future Hall of Famer. This time it was Babe Ruth, whose Yankees led Smith's Cardinals three games to none in the 1928 fall classic. Though play in the two leagues wasn't as drastically different as it would become in the days of the designated hitter, there were still differences in the American and National League rulebooks. The National League, for example, still allowed pitchers to "quick pitch" a batter. The American League, already laying its foundation as a hitter-friendly circuit, banned the technique and required that a pitcher wait until the batter was settled in before delivering.

The Cardinals led 2–1 when Ruth batted in the seventh inning against St. Louis twenty-one-game winner Willie Sherdel. Sherdel got two strikes on Ruth. Then Smith began bantering with the Babe in an attempt to distract him. It worked. While Ruth was jawing with Smith, oblivious to the St. Louis pitcher, Sherdel fired a fastball through the strike zone. But home plate umpire Cy Pfirman disallowed the pitch because commissioner Landis had decreed before the start of the series that the teams would follow the American League policy on quick pitches.

While Ruth, Sherdel, Smith and Pfirman argued at the plate, the Cardinals manager came charging out of the dugout to plead his pitcher's case. It was none other than Bill McKechnie. Once again, however, McKechnie and Smith failed in their bid to overturn a call in their team's favor.

Ruth homered a couple of pitches later, the second of three he would hit in Game Four as the Yankees completed another tidy World Series sweep.[33]

***

Though one wouldn't have thought so with the Pirates apocalyptic reaction to Rice's game-saving grab, there was another game to play the next afternoon. And, considering who was taking the mound for Washington, it was no wonder the Pirates were in such a foul mood the afternoon before. Walter Johnson had struck out ten of them in Game One, and he was on a World Series roll ever since his heroics in Game Seven the year before. Being down 2–1, Pittsburgh must have thought after Game Three, was the same as being down 3–1 with the "Big Train" waiting around the corner for them. And the Pirates were right.

11. The Catch

Johnson was as dominant as he had been in Game One, though in a different fashion. In the series opener, he had blown the ball by the Pirates all afternoon, with many onlookers believing that Johnson, at nearly thirty-eight years of age, summoned the best stuff he had ever delivered in his long illustrious career.[34] In Game Four, he was a model of cold efficiency. Johnson tiptoed through the first two innings, allowing a runner to reach scoring position in each, but settled into a groove after that. Beginning with catcher Johnny Gooch, who was spelling the still-steaming Earl Smith for the day, Johnson retired twelve consecutive Pirates from the second through sixth innings—none of them were by strikeout.

Meanwhile, the Senators' offensive outburst in the bottom of the third provided Johnson with a lead. Johnson himself singled to begin the inning, but was thrown out trying to advance to second.[35] Johnson must have feared that one run might be all the support he'd get against Pittsburgh's Emil Yde, a young left-hander who had won seventeen games during the regular season. But Johnson needn't have worried. Before the series, the Senators joked about the difficulty of pronouncing his unusual last name.[36] In the third inning, they'd show they had an easier time figuring out his pitches.

Rice singled after Johnson, his seventh single of the series. Bucky Harris reached on an error. Then Goose Goslin, again apparently feeling strengthened at the plate by the World Series stakes, ripped a three-run home run. Joe "Moon" Harris, the next hitter, also took Yde out of the park to make the score 4–0. Yde was pulled from the game after Harris's home run. Strangely, after two promising seasons to start his career, he'd never be the same again after the third-inning blow-up. Yde would appear one more time in the Series, as a pinch runner.[37] Within two years, his ERA soared to 9.71 and the Pirates let him go. He had a brief comeback with the Tigers two years after that, and that was it.[38]

Johnson's luck, of course, in Game Four was considerably better. Though he struck out only two, he didn't allow a run, and still is the oldest man to pitch a World Series shutout. In two starts in the 1925 World Series, Johnson had pitched eighteen innings, allowing one run and only eleven hits. He had won both starts.

Most importantly, he had pitched the once-lowly Senators to the brink of their second consecutive World Series title. Washington led three games to one, and no team had ever come back from that deficit to take the World Series. The Senators were just one win away, and they were red hot. Rice, in particular, was supplying steady offensive support for the brilliant pitching that the staff had been providing. He added another single in the fourth inning of Game Four, his eighth of the Series. Rice had two hits in each of the first four games.

He would actually collect two more hits in the next game, including, for the first time, a base hit to leadoff his team's half of the first. Rice came around to score later in the first. It seemed like a promising omen.[39]

Each manager made a significant decision for the fifth game. Harris, steadfastly refusing to give in and pitch one of his two star left-handers, started Coveleski, even though his back was hurting and badly in need of an offseason of rest and recuperation.[40] McKechnie finally decided to bench Grantham, is first baseman. It was curious timing, considering that Grantham had finally broken out of his terrible slump with a pair of singles in Game Four. But with the Pirates hanging on for dear life in the Series, he wanted a winner on the field, so he substituted the veteran Stuffy McInnis at first base.[41]

The missing Pirates offense reappeared quickly. Coveleski wasn't the same guy who had gone the distance in Game Two and lost. In fact, the Pittsburgh lineup picked up where it left off when it rallied in the eighth inning to steal Coveleski's first start from him. The Pirates won 6–3, also knocking Tom Zachary around for a spell after he entered in the eighth inning. Washington hung in for a while, cutting the Pittsburgh advantage to 4–3 on Rice's RBI single in the seventh, his tenth single of the Series. But the Pirates offense was more than good enough to give Vic Aldridge his second Series victory. Carey, Cuyler, Barnhart and Wright all contributed two base hits. Overall, the Pirates rapped thirteen hits. Though twelve of them were singles, the steady barrage was effective.[42]

The Senators had blown their opportunity to finish off the Pirates in Washington. Still leading the series three games to two, they weren't in bad shape. But things weren't nearly as sunny as they had been before Game Five, when a Washington coronation looked like a mere formality. Now the Pirates were beginning to hit like they had all season, and they were going home to Forbes Field.

* * *

Unfazed by Coveleski's subpar performance in Game Five, Harris sent another right-hander, Alex Ferguson, to the mound for the sixth game, another potential clincher. Ferguson had battled his way to a victory in Washington's Game Three victory, with a very important assist from Sam Rice, of course. Or, as Pittsburgh fans viewed it, from umpire Charley "Cy" Rigler.

The trip to Pittsburgh gave Pirates fans a chance to voice their displeasure over Rigler's out call en masse. As always, Rice led off the first for the Senators. Ring Lardner described the reaction in his syndicated column the next day: "The first batter to come up was Sam Rice. He was loudly booed by the crowd for no other reason than he made a good catch in Washington and robbed Earl Smith of a home run. He was booed every time he came up. The way not to get booed in Pittsburgh or perhaps elsewhere is to ignore fly balls or muff them."

American League official George Moriarty, hearing the abuse being directed at Rice, took up for Rice and Rigler: "The way that I saw the play from first base was that Rice made a fair catch of the ball," Moriarty said, "even though I was unable to tell what happened when he went into the stands. I did see this much. Rice caught the ball in his gloved hand over his head. Then he took a step or two as he ran back toward the bleachers and still had the ball in his hand. That was a momentary catch and that was all that was necessary. That is the way the play would have been called in an ordinary game without any protest. The fact that it was in a big series with everybody at tension doesn't change the play."

In Moriarty's view, whether Rice held onto the ball after he plunged into the bleachers was a moot point. He had maintained control of the ball long enough in full view to qualify the play as a catch. Just to show that he wasn't speaking with an American League bias, Moriarty added that a disputed play at home plate in Game Four, in which Bucky Harris was ruled out though it appeared he had slid under Smith's tag, was the correct call, as well. Comparing the two was somewhat comical — Harris had been called out with his team leading 4–0 and Walter Johnson cruising. Rice's catch was viewed, depending on what happened the next two days at Forbes Field, as a potentially decisive play in the World Series.[43]

***

In the game, Pittsburgh's McKechnie went with pitcher Ray Kremer, who had been knocked around for ten hits in the Game Three loss. Things again looked good for Washington from the outset. Goose Goslin cemented his World Series legacy with a first-inning solo home run, tying the record he had already shared with Babe Ruth for most homers in a single World Series. Whether the blast would cement Washington's second straight world championship was another matter.

Pittsburgh manufactured a pair of runs in the third to forge a 2–2 tie. Then, in the fifth, Eddie Moore homered to give the Pirates a 3–2 advantage in front of the home fans.[44]

When Joe Harris connected hard with a Kremer pitch in the ninth inning, it looked like another classic World Series contest might be underway. But "Moon" had lifted his blast to the wrong part of the ballpark — it clocked the center-field wall at Forbes, four hundred-plus feet from home plate. It was good enough to give him a double, but a precious few inches short of tying the game.[45] Still, McKechnie stuck with Kremer, who bore down to retire the innings final two batters, Judge and Bluege.[46] For the second October in a row, the Senators were going to play a Game Seven.

***

Puddles from a rainstorm soaked the Pittsburgh field the next day, and under normal conditions, another day's postponement in order to give the playing surface a chance to recuperate would have been in order. But the forecast for the next several days called for no break in sight, and Landis felt this was the best chance to finish the series, less than ideal as the conditions were.

"We are going to finish this game if it is humanly possible," he told both teams.

With two complete game victories already in the series Aldridge started the game for the Pirates. He wouldn't get out of the first inning this time. Unable to grip the ball or maintain his footing on the slick pitcher's mound, Aldridge allowed a single to Rice to begin the game.[47] After going hitless in four at-bats in the previous game, Rice was back in business with his eleventh base hit of the series, all singles. Aldridge started walking Senators after that, mixing in a wild pitch for good measure. When Joe Judge was walked with the bases loaded to bring Rice home with the game's first run, the anxious McKechnie had seen enough.[48] Had he thought things through, McKechnie may have thought that with the conditions being as they were, there would be plenty of opportunities for scoring on this day. But, then again, who was he to doubt Walter Johnson's ability in any conditions? The Pirates had been unable to touch him yet in his two starts. To keep his struggling starter in the game under the assumption that Johnson, too, would struggle was a calculated gamble that McKechnie was not prepared to take. Not after the way his team had battled back from a three games to one deficit to force this winner-take-all battle.

McKechnie brought in Johnny Morrison, who had thrown $4\frac{2}{3}$ innings of shutout relief in Game Four. He allowed three more runs to score. As he had in that fourth game, Walter Johnson had a 4–0 lead to work with.[49]

After the sixth game, Johnson had speculated about the opposing teams' differing mindsets. "I think that may be our team was a little overconfident after winning three of the first four games, and let down," Johnson said. "The team on the outside always fights harder than its rival."[50] That had been true the year before, with Johnson getting his second opportunity at glory after letting his team down in Game Five. It would be true in Game Seven of the 1925 World Series. If there was anything to be learned so far about the Pittsburgh Pirates, it was that they played their most desperate baseball when their backs were firmly against the wall. Trailing 4–0 before they had sent a batter to the plate in Game Seven, while facing perhaps the greatest pitcher to ever step on a mound: backs didn't get any more firmly to the wall than that.

If the weather didn't provide for the crispest form of baseball, it was a boon for the sawdust industry. Between innings, the grounds crew loaded up wheelbarrows full of it to dump on the infield and pitcher's mound. Even that wasn't enough for Johnson, who began hauling capfuls of extra dust to the mound in a losing battle to maintain his footing. "By the end of the game, he looked like he was covered with oatmeal," wrote Johnson's biographer (and grandson) Henry W. Thomas.

By the sixth inning, even Landis felt he had seen enough. With the capacity crowd filing in before the game, he would have been hard-pressed not to at least try to get the game in for Pittsburgh owner Barney Dreyfuss. At this point, however, an official game was already in the books. Dreyfuss could keep his payday. Washington, Landis decided, would get the world championship trophy.

"You're the world champions," he told Clark Griffith, seated next to him. "I'm calling this game."

Griffith, however, didn't want to win it that way.

"Once you've started in the rain you've got to finish it," he replied to Landis.[51]

Besides Pittsburgh fans, who wouldn't have wanted to see Johnson battle through the horrendous conditions and win his second Game Seven and third nine-inning complete game of this Series? Clark Griffith was not about to accept an asterisk on his team's triumph.

As the game moved on, McKechnie continued to utilize his entire pitching staff, while Bucky Harris chose to go with his best, Johnson, come hell or, literally, high water. Kremer, hurling on a day's rest after his brilliance in Game Six, was effective again.

With Kremer holding down the Senators through the middle innings, the Pirates tied the game 6–6 in the seventh. Max Carey popped a blooper into left field. Bluege, Goslin and Peckinpaugh all gave chase, only to fall short. They all believed, however, they had seen the ball land a foot into foul territory. They were shocked, then, when umpire Brick Owens called the ball fair. Goslin even attempted to prove his case by showing Owens a divot in the field where he claimed the ball had landed. On an afternoon in which the field resembled a minefield, however, one divot wasn't enough to convince Owens to change his mind. Eddie Moore scored to make the score 6–5.

Legit or not, it went down as Carey's third double and fourth hit of the game. Amazingly, he was providing his heroics while playing with a pair of broken ribs, an injury he had sustained two days earlier in a Game Six collision on the base paths.

Pie Traynor drove Carey in with the tying run with a triple deep to center field. Traynor actually tried to stretch the hit into an inside-the-park home run, but paid for his aggressiveness when he was thrown out at home plate.

Still, Washington briefly looked like it would prevail and avoid the embarrassment of blowing a three games to one series lead. Peckinpaugh hit a home run in the top of the eighth to put the Senators ahead 7–6. In the bottom of the inning, Harris stayed with Johnson rather than turning the game over to a fresh bullpen arm. He got the first two outs quickly, but he was racing against the elements, with the rain slamming Forbes Field as hard as it had all game. After the first two outs, Johnson called for sawdust reinforcement before continuing.[52]

Maybe the break stalled his momentum. The third batter, Earl Smith doubled. Then pinch hitter Carson Bigbee lifted a fly ball toward Rice in right. It was anything but routine in the conditions, however, and the ball sailed over Rice's head for the game-tying double.[53]

Peckinpaugh went from hero to goat in less than the time it took to play one inning when he nearly launched a toss to second base into right-center. Harris came off the bag to corral the ball, but the play kept the Pirates inning alive, with the score still tied 7–7.

Kiki Cuyler was now the batter, with the bases loaded and two outs. If Johnson had anything left after battling the elements the entire afternoon, he was going to have to find it here. It was a tense at-bat. The count went to 2–2, and Cuyler drew out the suspense by fouling off pitch after pitch. He took a close fastball, which the umpire ruled a ball. Johnson and the catcher Muddy Ruel were both frustrated by the call, having already taken a couple steps toward their dugout and thinking ahead to the ninth.

Perhaps suffering a letdown after thinking the inning was over, Johnson's next pitch drifted up in the strike zone. Cuyler jumped on it, rocketing a double down the right-field line. Only the Forbes Field ground rules—the ball had become temporarily stuck under the tarpaulin—kept the bases from clearing, but two runs scored to give Pittsburgh a 9–7 lead. After he finally induced the third out, Johnson waited for Peckinpaugh to pass by and put a comforting arm around him.

Soon everyone would need comfort in the Washington camp. Red Oldham, who three years before beat the Senators an astonishing eight times in one season, set Washington down one-two-three in the ninth, including a strikeout of Rice, to preserve the 9–7 Game Seven victory.[54]

After enduring the injury-plagued 1924 World Series, Peckinpaugh had waited a long year to take on the World Series at full strength. There are surely few examples in baseball history of a player experiencing such ecstasy and agony in the span of a single inning. Peckinpaugh made eight errors in the World Series, eight of the nine that Washington committed. The American League Most Valuable Player in the regular season was dubbed "the most invaluable player ever in a World Series" by Associated Press writer Robert Small.

James Harrison of the *New York Times* summed up the memorable afternoon perfectly:

(It was) the wettest, weirdest and wildest game that fifty years of baseball has ever seen. Water, mud, fog, mist, sawdust, fumbles, muffs, wild throws, wild pitches, one near fist fight, impossible rallies—these were mixed up to make the best and the worst game of baseball ever played in this country.[55]

For the second straight October, Bucky Harris faced criticism for keeping Johnson in too long in a key ballgame. The difference, of course, was that there was more baseball to play in 1924, and the team's rally had not only redeemed Harris's reputation. It had cast it in gold.

"Washington has a manager who is a genius in whom the recognized authorities on the game have never been able to find a fault," the *Sporting News* proclaimed just a few short weeks before the 1925 World Series.[56]

Similarly, Johnson's Game Seven performance the year before canceled out his abysmal Game Five loss. Asked after the Game Seven loss if his opinion on Johnson had changed, Harris shot back, "I think he's the greatest baseball pitcher of all time." That question came from a reporter, a Pittsburgh scribe. A telegram waiting for Harris in Washington hit a little closer to home. It came from American League president Ban Johnson: "You put up a game fight. This I admire. Lost the World Series for sentimental purposes. This should never occur in a World Series."

Sentimentality, Harris said in his return telegram, had nothing to do with the decision: "I have no apologies or alibis. I went down with my best." In Harris's mind, if Johnson couldn't hold down the Pittsburgh lineup, no one else at his disposal was going to be able to step onto the field, turned to mush by the late innings, and suddenly stop one of baseball's most feared lineups.

"Sentiment played absolutely no part in my decision to pitch Johnson," Harris told reporters in coming days. "He pitched wonderful ball. President (Ban) Johnson's remarks, if his telegram has been correctly quoted, are gratuitous and would have been better left unsaid."

Ironically, though it was the Pittsburgh Pirates that put up one of the World Series' most memorable disputes after Rice's game-saving Game Three catch, the Senators were the ones who griped publicly about the umpiring after the series. Commissioner Kennesaw Mountain Landis wasn't pleased at the display of sour grapes, and demanded a meeting and an apology.[57]

One person who didn't need to apologize for anything was Rice. He had twelve singles in the seven-game World Series, a record that remains on the books now eighty years later.[58] If it had been made in the television era, it would have been interesting to see how favorably Rice's catch would have been compared with Willie Mays's legendary grab in the 1954 series, Devon White's grab in the 1992 World Series or Endy Chavez's robbery of a sure Scott Rolen home run in the 2006 National League Championship Series. Of course, the fact the play wasn't recorded for dissection from multiple angles only adds to its mystique. Everyone in attendance, from the players on the field to the umpires to the vendors in the far reaches of the ballpark, had one chance to view the play, from one angle.

So did he hold on?

Only one man knew for sure, and he wasn't talking.

* * *

It had taken the Senators a long time to give Washington baseball fans, long-suffering even at the dawn of the 1920s, a proper thrill. But when they did finally come through in 1924 and 1925, they supplied enough drama to more than make up for all the last time. Both World Series were dissected again and again by fans and the press of the day, but in hindsight, the excitement and analysis was warranted. Eighty years after Walter Johnson shut down the New York Giants in Game Seven of the '24 Series, author Barry Levenson, in his chronicle of all the seventh games in World Series history, named the twelve-inning game the best Game Seven ever staged.

The 1925 deciding game? It didn't lag too far behind. Levenson placed it fifth of the thirty-five seventh games played to that point.

"Each seventh game is a saga that has already been told by countless thousands who have cherished the game of baseball and have shown their affection by retelling it to their children and grandchildren," Levenson wrote.[59]

And few could compare to the two Rice participated in.

***

Soon after Rice's World Series catch, the *Chicago Tribune* cooked up a feature story about the local boy made good. If an author is interested in creating the tale of an American hero, writer Frank Butzow suggests, he need "visit the little city of Watseka, seventy-seven miles south of Chicago, and in the pumping station, court house or the back room of Bernie Canavan's tailor shop get the story of Sam Rice."

Butzow goes on to describe Rice as "flashy," a laughable adjective for a workmanlike throwback playing in a period of boisterous superstars. But the article coming so closely on the heels of Rice's spectacular face dive into the bleachers, the writer can be forgiven for being caught up in the moment. This perhaps qualfied as the lone period of Rice's career when that label could accurately apply.

Besides supplying some folksy details about Rice's otherwise cloudy upbringing, the story is significant for one very big reason — the first known public unveiling of Rice's dark public secret. "The great tragedy of his life," as it is called, is curiously buried deep into the text of an otherwise very light, very breezy story. Rice's taste in beer rates a higher mention, as does his affinity for local pool halls.

Perhaps the *Tribune* incorrectly assumed that Rice's background was well-known to the Washington press and public. Perhaps he wasn't sure what to do with such unfathomable tragedy, particularly in a story that presumably was conceived as a celebratory feature story about Rice's shining moment, not an exposé about his hidden past. For whatever reason, the writer and paper downplayed the biggest revelation it had about baseball's man of the moment. And in those days, it was much easier for news to stay contained within a market than it is today, when the Internet sends stories bouncing around cyberspace like pinballs. Also helping keep the story of Rice's tragic past quiet was the fact the writer of the story, Butzow, wasn't regularly a baseball writer but covered statehouse politics out of Springfield. By the next day, he had returned to his regular duties covering the Illinois state government.[60] In the hands of a member of baseball's tight-knit fraternity of writers, surely Rice's secret would have spread like wildfire. Though it's possible that the more compliant sports writers of the era would have kept the story out of print at Rice's behest, the fact that Shirley Povich, the legendary Washington sports writer, didn't even write about the tornado until 1985 would seem to indicate that it wasn't being passed along as oral history.

Rice's catch brought him nation-wide attention, and momentarily drew the story of his tragic background to the surface. Apparently it was scarcely noticed, however, and wouldn't come up again until a decade after his death.

12

Back to Earth

The Senators had interrupted the "live-ball era" to win two American League pennants on foundations of lock-down pitching, airtight defense, and pesky, timely hitting that played well in their spacious ballpark. Opening day 1926, played at a bitter cold Griffith Stadium, seemed to be a continuation of the Senators' success via retroball.[1] As it turned out, however, the occasion merely marked their final gasp.

The matchup pitted thirty-eight-year-old Washington legend Johnson, ready to try to keep the magic going for yet another season, against Philadelphia's twenty-eight-year-old Eddie Rommell, a pitcher beginning to come into his own with more than eighteen victories in each of the previous four seasons, including twenty-one the year before.[2] What would develop would be a duel that remains one of the most captivating opening day pitching battles ever staged.

After appearing to tire in the seventh game of the previous fall's World Series, Johnson's arm awakened for the opener and he began shutting down the Athletics inning after inning. But so did Rommell. Rice singled in the sixth, then stole second base just under the tag of Athletics second baseman Max Bishop. But he ended up being stranded there, just like any other player that either team managed to sneak onto the base paths in the game's first fourteen innings.

It looked like the game might head into a sixteenth inning when Rice led off the bottom of the fifteenth with a line drive out, but somehow Bucky Harris, Goslin and Joe Harris followed his out with back-to-back-to-back base hits to push across the game-winner.

The giddy *Washington Post* predicted another American League pennant. "Take this if you wish," it said, "as an augury that Washington will defeat

Philadelphia once again, and if it pleases you further, that the third straight pennant will float over (Griffith Stadium) next year."[3]

One can't blame observers for getting caught up in the excitement, but the season didn't follow that script.

A frustrating summer ensued, particularly in light of what Washingtonians had gotten to experience the previous two years. In late July, the American League pennant for 1925 was raised over Griffith Stadium. By that point, the Senators were struggling to stay at the .500 mark. The New York Yankees had long before lapped the American League field, reeling off sixteen consecutive victories in late May.[4]

It wasn't tough to figure out where things went wrong for the Senators in '26 — the reliable pitching of the World Series years was no longer up to pennant-caliber. The ageless Johnson, having put in such an incredible opening day performance, posted a losing record while giving up nearly twice as many home runs as he had the season before. Dutch Ruether's ERA soared a full run.[5] But the team may have been able to absorb those dropoffs, perhaps not enough to catch the Yankees but enough to put up a respectable season, if Griffith hadn't tried to get a little too cute on the offseason trading market. He sent Tom Zachary to the St. Louis Browns for pitcher Joe Bush and backup right fielder Jack Tobin. Both bombed in Washington and both were gone before August.[6]

The usually reserved Walter Johnson lashed out as what he felt was an underachieving, complacent bunch.

"Johnson told how he didn't think his supporters were taking the game seriously enough," one account of the late August blowup said. "He named names and told facts as he saw them.... Johnson fights for every last advantage in a ball game. He always goes down with his colors flying. He doesn't like to see his teammates resting because of a long lead, but insists on their going through at top speed."[7]

Whatever could go wrong did so. The Senators played an exhibition game on an off day in mid-June, and Earl McNeely hurt his foot.

"These extra games are worse than war, pestilence and famine," one writer vented.[8]

In August, rain wiped out a full week of the Senators' schedule.[9]

Without a pennant race to follow this year, the Washington press had some idle time to chase around rumors. When American League president Ban Johnson was laid up for a few days with a foot infection, word leaked that he would have to get the foot amputated, and even give up the league presidency. Clark Griffith seemed like an obvious front-runner.

It wasn't true, however, so Griffith had to keep trying to clean up the mess.[10] One of his moves to that effect illuminates the contradiction that sometimes was Clark Griffith. In July, while signing just about anybody that would helps his team steady the ship, Griffith acquired minor league pitcher Emilio Palmero, who hadn't appeared in a major league game in five years.[11] Though playing in the United States at the time, Palmero was from Cuba. And although baseball's color barrier would remain erected for two more decades, that didn't dissuade Griffith from putting Palmero on his ballclub's roster. In fact, he had signed the modern game's first two Cubans back in Cincinnati when he had acquired Rafael Almeida and Armanda Marsans. Years later, Griffith would sign even more Cuban players for the Senators. Noticing this, a black sports writer in Washington, D.C., Sam Lacy, lobbied Griffith to employ an American black. "I am not sure that time has arrived yet," Griffith said. "A lone Negro in the game will face rotten, caustic comments. He will be made the target of cruel, filthy epithets." Of course, so were the Cubans Griffith signed. The suspected real reason Griffith didn't want to sign a black wasn't concern for their safety or emotional well-being, nor was it bigotry on his part. He worked to keep black players out of the majors for the same reason he accepted Cubans into his fold—his own financial gain. While the Cuban players came cheap, Griffith stood to gain by keeping the Negro Leagues operational because he lucratively rented out Griffith Stadium to the local team.[12]

However Cuban players might help the team in the future, Emilio Palmero wasn't the answer in 1926. He was signed, given a shot, and released within about a month.[13]

Through all the team's difficulties, Rice just kept on playing at a high level. While the Senators floundered in June, he put together a fourteen-game hitting streak in which he batted .400—in eight straight games during the streak, Rice had at least two hits.[14]

The Senators needed a late-season surge to climb out of the American League's second division, and even then Joe Judge's late-inning home run on the season's last day was the only thing that vaulted them into fourth place.[15] But Rice was exempt from any blame for the tumble. He hit .337, finishing what would turn out to be the best three-year run of his career. From 1924 through '26, he batted .340. His 216 hits in 1926 gave him three consecutive seasons of at least two hundred.[16]

But without a title to play for, an empty feeling draped Washington, D.C. For at least the time being, the glory days had ended. That would become even more evident soon as the Senators unsuccessfully tried to get things back on track in 1927.

Continuing where they had left off the season before, things went sour from the outset of spring training for the Senators in 1927. In Tampa, Florida, before an exhibition game, Johnson was throwing batting practice to Joe Judge. Judge ripped a line drive back through the middle, striking Johnson in the right leg. The Senators had seen this before, Johnson being dusted by a line drive through the middle. Usually, he rose to his feet, brushed himself off, then, like clockwork, turned in three hundred-plus innings and twenty-five victories. In fact, just a few days before, Judge had lined a ball off of Johnson's other leg with no damage done. So used to the scene were Johnson's teammates, and desensitized to the sight of Johnson sprawled out after a hot smash off of some seemingly indestructible body part, that jokester coach Al Schacht hustled out to the mound and jokingly gave Johnson an animated ten-count.[17]

This time would be different, though. Just two years removed from his twelfth twenty-win season for the 1925 American League pennant winners, Johnson would battle back onto the field, but posted just a 5–6 record in eighteen appearances, along with an ugly 5.10 ERA. Johnson turned forty about a month after the end of the season.[18] He never pitched again, though that didn't mean his role with the franchise had ended—far from it.

For the time being, even with Johnson sidelined to begin the campaign, there were still reasons for optimism. After seeing the mini-dynasty come to an end in 1926, Griffith didn't stand pat and wait for the team to magically turn itself around. For better or worse, he aggressively sought to make additions to the roster that he thought would help lift the team back to its previous heights.

For one thing, the 1927 Senators outfield would consist solely of future Hall of Famers, for Griffith had obtained Tris Speaker in the offseason. Initially, the move was made to give McNeely an occasional respite—Speaker's performance had dropped off in 1926, and he was rapidly nearing the end of his playing career. But it wasn't a move made without a degree of controversy. At the end of 1926, Speaker had been involved in baseball's most lurid gambling scandal since the 1919 World Series fix, a scandal that had it shaken out the way it was initially presented, threatened to eclipse even the 1924 pre–World Series scandal.

A player-manager who had led Cleveland to the 1920 World Series championship, Speaker raised suspicion among fans by resigning unexpectedly in late November. Less than two weeks earlier, Detroit's Ty Cobb had done the same thing. Something seemed to be going on, and it was. In December, commissioner Landis announced that he was investigating both players for allegedly fixing a game on September 19, 1925. According to the account being given by former Detroit pitcher Dutch Leonard, four players—himself, Cobb, Speaker and "Smokey" Joe Wood—met discreetly after the previous day's game between the Indians and Tigers. The Indians were firmly entrenched in second place behind the White Sox at that point, while the Tigers were battling for third place and a share of baseball's postseason money. According to Leonard, Speaker and Wood were willing to throw the game, helping ensure Detroit third place, in exchange for Cobb and Leonard involving them in a sizable bet with a bookie on the contest.

(One thing Speaker had going for him — he had hit two triples and a single in the game in question, hardly the tell tale performance of a fix being in.)

The American League, which had reportedly paid Leonard between $15,000 to $25,000 for a cryptic letter from Cobb that supposedly confirmed the incident, suspended both players while Landis investigated. The disclosure of the existence of "friendship games" late in the season, in which players from one team offered players from another fine clothes and/or cash to try extra hard against a team they were battling for final position, was one revelation that came out of the investigation which embarrassed baseball. But on the whole, people came to the two living legends' defenses, no small feat considering some of the feelings about Cobb that existed.

"I want the world to know that I stand with Ty and Tris," wrote syndicated columnist Will Rogers. "I've known them for fifteen years. If they have been selling out these years, I would like to have seen them play when they weren't selling."

After a series of interviews and inquiries, Landis acquitted both players.

Griffith made a run at Cobb, but was outbid by Philadelphia's Connie Mack, who offered the outfielder a blank check (which Cobb cashed in for $85,000). Griffith was able to secure Speaker for about $30,000.[19]

The acquisition of Speaker worked out fine. While McNeely faltered, Speaker stepped in and rebounded with a .327 average and forty-three doubles.[20] But it was the Senators' other major offseason deal that did serious damage to the team's hopes to challenge for the pennant — and Speaker was actually the man who initiated the deal. When Buddy Myer, who had a promising rookie season in 1926, started slowly in '27, Speaker and Harris talked Griffith into dealing him to Boston for veteran Topper Rigney. Rigney struggled with Washington, earning his release before the season was over, while Myer continued to show his potential, including a well-honed batting eye that helped him reach base often.[21] The wrong would eventually be righted, with Myer returning to Washington for the bulk of his seventeen-year career and even winning an American League batting title in 1935.[22] But in the meantime, the franchise had to live with a trade that Shirley Povich would call "the most colossal error in the trading market in the history of the club." Griffith himself concurred, saying it was, "the worst deal I ever made."[23]

Griffith's offseason manuevering was no match for the plague of injuries that swept through the Senators' roster, which *The Sporting News*, in less politically correct times, had begun calling "Harris' Cripples" barely a few days into the season.[24] Harris played opening day with a broken finger in "an effort to buoy the spirits of his team."[25] Bluege battled a strained leg muscle.[26] Worst of all Goslin was stricken with pleurisy, spending four days in a Pittsburgh hospital as the Senators made their across the Midwest on a road trip.[27]

Meanwhile Rice, one of the Senators actually healthy enough to take the field day after day, struggled with health problems of his own, something he tried to fight through at first. Rice developed headaches, then difficulty with his eyesight, complaining that he was having trouble following anything while he was in motion.[28]

In 1927, the American League as a whole would bat .286 and score almost 6,100 runs. Babe Ruth would slug 60 home runs, while he and teammate Gehrig would both drive in more than 160 runs. Detroit's Harry Heilman (.398) and Philadelphia's Al Simmons (.392) both challenged the .400 mark into the season's final few games.[29] Yet a week into June Sam Rice, one of the era's most bankable hitters, was struggling along with a .194 average.

As the Senators treaded water at around the .500 mark, Rice did little to help pull them out of their early-season sleepwalk. During one particularly ugly stretch, Rice went just 3-for-40, his average plummeting from .257 on May 7 to .195 after the first game of a May 30 double header against the Red Sox (a 3–0 Boston shutout).

Something was clearly wrong. Even when his team was good, Rice was bad. On May 17, Washington drubbed the Cleveland Indians 12–0. Speaker and Goslin combined to go 7-for-7 — a sweet afternoon, surely, for Speaker against the team that cut him loose rather than see him through a potentially damaging scandal. Meanwhile Rice, mired in the worst slump of his career, went 0-for-6. All the while, with the exception of a brief spell in the number two hole, Harris kept leading his veteran off. While the powerful Yankees began to run away with the American League, Washington was led off every game by a player who was struggling to bat .200.[30]

In mid–May, an explanation for Rice's plate struggles arose. He was suffering from what he believed to be sinus headaches. The problem actually first flared up in late April, forcing Rice to the bench for a couple of games, but seemed to be under control.[31]

When the headaches returned in late May, Rice knew it was time to visit a doctor. The severity had increased, along with the area in which Rice felt pain. Whereas the discomfort was initially confined to his forehead, causing him and others to attribute the pain to simple sinus difficulties, a sore throat convinced him that something further might be wrong.

An exam revealed three infected teeth, which "had poisoned his entire system." He had them extracted.

But the good will Rice had accumulated during the three years of his mid–1920s prime, climaxing with his World Series catch, had apparently expired by this point. Playing through pain? It was a heroic act when a man continued to hit to his standards, a selfish one when his performance dipped as Rice's had.

"While his gameness should be commended, he really handicapped his team by his action," Frank H. Young wrote in the *Post*.[32]

The Sporting News, noting Rice's advancing age, cautioned that, left untreated, Rice's teeth and gum infections could jeopardize whatever future in the game he still had left.

"It would be wise," read the story, "for this ailment, if allowed to get a hold, could end the career of a veteran."

The same article pointed out that the Senators would be all right without Rice for a few days, because his backups were capable, but losing him in the long term would be a blow the '27 Senators probably couldn't recover from.

"It takes at least four pretty sweet players to equal one Sam Rice," the story said.[33]

Removing a few bothersome teeth was kind of a catch-all solution in the rudimentary sports medicine era of the 1920s, but in Rice's case, it seemed to work.[34] Relieved of the pain and accompanying sluggishness on the field, Rice's batting average began a steady climb. So did the Senators, though an Independence Day massacre at New York probably killed any delusions of a return to championship form (the Yankees drubbed Washington 12–1 and 21–1 in the same afternoon).

At the same time, Rice entered one of the most blistering stretches of his career. Over a sixteen-game span, he hit .467. Finally, on the last day of July, Rice reached the .300 mark for the season, a remarkable turnaround considering his career appeared to be in serious jeopardy just a few short weeks before.[35]

Yet at the same time, Rice's days in Washington appeared to be numbered, a rumor apparently leaked to the *Post* by franchise insiders. By this time, Rice's slow start at the plate was no longer the problem — he was hitting again, and those previous difficulties had long since been explained away as being in large part due to the string of nagging health issues he had battled through from spring training on into midsummer.

It was Rice's attitude toward fielding and base running, two areas of the game in which his commitment was never in question in the past, that had thrown up red flags about his future with the Senators. In the past, Rice's difficulty picking ground balls from the outfield grass had been an annoyance at times, but something that the fans and the organization could live with because the rest of his game was so honed.

Particularly alarming was Rice's sudden reluctance to track down fly balls in the deepest parts of the ballpark.

"The slightest shadow seems to be a stop signal for him," it was noted.

Baseball people called this being "fence shy," and it was a disturbing development coming from a man who less than two years earlier had sacrificed his body tracking a fly ball headlong into the right-field bleachers. Now the winter of platitudes that the famous World Series catch drew him from the local and national press, along with his peers, seemed like a distant memory.

"This does not necessarily mean that he will drop out of the big league picture, for he is a better player than many regulars now on other teams in the majors," a report in the *Post* stated, tellingly faint praise, "but remarks made here and there by those 'in the know' indicate that Rice's stock with the Washington bosses is dropping fast."[36]

Pressed about the issue during a Senators' series in St. Louis, Harris admitted that he was seriously examining other options for the 1928 season.

"With Sam fielding as he is at present, I would hate to think of him being in right field all of next season," the manager said.

Two outfielders, Sammy West and Ollie Tucker, were being looked at as potential replacements for Rice. In fact, Harris indicated he wished he could make the move immediately if he could have trusted that West would be able to hit adequately — but with his playing time so sporadic, he felt he wanted him to take over the job under conditions more conducive to his success, presumably after a spring full of at-bats. Meanwhile Tucker, who was getting consistent at-bats, was batting at a .379 clip at the Senators' affiliate in the Southern Association.

Harris may have been trying to light a fire under Rice, but as prospects, West and Tucker were not exactly slouches.

"Of course," Harris continued, "this is no final decision, for Sam has been a great fielder in his day and may come out of his 'trance' almost overnight."[37]

Meanwhile, Rice's production at the plate steadied and he ended the season batting .297 with ninety-eight runs scored, including at least one in sixteen consecutive games down the stretch.[38] The Senators won eighty-five games, good enough for third place. It was nothing to be ashamed of. No team, possibly in the history of the game, would have beaten the 1927 Yankees out for the American League title.

They capped the 110-win regular season with a four-game sweep of overmatched Pittsburgh in the World Series.[39]

It was, at least, an entertaining ride that the Senators took their fans on in 1927. Though Johnson was rarely healthy enough to pitch effectively, when he was able to go at all, the club marked his twentieth anniversary with the franchise with World Series-style fanfare on August 2. Johnson appeared in his final major league game on September 30, pinch hitting of all things. It was a historic afternoon in more ways than one — an inning earlier, Babe Ruth had hit his sixtieth home run of the season, victimizing Tom Zachary. And adding to the theme established for the team early in the season, Speaker, not wanting to miss his fellow great's grand day, played despite an injured wrist.[40]

Soon after the 1927 season concluded, the Senators began adjusting the roster for the next season. Rice's starting spot in right field, and any spot on the Washington roster whatsoever, appeared to become safer as the offseason progressed. McNeely, the hero of the 1924 World Series just a few years before, was dealt to the St. Louis Browns for pitcher Milton Gaston.[41] Gaston had won thirteen games and lost seventeen the season before, posting an unsightly 5.00 ERA. But he had thrown 254 innings, the kind of workload the team was going to need now facing the prospect of life without Walter Johnson for the first time in twenty years.

If the Senators were to hand vaunted prospect West a starting outfield spot, however, they would still have to either trade or release one of the remaining starters, Rice, Goslin or Speaker. As Goslin had batted .334 with 120 RBIs in 1927, he was the least likely to go.[42] On the other hand, trade and release rumors dogged Rice all through the 1927 season, even after his health and hitting picked up over the second half of the summer. Rumors that began to circulate heavily right after the season, about the same time Griffith was working out the deal to ship out McNeely, seemed to indicate Speaker, not Rice, would be the odd man out of the Senators' outfield in 1928. Though both parties denied it, there were reports that the Boston Braves were pursuing Speaker as their new manager.[43] A year removed from the gambling scandal had allowed Speaker's reputation to recover sufficiently that a team would again consider placing him in charge. However, the Braves preferred a younger manager who still had a lot of his playing days ahead of him, and eventually settled on Rogers Hornsby, eight years Speaker's junior.[44]

By December, the New York Giants were pursuing Speaker. And since his performance didn't quite live up to his salary in 1927, Griffith was beginning to make it clear that he wouldn't stand in the way if Speaker could work out a deal elsewhere.[45] Every few days seemed to bring a new rumor about where Speaker might be headed, including the St. Louis Browns, where he and Ty Cobb would supposedly sign on to play a season in the same outfield, as well as International League teams Montreal and Jersey City.[46] Griffith finally put an end to the melodrama in late January, granting Speaker his unconditional release (he eventually signed with the Philadelphia Athletics for his final season, playing in just sixty-four games but indeed sharing a dugout with his partner in notoriety, Cobb).[47]

Speaker and McNeely were both now gone, opening at least one Washington outfield spot for one of the team's farm league up-and-comers. Regardless, Rice's starting position still wasn't guaranteed.

Reported the *Washington Post*: "It is no secret that the veteran, Sam Rice, will report at next spring's Tampa training camp with the knowledge that he is merely a candidate for the right-field job and hasn't a stranglehold on it, as has been the case in many previous seasons."[48]

But Rice did win his spot in the lineup, and soon showed why he deserved to still be out there.

12. Back to Earth

By July, the Senators had long been an afterthought in the American League pennant race, and faced the prospect of nine games in five days. Somehow, Washington managed to string together five straight victories during that time.[49] Rice was the hottest Senator of all. The stretch included four double headers, both pairs coming on consecutive days, yet Rice didn't miss an inning. Not only that, but he was flat-out torrid at the plate, collecting sixteen base hits over the five days.[50]

Though his team struggled for the entire season, prompting ever louder calls for Bucky Harris' firing or resignation, the once-again healthy Rice was enjoying a sort of renaissance season a year after his worst overall season since he became a full-timer in the big leagues.[51] On September 5, he was batting .340.[52]

With his team long out of the American League race — again — September was turning out to be a very good month for Rice. On the thirteenth, a fortuitous off day for the Senators, Rice competed in the District of Columbia left-handed golf championship at Indian Spring. Rice not only won, he lapped the field. The tournament was split into a pair of rounds, on in the morning and one later in the afternoon. By the time Rice headed into the clubhouse after carding a morning seventy-six, he held a ten-stroke lead over his closest competitor. On cruise control, he slipped to an eighty-three in his second round — his worst round of the year, actually — and waltzed to the finish with a five-stroke victory over Byrn Curtis.[53]

A few years before, of course, it had been the popular opinion around baseball that golf interfered with player performance, as it supposedly sapped their energy and altered their natural swings. Rice seemed to come out of his thirty-six holes of competitive golf just fine, though. When the Senators returned to action two days later, in Detroit, he had three hits in a 12–2 victory. The next day, Washington won again, 11–7. And again, Rice had three hits.[54]

If anything, the mid–September golf tournament had helped his batting, strange as it may seem. After peaking at .340, Rice had gone into a little bit of a tailspin, with just two hits over his next twenty-four at-bats before the golf tournament at Indian Spring.[55] After getting away from baseball for a few days—the golf championship coincided with a four-day respite from action for the Senators— Rice closed the season by hitting safely in eleven of the final thirteen games he played.[56]

In saying goodbye to McNeely and Speaker, and not rushing one of the other minor leaguers to the major league outfield, the Senators had made the right move. Rice was back to his old self in 1928. "Sam expects to stage a comeback," *The Sporting News* had reported in January, right when it appeared Griffith would choose to keep him instead of Speaker to fill out the Washington outfield for 1928.[57] The newspaper was correct. By mid–May, while the Senators performed a nine-game freefall into last place in the American League standings, Rice's average had risen to .359 and the publication updated his season enthusiastically: "Sam Rice is doing the best batting of his career."[58]

There was a late April scare that Rice's sinus problems, or whatever they were, from the season before were creeping back up, but that turned out to be nothing more than a common cold.[59] Otherwise, while the team mostly struggled, Rice had a terrific season, batting .328 with 202 hits. He had fifteen triples, the second-highest total of his career, and his thirty-two doubles gave him more than thirty doubles and ten triples for the eighth consecutive season. Perhaps one of the few signs of aging was Rice's sixteen stolen bases, his lowest total in a full season since he had been in the big leagues. But Rice was stealing smarter these days, only getting thrown out three times two seasons after he was nailed twenty-three times.[60]

While Rice was back to putting in his usual steady season, the Senators were not short on melodrama in 1928. Goslin led the American League with a .379 batting average, winning an exciting three-man race between he, St. Louis' Heinie Manush and New York's Lou Gehrig.[61] But he also caused the organization great consternation with a throwing arm injury in spring training that could have been easily avoided. One day, Goslin wandered over to join a high school track team practicing in a nearby field. He picked up the shot put, out hurling all of the high school kids, but throwing out his arm in the process. In those days before the designated hitter, Harris was forced to keep him in the lineup, ordering shortstop Bobby Reeves to venture deep into left to take Goslin's short, soft relay throws any time the ball was hit that way. Harris remarked that Goslin was "the only outfielder in history with a caddy."[62]

After the horrible start, the 1928 Senators finished the season in fourth place, 75–79.[63] The recovery wasn't enough to save Harris's job, though, as the summer-long rumors regarding his tenuous status turned out to be true. As soon as the season ended, Griffith terminated Harris, who, rumor had it, had taken up quite the D.C. social life after his marriage to Elizabeth Sutherland, the daughter of a West Virginia U.S. senator. But Griffith didn't dismiss the man who had led the franchise to its greatest heights without regard for his employment status—he helped set him up with the open managerial position in Detroit, literally within the hour.

Though the team's recent lack of success prompted Harris's dismissal, overall Griffith had been pleased, of course, with the results of appointing a manager from within the ranks of his roster. The hire of Harris had been a risk at the time, considering his age, but it had brought immediate dividends in the form of a World Series championship. It also brought a period of serenity to the franchise after several years of instability in the dugout leadership. So while

12. Back to Earth

now looking for Harris's replacement, Griffith's first inclination was to examine the Senators' current roster for a player who could fill the role.

Three men jumped out — Rice, Judge and Bluege. All were proven winners. Judge and Rice had been part of the organization for a long time. But ultimately, Griffith judged all three to be "uninspiring." Which made his eventual selection for the job, Walter Johnson, curious.[64]

In mid–October, Johnson signed a three-year, $25,000-a-year contract to manage the franchise that he had served as the face of for so long. Washington fans were delighted. Griffith, having executed a brilliant public relations move, now went about the business of trying to convince the press that Johnson had the personality to lead in his new capacity. The former pitcher's year as a minor-league manager in Newark, Griffith explained, had helped dispel any doubts he may have previously had. Not only did Johnson gain the experience of making decisions to guide a team through a full schedule of games, he had also shown himself capable of playing the disciplinarian role when necessary, suspending two of the team's stars late in the season after they violated team rules.[65]

While Johnson, after a year of training in the bushes, had moved forward into his next career, Rice was spending the offseason contemplating his next move. At age forty, his life had reached a possible crossroads.

Rice and Edith were spending the winter in San Diego.[66] As usual, Rice was taking advantage of the warm Southern California climate to work on his golf game (an article of the time identified Rice, Brooklyn's Arnold Statz and Chicago Cub "Speed" Martin as baseball's best golfers). Having played in serious amateur tournaments for years, Rice was beginning to become even more serious about the game. He helped form, for example, a Pacific golf association for major leaguers spending the offseason in California.[67]

Rice had always been serious about his golf game, but now the lure of the links was pulling him harder than ever. Rice, nearing his fortieth birthday, was giving serious consideration, despite his success the season before, to retiring from baseball.

What frightened Griffith and made him believe that Rice might carry through with his retirement comments wasn't just his advancing age, but how well Rice had managed his meager salary through the years. The Senators' boss was well aware that Rice had taken care of his money and invested it wisely. Any return to the baseball field wouldn't be undertaken out of financial necessity, that was for sure.

Griffith also feared that Rice might want choose to leave the game on top after his return to form in 1928.

The drama began to build in late January, and finally came to an end a few days later, when Rice ended the speculation by signing his Senators contract for the 1929 season.

"I know Walter Johnson will be tickled when he hears this news," Griffith said. "While we both felt that Sam would not retire as had been reported, there is always the possibility that such a contingency will arise, and we need Rice this year."

In the end, the urge to play trumped the urge to walk away.

"The 'old fever,'" Griffith said, "just cannot be controlled.... That is what gets 'em, the old fever; the urge to stay in the game which has been their life's work and they seldom want to leave while they still are capable of playing good baseball."

But just because Rice was returning to the roster didn't mean that he was promised his traditional starting spot in the Senators' outfield.[68]

Unbelievably, despite the fact he would be playing for his longtime teammate, Rice's .328 average and 202 hits in 1928 weren't enough for him to secure a starting outfield spot for the following season. For the last few years, the Senators had constantly been acquiring a parade of young outfield prospects who were supposed to push Rice out of his accustomed patch in right field. As the 1929 season approached, the brain trust of the organization thought they had finally found one up to the challenge — Red Barnes.

"If Barnes presses Rice for the position, it should be an incentive for Sam to 'bear down,'" Griffith explained. "I would not be surprised to see him repeat his 1924 and 1925 years, when I honestly believe he was about the best ball player in the league."[69]

Initially, Barnes was looked at as competition with West for one of the Senators' outfield slots, but when both had productive seasons in 1928, the organization began to look at them as dual cornerstones of a possible outfield of the future — and present — for the Senators.

Rice had other ideas.

It was one thing to talk about an outfield youth movement, another thing entirely to take drastic leap of replacing a franchise mainstay like Rice while he was still, despite advancing age, at the top of his hitting prowess. But in late March, with the season still weeks away, that's what Johnson did.

"Rice is a great player and no doubt will see plenty of service with us during the coming season," said Johnson, trying to dress up the blow. "But we are looking toward the future as well as the present in our plans, and unless either West or Barnes flivver they will be our regulars."

To that point, Barnes had hit about .400 during an extended look during the spring. Rice, meanwhile, had appeared in just two games, hitting well in both of them.

"I know that Rice played one of his best games last year, hitting .328, and it is a lot of satisfaction for me to have a fellow of his type around," Johnson continued.

After a two hundred-hit season, Rice had been demoted to utility man. But Johnson's decision came with a caveat — if either West or Barnes failed to perform at the kind of pace they had set during their torrid springs, he would replace either of them with Rice.[70]

It took all of five games for Rice to earn his old job back. After making only a pair of pinch-hitting appearances in the first four games, including three Senators losses, Rice was back in the lineup on April 23 at Philadelphia. He played right field and batted third. Barnes' slow start was attributed to a knee injury he suffered in a late exhibition game in Charlotte.[71] But whatever the reason, as it turned out, Rice was back in right field to stay. He wouldn't miss another game until August 17.[72]

Rice had secured his short-term future, but by 1929, his tenure with the Senators was clearly a season-to-season proposition. A couple of factors were threatening to push him out the door. For many years, ever since home runs began leaping off the bats of American League hitters beginning in 1920, Griffith had watched sluggers like Ruth and Foxx and longed for his own power-hitting outfield bat. Rice was a hit machine who played a terrific right field, but his power stroke was nearly nonexistent. During the 1929 season, Griffith was interested in, for example, New York's Ben Paschal. Though he hadn't matched the output since then, Paschal had hit twelve homers for the Yankees in 1925. He was struggling and very much available in 1929.

Paschal had another quality Griffith wanted for the Washington lineup — he was a right-handed batter, unlike Rice and the rest of his Senators outfield mates.[73]

But Paschal ultimately wasn't a good fit, mostly because, at age thirty-three, he didn't possess perhaps the most important attribute Griffith was searching for — youth.[74]

"The Washington club," the *Sporting News* reported, "is scouring the bushes for new talent on the principle of catching them while they are young."

Griffith was, the paper continued, "not interested in athletes whose lease on baseball life under the big tent is past its early stages."[75]

Griffith had done a great job scouring America's various minor leagues to assemble the core of the 1924 and 1925 American League pennant-winning teams. But what was left of that core, including Rice, was now beginning to age. His desire to begin work on a new nucleus to perhaps prepare the Senators for another run in the 1930s was fairly obvious.

Besides Griffith's desire to see Barnes and West worked into the regular outfield, he also appeared determined to establish a farm system for the Senators. Branch Rickey would eventually establish the first such system for his St. Louis Cardinals in the 1930s, but in 1929, Griffith was pursuing a very controversial and widely unpopular system.[76] He pushed ahead, though, and was on the verge of purchasing the Atlanta Crackers of the Southern League for an eye-popping $600,000.[77]

The transaction was imminent, hours away even, when Southern League president John D. Martin intervened, invoking a league rule that said three-fourths of the franchises in the Southern League would have to approve the sale of another to a major league team.

Griffith, not wishing to politick, withdrew the offer.

This was good news to baseball purists, who felt that the implementation of a true farm system in major league baseball would hurt lesser franchises who wouldn't be able to afford to stockpile players in the manner of the more successful franchises (why the balance of power would be any more skewed than it already was because of the bidding wars of the time was not adequately answered by these opponents).

"Carried a little further," the *Sporting News* said, "one can visualize future baseball scouts choosing recruits in the cradle."[78]

Griffith eventually tried to work his way around the resistance, as his number one scout Joe Engel purchased the Chattanooga franchise in the Southern League for $50,000 (facilities were not part of the price tag, unlike the proposed Atlanta acquisition).[79]

It was an active summer for Griffith. As the Senators struggled into late July, he ventured into the team's clubhouse and gave the team a fiery speech in reaction to their poor play, his first such lecture since he gave up the managerial reins in 1920.

He also had the usual firing and trade rumors to deal with. The hottest ones had him relieving Johnson of his duties less than a year into his tenure. Griffith denied them. He also denied that Rice, Judge and Ruel were on the trading block.[80]

As usual, the most interested suitor was said to be the New York Yankees.

"Based on the assumption that all outside interests must pay tribute to New York," said one Senators beat writer of the rumors, "they usually have Washington disposing of all its desirable players, most of them headed for Gotham.... The New York stories that Rice, Judge and (Sam) Jones will be traded can be dismissed as beautiful dreams of dope purveyors who deem it the proper thing for other clubs to hand over their stars for New York's discards."[81]

Griffith also had to battle the specter of gambling in baseball, which reared its head when three men were arrested in Boston during a Senators series there for taking bets on the series. To combat the scourge, he hired eight D.C. headquarters detectives and six Eighth Precinct officers to staff Griffith Stadium for games.[82]

And, finally, he spent the later part of the summer looking for a new spring training home for the Senators, who were planning to move out of their long-time February and March home in Tampa.[83]

12. Back to Earth

Through all this turmoil, one thing was very clear as the 1929 season progressed — the brief demotion of Rice to a reserve role was a very big mistake. While his team slumped badly — Goslin followed his batting title with a mystifying .288 average, the worst of his career — Rice picked up where he had left off the year before.[84] By mid–June, he was hitting .362, ninth in the American League.[85] Rice wouldn't keep that pace up all summer, but he eventually settled into a nice groove and his average stayed right at around .330 the entire summer.[86] He finished with a .323 average with thirty-nine doubles and ten triples (again topping thirty doubles and ten triples). He finished just one hit short of two hundred — a hit he certainly would have picked up had he been in right field to start the year instead of Red Barnes, who batted .200 in 130 at-bats and was finally given up on by the organization the following summer. Perhaps most amazing of all, at an age when his bat was supposed to begin slowing down and a major league fastball should have been tougher and tougher to catch up to, Rice struck out a career-low nine times in 616 at-bats.[87]

These were good times for Rice and good times for baseball as a whole. American League president E.S. Barnard boasted that attendance had increased by a total of about 480,000 fans from 1928, resulting in the third-highest total in the history of the American League. National League fans were not adverse to spending money on tickets, either — the Cubs had to actually refund $1.5 million to would-be World Series ticket buyers, so great was the demand (as it has every year since then, October ended without a Cubs World Series victory, as the Philadelphia Athletics took them in five games).

In Cleveland, the Indians were dreaming excitedly about the future, and not just on the field. General manager Billy Evans had to turn away an airplane company that attempted to sell him planes to fly the team from city to city. But he said, surely with an optimistic gleam in his eye, that the day would come when all major league teams would be whisked from city to city by air.[88]

13

GRANDPAP OF THE POTOMAC

Rumors that the American economy was heading for a down period began to circulate in early autumn of 1929.

While baseball executives were dreaming of a future of flight and boasting about their terrific ticket sales, one respected American financial expert, Roger Babson, urged caution.

"Sooner or later," he explained, "a crash is coming. And it may be terrific." He was right.[1]

In October, the World Series between the Cubs and Athletics played in front of full houses. Fifty-thousand fans crammed into Chicago's Wrigley Field, far exceeding the ballpark's capacity. The final three games, concluding with Philadelphia's clinching 3–2 victory on October 14, drew capacity crowds to Shibe Park, all announced at 29,921.[2]

By the time the game reconvened in the spring of 1930, the nation was a changed place.

This wasn't the smooth transition from 1919 to 1920, with symbolic changes in science, leisure and sport only making themselves clearly visible with the benefit of hindsight. The Roaring 1920s crept up on America. But they ended with a crash.

Uneasiness on Wall Street began on October 24. The system essentially ground to a halt a few days later, on October 29, Or Black Tuesday.

After he was released by the Senators following the 1934 season, Rice caught on with the Cleveland Indians, where he played one productive season for former teammate Walter Johnson. (National Baseball Hall of Fame Library, Cooperstown, N.Y.)

"They roared like lions," explained one report from the time. "They hollered and screamed, clawed at one another's collars. It was a bunch of crazy men. Every once in a while, when shares in radio or steel took another tumble, you'd see some poor devil collapse and fall to the floor."

Sixteen million shares were traded during the frenzy of panic selling. Investors lost $8,000 million. In that one day, shares in Union Cigar free fell, from $113 at the beginning of the day to $4 by the close of trading. The company's president committed suicide by jumping off a window ledge.

By no means was this a singular story.

In the meantime, baseball and the Washington Senators carried onward, facing a rough decade ahead. Rice, in fact, seems to have survived the Depression just fine. His broker and friend Bill Birely remembered Rice as a conservative and sharp investor.

"He had quite a holding," said Birely. "He had quite a portfolio."

And, Birely said, Rice was very cautious with his money. He allowed himself one major luxury — Studebaker cars. But he made up for that by skimping on the maintenance.

"He never changed his oil," said Birely. "He maintained that it was a waste of money. I wouldn't say that he was tight. I would say that he wasn't a big spender."[3]

While Griffith was rejecting overtures from the Browns for Goslin (the teams would eventually consummate the deal less than two months into the 1930 season), Rice was sending signals that he intended to bounce back from the drop-off of 1929. And he wasn't going to be content just to arrive in Biloxi for spring training and expect it to happen as if by magic or the force of his will. After the '29 season ended, he asked for and received permission from Griffith to spend two weeks in Hot Springs, Arkansas, prior to the opening of Senators camp, putting his body through a workout regimen of "mountain climbing, golf and baths so that he'd be ready to hit the ground running in March."[4]

"(Rice) has promised Johnson another two hundred–hit season next year," Paul W. Eaton wrote in *The Sporting News*. "(And he) is overlooking no opportunity to be on edge."[5]

So it was that while in 1929 the Senators had attempted to bench Rice, but in 1930, he spent a good portion of the summer as the best hitter in the American League.

It began inconspicuously, with a single in four at-bats on opening day in a 4–3 loss to the Red Sox.[6] By the time April rolled into May, the Senators were 11–3 and Rice was hitting at a .380 clip, good for seventh in the league. What's more, he had hit safely in all thirteen games he had appeared in to that point. Then Rice really got hot. He had three hits each in three games from May 8 to

10, the first against the White Sox and the next two against the Tigers. All were Washington victories. The next day Rice slumped — he managed just two hits in four trips to the plate. So did the Senators — they actually lost a game, falling 5–3.

It seemed a magical season was underway in Washington, for both Rice and the Senators. On May 30, the team headed to Philadelphia for three games against the team trailing them in the standings by three full games. The team, picked almost universally to finish in the American League's second division, was 27–11. Rice, meanwhile, had risen to the top of the league batting leaders with a .410 average. The week before, he had ripped six hits in seven at-bats over two games against the Red Sox.

Rice started the season on a twenty-eight-game hitting streak, and the Senators were equally hot.[7]

"Watch our smoke," the usually soft-spoken Johnson publicly boasted at one point.[8]

Things couldn't go that swimmingly forever, though. While Rice kept hitting — safely in forty-four of the first forty-five games he played in, as a matter of fact, after he immediately followed the end of his first hitting streak with a sixteen-gamer — the Senators allowed the Athletics to make up that ground in a hurry. They lost all three games in Philadelphia. Then, when the teams returned to Washington the next day for a single game, they lost that one, too.

Still, the Senators continued to keep pace with the Athletics, and on July 8, after Washington had won eight games in a row, all on complete games by Senators starting pitchers, the teams were in a virtual tie for first place. From that point on, however, Philadelphia, the defending World Series champions, began to play like it, and the Senators began to steadily lose ground in the American League standings. By late July, the Athletics held a 6½-game lead.[9]

All the while, however, Rice continued to flirt with the .400 mark and the American League hitting lead well into June, but at forty years old, playing every day, sometimes twice a day, was bound to exact a physical toll. And that it did, as he suffered a bruised knee in a series against the White Sox.[10]

Rice's knee forced him out of action at precisely the right time. Rice had come to the plate once in a game against the White Sox on June 22 when he left the contest. So Sam West and Dave Harris were in the outfield when, they reported, shots of some sort rang out and whizzed past their ears. Both reported seeing turf dug up in front of them, and reported the incident to the Washington police. Harris had replaced Rice in right field — it was his first game as a Senator.[11]

Rice returned to the lineup a couple days later and continued to it, not falling into any kind of prolonged slump until late July, when he fell into a miserable 3-for-39 slump. At that point, Rice was beset by stomach problems, but with his team trying to claw back into the pennant race with the Athletics, and offense difficult to come by, Johnson had no choice but to keep penciling Rice into the lineup game after game. Between July 25 and August 8, Rice lost thirty points from his batting average.[12]

"Rice," read one report, "is beginning to feel the effects of his long service and cannot be counted on to play through an entire season at top speed."[13]

One place where physical weakness, and perhaps age, seemed to take its toll on Rice was on the base paths. On July 17, he led the American League with thirteen stolen bases. That was precisely the number he would end up with for the season.[14]

Rice had been in Washington since 1915, and even as he banged out hits at his old rate — 207 in 1930, his sixth and final season over the two hundred mark — the world around him began to change.[15] In midseason, the Senators were playing a series at St. Louis when Rice's roommate Goslin left the hotel to visit a zoo in the city. When he returned, Rice had news to deliver.

"Hey, you're in the wrong hotel," Rice told him.

Goslin was confused.

"I tell you, you're in the wrong hotel," Rice continued.

"What are you talking about?" Goslin asked, confused.

"Don't you know," Rice said, "that they traded you to the St. Louis Browns?"[16]

The way the game was presented was in a transition period, as well. The sporting papers of the day were filled with advertisements from sporting good companies like Louisville Slugger and Spalding. But by 1930, they were also earning advertising revenue from companies such as General Electric and the Giant Manufacturing Co., producers of powerful flood lights that were being used to illuminate minor-league ballparks around the country — night baseball, the experiment, was beginning to get a footing in the bushes.

"Flood lighting will work a revolution in professional baseball," a GE ad in *The Sporting News* read. "It will bring out crowds who can't go in the afternoon; it will re-establish baseball as a consistent profit-maker by fitting it into America's amusement hours."

What GE and others were selling, Griffith, for one, wasn't buying. He had taken in a minor-league night game in Newark, N.J., and left unimpressed.

"(There is) nothing to it for anyone who wants baseball instead of a mere show, and I believe fans prefer their baseball," Griffith said. "I am satisfied it will be many years before the big leagues take to night baseball, if ever."[17]

Griffith held on longer than most — when the Senators finally flipped the on-switch at Griffith Stadium in 1941, they were the eleventh of the sixteen franchises to finally play a home game under artificial illumination.[18]

Griffith wasn't completely anti-progress, though. In early September, he installed a public address system at the ballpark, and fans were greeted not only to announcements of who was batting and pitching, but also explanations of the intricacies of confusing plays on the diamond.[19]

Ultimately, it was a nice consolation prize for Washington fans, who were treated to a surprising second-place finish in 1930 by the "Grandpaps of the Potomac," as one clever sports writer nicknamed them.[20] But Philadelphia's 102 victories were too much to keep pace with, and the Senators' ninety-four victories, two more than they won during the 1924 championship season, still placed them eight games back.[21]

The season was notable not just for the ninety-four victories, but the manner in which an energized Griffith had coaxed it out of his organization's roster. He was an active man at the trading deadline, and though sentiment had played a part in his hiring of Johnson as manager two winters before, it seemed to be the furthest thing from his mind when he traded Goslin to St. Louis for Heinie Manush. Goslin was batting .271 at the time of the trade. Manush bolstered the Washington attack instantaneously, hitting .362 the rest of the way. Griffith also received Alvin Crowder in the trade, and the pitcher won fifteen games in a Washington uniform — before long, he'd develop into the ace of the Senators pitching staff. Griffith also dealt Rice's one-time replacement Red Barnes for another outfielder, Dave Harris (who would actually become his future replacement).[22] And to end the flurry of trading activity, Griffith acquired first baseman Art Shires from the White Sox — this was an attempt not only to shore up the team's depth at that position, but to provide some competition for Judge, which Griffith had observed was a productive way to get Judge's best out of him.[23]

While the Senators' season was merely a step forward — a huge one at that — Rice's 1930 campaign was historic, and remains so to this day.

After flirting with .400 well into the summer, Rice's average plummeted for a while, then leveled off at around .350 for the season's final two months.[24] He batted .349. Only Ty Cobb, who hit .357 in 1927 at age forty, hit higher for a season after that birthday among players who qualified for their league's batting title (3.1 plate appearances per game).[25]

Rice's 207 hits in 1930 put him in even more select company. As of 2006, he remains the only player in baseball history to reach the milestone at age forty. Paul Molitor actually had 225 hits in 1996, but he turned forty during August of that season (Rice is actually also the third-oldest player to reach two hundred hits, having reached 202 in 1928 at the ripe old age of thirty-eight.)[26]

The 1930 season was actually a good one for old geezers like Rice. On June 27, Philadelphia pitcher Jack Quinn hit a home run. He was eight days shy of his forty-seventh birthday (Julio Franco finally snapped his record as the oldest major leaguer to hit a homer when he connected on April 20, 2006 at age forty-seven). Quinn was just getting started, though — he'd move to Brooklyn after the season, and lead the National League in saves two straight years, finally retiring after the 1933 season, at age fifty.²⁷

It's one thing for modern players like Molitor or Franco, with all the modern amenities available to them to stay in playing shape at an advanced age, to continue to perform. Rice had his season in an era when it was virtually unheard of — Quinn excepted — for star players to continue to play at a high level, let alone put in what can arguably be considered a career year, after their fortieth birthdays.

Among Rice's peers: Babe Ruth struggled to a .181 average as a forty-year-old. Tris Speaker batted .267 in just sixty-four games. Rogers Hornsby, as a player-manager for the St. Louis Browns, had just five at-bats as a forty-year-old. Goslin was three years into retirement. Joe Judge logged fifteen at-bats for the Red Sox.

By the time he would have been forty, Lou Gehrig, sadly, had already been dead for two years.

Rice, in 147 games no less, had thirty-five doubles and thirteen triples to go along with his other numbers, so his legs had life in them, too, not just his bat.²⁸

But that didn't mean he was intent on returning for another go.

"Sam, who is pretty well fixed with this world's goods and doesn't have to labor out there under the hot sun," the *Sporting News* reported, "has had a notion for some time now that he would like to confine his exercise to golf. He was on the verge of quitting the game for good last winter, but finally reconsidered, and now again is talking of hanging up his glove for all time."²⁹

And even if Rice did decide to return, Johnson wasn't counting on another season like the one he had just put in.

"Both of these veterans," said Johnson, referring to Rice and longtime teammate Judge, "played as well, if not better, than they ever have, but they've reached that stage when I have to be protected in case they start slipping."³⁰

As he had every other time he had contemplated retirement, however, Rice did return. And as the 1931 season dawned, he remained the Senators' regular right-fielder, at least temporarily.

But just a few games into the season, that status already seemed precarious, particularly in light of the concerns Johnson had expressed the previous fall about Rice's age. In late April, Rice and Judge were both mired in slumps, though Johnson tried to dress it up as best as he could, explaining that both were hitting the ball hard, but just right at people.³¹

On April 27, Rice came to bat with the bases loaded against the Yankees in the bottom of the twelfth inning. There were two outs in an 8–8 game, and Rice, in conditions described as "football-playing weather," took a pitch off his wrist to win the game.³² A couple of weeks later, he made one of the six bases he would steal on the season an exciting one. After doubling to lead off against Cleveland's Wesley Ferrell, Rice moved to third base on a groundout, then stole home when he noticed that Ferrell was slow in his delivery to home plate.³³ Rice's legs may have been slowing down, but he certainly still had his baseball wits about him at age forty-one. It was the eleventh of twelve steals of home Rice would have in his career, the first one coming on August 2, 1917 when he was a spry twenty-seven-year-old, the final one coming more than a year later, at age forty-two.³⁴ Rice is twenty-sixth all-time in career steals of home (though research into the category is ongoing). Tied with him? His favorite manager — Donie Bush.³⁵

In June of 1931, Judge missed several games after undergoing an appendectomy.³⁶ And by the end of the month, both he and Rice were in serious danger of losing their everyday status.

"Scribes have been singing the swan song of both for some time," the *Washington Post* wrote, "and had been proven wrong so many times that they finally had forgotten both words and music, but they are now seeking the copyright owners with a view toward popularizing the song again."

Rice's situation wasn't helped by the fact that Dave Harris, who had watched a bullet whiz past him while filling in for Rice in 1930, was hitting as well or better than Rice, and was ten years younger.

"As long as Harris shows ability to clout, he will get the first call," the *Post* reported.³⁷

That Rice was itching for his old regular role back was obvious. In a July game against the Red Sox, he ran out to the batter's box, attempting to pinch hit for Firpo Marberry. The pitcher had other ideas, though — wanting to finish his start, Marberry sent Rice back to the dugout and took his own cuts.³⁸

Rice played in 120 games in 1931, by far the lowest total since the season he had lost thirteen years before while serving in World War I. He batted a respectable .310. He spent most of his time in right field, but even played some of the first few games of his career in left field as Johnson tried to use him as much as he could without sacrificing Harris's time. The Senators won ninety-two games, including twelve in a row at one point, but it wasn't enough in a tough American League, as they still finished in third place and well, well behind the pennant-winning Philadelphia Athletics.³⁹

In no time after the season's conclusion, Rice had returned to his beloved golf links, playing competitive tournaments while the World Series was still going on.⁴⁰ Later in the month, he unsuccessfully tried to defend his District of Columbia left-handed title at Indian Spring.⁴¹

During the offseason, Clark Griffith believed he had found the long-range answer in right field for the ballclub, acquiring Carl Reynolds in a trade with the White Sox. Just two seasons before, Reynolds had batted .359, third in the American League. He had also driven in 104 runs, and hit twenty-two home runs. Reynolds' production had dropped during an injury-plagued 1931 campaign, but Griffith believed he had the solution: Reynolds' injuries often came during collisions at home plate. To avoid injuries, he just had to learn how to slide properly.[42]

Shirley Povich, the *Washington Post* columnist, worried both Rice and Judge would not be able to perform well in limited roles, and suggested that the Senators ought to look into trading the pair to teams that could use them every day while their games still had some life.

"Players of their age require constant duty to be in top form and their value to the club probably will be considerably impaired as a result of the benchwarming," he said. "...In justice to their long services with the Washington club, it would be fitting to trade the pair to a team on which they would see service every day."[43]

There are many reasons why Rice did not reach three thousand hits for his career, his late start due to the family tragedy and the lost 1918 season being the top ones. But a rule passed before the 1932 campaign by baseball's executives, at their annual Chicago meetings, probably helped shorten Rice's career by at least a year. With the financial crunch of the Great Depression starting to close in on the game, a vote among owners reduced roster sizes by two spots, cutting the number of active players at any one time from four-hundred to 368. The market for aging, expensive outfielders had just tightened considerably.

A few months later, when only 121,000 fans showed up for the eight season openers, it was clear that the Great Depression was having its effect on the business of baseball. And a month later, figures indicated that attendance at major league games had dropped forty-five percent from the same time the season before. Owners would lose more than $1.2 million, collectively, in 1932.[44]

On April 13, the Senators opened the 1932 season in Boston, with Reynolds as the starting right fielder and Joe Kuhel supplanting Joe Judge at first base.[45] Both veterans Rice and Judge were in subordinate roles, even though Povich had lobbied in print for a trade of Judge to Detroit just a few days before the season opened.[46] Rice pinch-hit in the game, grounding out.[47] Three days later, Rice pinch-hit in the top of the ninth inning in a game the Senators trailed in Philadelphia, 4–2. The tying runs were on base with two outs. But Rice, with a chance to be the hero, struck out.[48]

But just because Rice was mostly out of sight in 1932 didn't mean he was out of the minds of the team's loyal fans. On May 4, members of the Washington, D.C., Optimist Club pitched a "Sam Rice Day" for later in the season, targeting July 20 or 21 as potential dates. The club urged Rice fans to attend a meeting at the Hamilton Hotel later in the week for the formation of a "Sam Rice Day" committee.[49] At that meeting, attended by representatives of many of the more prominent members of Washington's business society, it was decided that "Sam Rice Day" would be held July 19. The date wasn't random — Bucky Harris would be in town that day with his Detroit Tigers. Then, in the midst of all this talk about a day to honor Rice, as if on cue to remind the world that he did indeed deserve the honor, he doubled and tripled in consecutive pinch-hitting appearances.[50]

When the day arrived, various acts kept the crowd entertained until the proceedings began. The Elks Boys Band and Almas Temple musical unit provided the soundtrack. Comedic coaching team Nick Altrock and Al Schacht entertained the spectators in their usual fashion.

Rice was showered with gifts during the ceremony, beginning with $2,235.09 in cash. Initially, Rice was to be given the profits above a normal Tuesday gate. However, a disappointing crowd of 5,093 fans showed up, topping the Tuesday average by just ninety-three people. The Great Depression clearly affected interest even in the most worthy of diversions, especially if they cost any money whatsoever. The Senators, however, weren't about to just give their seventeen-year veteran $93.

Clark Griffith put in a call to Detroit president Frank Navin, and the two agreed to base Rice's share upon a revised expected crowd of three thousand spectators, rather than the originally agreed-upon five thousand.

On top of the cash, he was given a Studebaker automobile, a large engraved loving cup, a silver service from the Senators organization, a Bulova electric clock from Ross Co., a wicker set made by the wounded war veterans of Walter Reed Hospital, a wristwatch from the Kay Jewelry Co., a portrait of himself painted by local artist Frank Hall, a silver service set from Alma Temple, a set of golf clubs from the Indian Spring Club and floral arrangements from two D.C.–area florists.

Besides the two teams playing, three other American League teams sent representatives—Herb Pennock of the Yankees, Ed Rommel of the Athletics and Milton Gaston of the White Sox attended the ceremony, in uniform.

United States President Herbert Hoover wrote Rice a congratulatory letter:

My dear Mr. Rice:

You have given all of us who love baseball so much pleasure that you have richly earned the honor of a "Sam Rice Day." I heartily congratulate you upon your seventeen years with the Washington Baseball Club and with your every success in the future.

Yours faithfully
Herbert Hoover.

Rice was so touched by the outpouring that he could barely muster words when called to the microphone. "Thanks, folks. This is the greatest day in my baseball career," was all he said as he addressed the Griffith Stadium crowd. He had collected his thoughts to express himself in greater detail in a letter he distributed to the local newspapers the night before, to be published the day following the event.

"Please accept my grateful thanks for the wonderful tribute paid me by the fans and sports writers," Rice wrote. "Will you say for me that I appreciate my day at the baseball park and the many beautiful gifts but, above all, the sincerity of the fans in remembering me. Mrs. Rice joins me in thanking you."

Shirley Povich deemed Rice's sentiments sincere in his column:

> Those tears that welled in the eyes of Sam Rice as he stood at home plate to receive the tributes of a grateful fandom were no phonies. Those salty crystals that coursed their way down the cheeks of the Nats regular outfielder of seventeen years of regular service were no studio trick. Sam didn't bring the prop onion along for the occasion.

He told them it was the happiest day of his baseball career. That was his speech and with each succeeding tribute of the hometown fans there was no doubt that he meant it. Stolid old Sam Rice, fazed by the swift of no pitcher, almost broke down under the homage of an admiring fandom.

Rice had made a career of blocking out distractions and performing at a high level, so it came as no surprise when, in his first at-bat of the afternoon, he lined a single to left field. Unlike the 1925 World Series catch ball, which Rice would come to regret not hanging onto, the ball was tossed out of play to the Washington dugout, where Johnson held onto it for safekeeping.[51]

14

End of the Line

The Senators won ninety-three games in 1932, but finished fourteen games behind the American League pennant-winning Philadelphia Athletics. But Griffith felt he had to make a managerial move before the 1933 season, and not necessarily because Johnson had done a poor job. In fact, he had averaged ninety-three victories a season over the last three of his four-year tenure.

But the Depression was setting in even deeper by the time the 1932 season ended, evidenced by the drop in attendance at Griffith Stadium from 614,000 in 1930 to just 371,000 two years later. Johnson's salary, particularly without a pennant to show for it, just wasn't something the "Old Fox" could pay any longer.[1]

As they did in 1928, when Griffith eventually brought back Johnson to lead the team, the Washington media speculated that the hire would come from the Senators' nucleus of veterans. They zeroed in on the longtime teammates, Rice and Judge, as well as shortstop Joe Cronin. Though only twenty-six years old, Cronin seemed like a viable candidate mostly because he resembled Bucky Harris in age (Harris was twenty-seven when he led the 1924 Senators to the World Series victory) and disposition.

"I like these young, peppy scrappers," Griffith had said of Harris, and Cronin also fit the mold.[2]

The *Washington Post* conducted a fan poll to determine who Washingtonians felt should next manage the team, with Judge leading the voting at 33.7 percent, with Cronin coming in next at 15.5 percent and Rice finishing third among Senators fans at 4.6 percent.[3]

A couple of days later, Griffith selected shortstop Cronin, who became the youngest manager in major league history.

"Cronin's a scrapper," Griffith said. "He thinks nothing but baseball. I like these young fellows who fight for everything. I made no mistake with Bucky Harris. I think I have another Harris."

Cronin didn't expect to make up the difference between his team and the teams at the top of the American League through sheer force of personality. He wanted to fine tune the roster, and was straight-forward with Griffith about who he wanted him to pursue at the winter meetings, appealing to Griffith's self-image as a skilled wheeler and dealer.

The Senators had posted a 4.16 team ERA in 1932, third in the American League and not good enough, in Cronin's estimation, to close the gap between his team and the Yankees and Athletics. But he didn't just want Griffith to round up the best pitchers available in the trade market. He strategically targeted three pitchers. Earl Whitehill of the Tigers and Walter Stewart of St. Louis, Cronin felt, matched up well against the Yankees because they were left-handed. And Cronin felt if the Senators were to close the gap in the American League, they'd need to do a lot of the work themselves and have success in their twenty-two games against New York. The third pitcher Cronin targeted, Cleveland right-hander Jack Russell, the new Washington manager wanted because he had been successful against the Senators themselves the past few seasons, and Cronin wanted to take him out of the opposition's hands.

Griffith traveled to the meetings and came back with all three pitchers and more. In fact, it was the other players he acquired along with St. Louis' Stewart that pretty much relegated Rice to even more of a role on the bench for the 1933 season than he had been filling the previous two seasons. It was to be his last in a Washington uniform.

When Johnson was fired in October, Goose Goslin had contacted Griffith, expressing interest in returning to Washington. He and Johnson had their differences as teammates, and now that the "Big Train" was out of Washington, he wanted back in.

"You've never won a pennant without me," Goslin reminded Griffith.

Griffith was able to swing the deal, a large one that included six players. He shipped fifteen-game winner Lloyd Brown to St. Louis, along with Sam West and Reynolds, the two men who had shared the right-field playing time with Rice in 1932. However, in return came Goslin and Fred Schulte. Schulte was a born center fielder. With Manush already anchored in left field, Cronin and Griffith felt they could switch Goslin, ten years younger than Rice, from his longtime spot in left over to right.

The Washington outfield was set, and Rice wasn't much of a part of it.

Griffith had filled Cronin's wish list and more, filling any holes he had uncovered along the way.[4]

In late January, Rice signed what would turn out to be his final contract with Washington. He took a paycut to stay with the organization in 1933, a product not only of his own diminishing role in the Senators' outfield, but also a reflection of the downward trend of all baseball salaries during the Great Depression.[5] A few weeks later, Rice told a reporter that he was unimpressed with the American League's crop of young outfielders, half-joking that, even at age forty-one, he wasn't especially concerned about his job security when he looked around.[6] But Rice also said during spring training that the team Griffith had assembled for the 1933 season was the best in franchise history.[7]

And if Rice came off bitter or as a bit of a crank about the game's young players, at least he was willing to pitch in to try and foster their improvement. He helped spot a flaw in the batting style of rookie shortstop Bob Boken (he was holding the bat handle too close to his stomach, Rice observed). And though it had been nearly two decades since Rice had last taken the mound as a young pitching prospect for the Senators, he had retained enough of his knowledge about that craft to help bring along 6-foot-4 mound hopeful Bob Cassell, who Rice felt was throwing the ball "like a shotput." Rice's input didn't end up doing much for either's big-league career prospects. Boken batted .247 in two major league seasons with Washington and the White Sox. Cassell never appeared in a regular-season big-league game.[8]

Rice's stronghold on a regular outfield spot was gone, but on the golf course, he had retained his place as the team's top player, despite game challenges from Earl Whitehill and Luke Sewell. Golf was actually a hot topic for the 1933 Senators, who became miffed that Biloxi Golf Club was charging them regular daily greens fees of $1.50. The players, about a dozen of them, felt that they should be granted a discount as frequent customers.[9]

While Rice wasn't seeing much playing time in April, he presumably was at least a bit player in one of baseball's ugliest brawls—before it was all over, most players on both teams were, as well as a good portion of the seven thousand fans present at Griffith Stadium.

Bad blood between the Senators and Yankees dated back to the summer before, when Senators outfielder Carl Reynolds bowled over Yankees catcher Bill Dickey at home plate. Dickey hopped to his feet and slugged Reynolds as hard as he could, breaking his jaw with a single punch.

"It was hot and the games had been close and I had been banged around for day," Dickey later said. "When Reynolds came at me high, I just had to hit somebody."[10]

The 1933 brawl, taking place during a 16–0 Yankee victory on April 25, all began on a double-play ball, with New York "hot-tempered Alabaman" Ben Chapman sliding spikes high into a fellow Southerner, Washington's Buddy Myer.[11] Reacting immediately, Myer began kicking Chapman in the back. Fending off the assault, Chapman hopped up and started swinging at his combatant. Meanwhile, both dugouts emptied.

Umpires and the dozen uniformed police officers in attendance at the ballpark broke up the brawl, and order seemed to be restored as Chapman exited the field after being thrown from the game. But Chapman had to exit through the Washington dugout to get to his clubhouse, and was subjected to the harassment of the Senators players as he made his way through.

Whatever it was that Washington pitcher Earl Whitehill added to the insults, it particularly set Chapman off. He slugged Whitehill in the left eye, then followed with a second punch to the right side of the pitcher's face before Whitehill's Washington teammates could join in.

This time the brawl really became ugly, with three hundred fans storming the field to join in. Luckily, an anonymous call had been put into the District's Second Precinct police station, and reinforcements arrived to assist the overmatched officers already assigned to work the game. New York's Gerald Walker punched both police and civilians. Teammate Vernon Gomez struggled as police attempted to subdue him, as well. Yankees surrounded Chapman, trying to protect him, but fans broke through the barricade, pummeling him before police jumped in and arrested several of them.

The brawl, said the *Washington Post*, "transformed Griffith Stadium's diamond and the Washington dugout into a seething melee of flying fists."

The entire second brawl had taken place right in front of the field box of United States Vice President John Garner, who had showed up to enjoy an afternoon of baseball, and was instead treated to the ugly display, a scene that had to resemble the infamous brawl between the Indiana Pacers and the Detroit Pistons of the NBA in 2004.

In the aftermath, Yankee brawler Chapman played the role of the proud warrior, fielding questions from reporters sporting "dull red" bruises across his upper body and a "ripe-red cut" on his cheek.

"That's baseball and always has been, breaking up double plays," he said. "That's what I'm in there for when I'm running. If this game is ping pong, I don't know anything about it. I'm playing baseball."

Chapman also said he didn't regret starting the second brawl in the Senators' dugout, and said he knew what he was in for as soon as he threw the punch at Whitehill.

"I knew whose dugout I was in and I knew what was going to happen if I punched him," he said.[12]

(It would be quite a summer for Chapman, whose wife would soon file suit back home in Alabama against him, charging desertion.)[13]

At least the brawl brought a little life to the dugout, Rice's home for almost every inning of the 1933 season to that point. He didn't get his first start until May 10, the team's twenty-third game of the season.

In just his third start of the season ten days later, Rice was able to, for one day, conjure the past. Leading off and playing center field against the White Sox, he had four hits, scored three runs, drove in three more and spearheaded a 7–0 Senators victory. He did so in the absence of Schulte, who had injured a finger on his left hand in a recent collision with Cronin.

"The White Sox forgot how to hit, the (Senators) forgot how to lose and Sam Rice made everybody forget Fred Schulte," Povich wrote in the next day's paper.

The Rice-led victory moved the Senators within a game of the first-place Yankees, in sole possession of second place in the American League a full game ahead of the third-place Indians, who had dropped their contest that afternoon.

Newly elected vice president Garner was back in attendance, apparently not completely turned off by the theatrics at his prior appearance at Griffith Stadium, and sat alongside Senate majority leader Joseph Robinson. With Monte Weaver earning the impressive victory in his first start in two weeks, and Rice rising from the bench to lead a Senators victory, the *Washington Post* played off the Democrats' 1931 campaign song, a tune of the day called "The Forgotten Man."

"Old Sam Rice went back to the scene of his former triumphs in the outfield and he dug up fond memories of his heyday feats with a flawless game in the field and a double, triple and two singles," the paper said.[14]

Rice's "triumphs," however, along with his playing time, would be rare in '33. He seemed to be good-natured about it, though, throwing batting practice to his younger teammates every day, and joking that he felt like his arm was in good enough shape that he could really pull a page from the past and win one on the mound if the team needed him to.[15]

The new-look Senators, after all, were doing just fine without Rice in the everyday lineup, surging to forty games over .500 at 82–42 on August 29.[16] That day, Rice found himself confined to a Cleveland hospital bed with a stomach ailment.[17] The stay in the city wasn't all bad, however — in a 14–1 victory over the Indians the day before, Rice had slammed a rare pinch-hit home run into the right-field bleachers at the Indians' new ballpark.[18]

Cronin's plan to secure the American League pennant worked. Behind the revamped pitching staff and outfield, along with the new life he brought to the dugout leadership, the Senators took fourteen of twenty-two meetings with the Yankees (though they did lose the Myer-Chapman brawl game, 16–0). By early September, they built a nine-game lead over the Yankees, then cruised to the finish by seven games, winning a franchise record ninety-nine games.[19] For the second time in his career leading the organization, Griffith had struck gold in finding a young, energetic leader on his roster. Both Harris and Cronin had won American League pennants with their first team.

And as Harris' 1924 team did, Cronin's Senators would face the New York

Giants in the World Series. Like Washington, the Giants were a different team than they were nine years before. Gone was franchise face John McGraw. The feisty long-time manager had retired the year before. The Giants, like the Senators, were now led by a hard-hitting player-manager, first baseman Bill Terry.

The first game was October 3 at the Polo Grounds, and Giants manager Terry had no doubts about who he would send to the mound to give his team a 1–0 series edge.

It's kind of a shame that nearly every biography of Hubbell's begins with a feat he managed at the 1934 All-Star Game, the consecutive strikeouts of five Hall of Famers in front of the home crowd at the Polo Grounds (for the record: Babe Ruth, Lou Gehrig, Jimmy Foxx, Al Simmons, and Cronin).[20] Because he accomplished so much more than that over the course of his career.

From 1933, when he really came into his own, through 1937, his last great year, there was hardly a more dominant pitcher in the game. When Terry sent Hubbell to the rubber for Game One, he wasn't just sending out the best pitcher in the National League. He was putting the ball in the hand of the N.L.'s Most Valuable Player for that season.

Hubbell won twenty-three games and lost twelve, and also pitched more than 308 innings.[21] He went the distance in an eighteen-inning, 1–0 victory over the St. Louis Cardinals. He did not walk a batter in the shutout, one of his ten on the season.

Not only was Hubbell incredible on the mound in 1933, but he cut a figure that Depression-era fans could relate to, particularly those from his native Great Plains states.

"He was an ideal hero for that age," one writer said of Hubbell, "a gaunt, hungry-looking Oklahoman, so lean he looked as though he might fall apart before he finished his game."[22]

Hubbell continued the mastery of the regular season in the start against the Senators, striking out ten in a 4–2 victory. Both runs by the Senators were unearned, and the game was never really in doubt, as New York surged to an early 4–0 lead.

For the first time in three postseasons, Rice watched an entire World Series game from the dugout. Dave Harris was the only pinch-hitter Cronin used in the game. His eighth-inning walk, however, did not lead to anything larger for Washington.

While Terry had no doubts about who he would go to in the first game, Cronin's pitching choice would go down as his first strategic blunder of the series. While Terry announced that Hubbell would start well in advance—no surprise there—Cronin kept his selection close to the vest. The morning of the game, he surprised almost everyone, passing up twenty-four-game winner Alvin Crowder and twenty-two-game winner Whitehill, who had the staff's best ERA, and instead went with Walter "Lefty" Stewart. None of Cronin's pitchers had started a postseason game until October, 1933.[23]

Though Hubbell was clearly the Giants' ace, they certainly weren't a one-man staff, and in Game Two the next day, Terry called on Hal Schumacher to go for the club's second victory in a row. Crowder, who probably should have been the Game One starter, got the nod this time from Cronin.

Game Two would finally see Rice get into a game in this series. Unfortunately for him, the outcome was in little doubt by the time he grabbed a bat to pinch-hit for pitcher Tommy Thomas in the seventh. For most of the game, everything had been going well for the Senators, with Goslin breaking through for a home run and a 1–0 lead off Schumacher in the third. Three innings later, the Senators really had an opportunity to put the pressure on the Giants. But Bluege struck out with the bases loaded to end the inning.

It was the momentum shift the Giants were waiting for. In the bottom of the inning, they exploded, scoring six runs on eight hits. All the damage had already been done by the time Cronin finally replaced Crowder with Thomas to get the last out. The inning was a nightmare for the Senators, but it could have been even worse — the Giants left the bases loaded.

In the bottom of the inning, Rice singled in his pinch-hitting opportunity. Of course, with the Giants sitting on a large lead and Schumacher finding his groove by that point, it mattered little. But the two games to one lead wasn't insurmountable, especially with the series heading back to Washington the next day for the first time in eight years. Rice had to figure he would get another opportunity to make a difference before it was all over with.

His manager had other ideas.

Sure the Senators couldn't wait to exit New York. It had been a nightmarish two days for them all the way around. Cronin's every move seemed to backfire on him. Off the field, on the way to the Polo Grounds for Game One, Buddy Myer had witnessed a truck kill a pedestrian. Shaken up, Myer made three errors in the game.

In Game Three, Cronin's luck began to turn. He gathered the men in the clubhouse before the game, delivering his one and only pep talk of the week.

"He said he hoped they were as ashamed of what had happened in the first two series games as he was," Shirley Povich later recalled. "He told them they were a better ball club than the Giants, and now was the time to show it to a city that had supported them all season."

For one day at least, the Senators did look like the better team. Whitehill started and shut the visitors from New York out by a 4–0 score. The rainy weather and the Senators' first two losses in New York had kept the crowd to sub–World Series levels, but faced with a desperate situation, the Senators came through.[24] But to realistically remain in the series, they'd have to do it one more day.

Taking the mound for the Giants in the all-important Game Four would be Hubbell, the masterful starter from Game One. The hungry-looking Oklahoman was on his game again, setting the Senators down in order until Goslin singled in the fourth inning. Terry had homered in the top of that inning to give the Giants a 1–0 advantage, and it began to look like it might be the only run the Giants ace would need to stake his team to a three games to one lead in the series.

As it would turn out, Hubbell's pitching wouldn't be the problem for New York. A fielding blunder would be, extending the game as well as the Senators hopes.

In the bottom of the seventh, still trailing 1–0, Washington's Joe Kuhel tried to bunt his way on base with one out. Hubbell made an error on the play, though, giving Washington hope. After a sacrifice bunt moved Kuhel into scoring position, Luke Sewell came to bat, facing perhaps the Senators last chance to tie the game and try to win it in either the eighth or ninth or extra innings.

He came through, singling to center. The game was tied, and with Weaver continuing to pitch through trouble, the energized Senators had reason to think it might just be their day after all.

The Giants scored a run in the top of the eleventh, putting the Senators' backs against the wall one more time.[25] They wouldn't go down without a fight, though. And if the situation called for it, Cronin had reinforcements on the bench, including Rice. He had been a World Series hero eight years before. Could he do it again? Would he even get the chance?

After the Giants were finally set down, the bottom of the eleventh began. It was an inning that would haunt Cronin all offseason and perhaps for the rest of what would turn out to be a brief managerial stay in Washington.

Cornered into a desperate situation, Schulte got Washington hopes going, singling to left field to begin the inning. Kuhel, who had started the fourth-inning rally with a bunt that Hubbell mishandled, laid one down again. And he was safe again, a bunt single that put two men on base with nobody out.

Bluege, up next, made the first out of the inning on a sacrifice bunt. It was Cronin's first strategic call of the frame. It wouldn't be his last.

The Senators now had runners on second and third with just one out. A base hit would likely win the game and knot the series at two games apiece. But now it was time for Terry to counter Cronin's move, and he intentionally walked Sewell to load the bases.[26] He made one more key move — though he was in trouble in the eleventh, Terry, after consulting with his ace, decided to stick with Hubbell.[27]

Now it was decision time for Cronin. The pitcher's spot was up, and the young manager scanned his dugout for a man who could come up clutch with the season potentially on the line. Dave Harris had already entered the game earlier, taking over for Manush in left field. His choices came down to Rice and catcher Cliff Bolton.[28]

Cronin settled on Bolton. Almost immediately, Giants coach Charley Dressen hopped out of the dugout, consulting with shortstop Blondy Ryan. Dressen had remembered Bolton from the days when the both were in the Southern League, and instructed his shortstop to shade toward second base — Bolton was a dead-pull hitter.

The positioning was perfect. Bolton hit a sharp grounder directly to where Ryan was standing, and the shortstop scooped up the ball and started a game-ending double play. The Giants lead was three games to one, and they would go for the clinch the next day.

If Cronin's selection of the seldom-used Bolton over Rice in Game Four wasn't enough to symbolize the end of Rice's long tenure with the Washington organization, the next day would see to it. Though fighting for their postseason life, the Senators battled to a 3–3 tie through nine innings, and the game again went into extra innings.

In the tenth, Mel Ott lifted a fly ball to deep center field, and Schulte moved back on it. As he neared the wall, Schulte got his glove on the ball. But as he crashed into the fence, the ball squirted out of his glove and the ball landed in the first row of seats for what would turn out to be a game-winning and World Series–clinching home run.

In the 1925 World Series, Rice had tumbled into the bleachers to rob Pittsburgh's Earl Smith of a sure home run. Eight years later, one of the men who had squeezed him out of the Senators outfield had not only been unable to duplicate the feat, he had actually knocked the ball into the stands.[29]

With Rice watching from what had become his customary spot on the Washington bench, his teammates went down quietly in the bottom of the inning.[30]

* * *

Under the subheading, "Cronin the goat of the series, plays hunches in crisis," *The Sporting News* absolutely excoriated Cronin for batting Bolton instead of Rice in the situation.

Cronin had overextended himself, the paper said, repeating the criticism the young manager had endured while he was slumping early in the season. He had tried to be a great hitter, shortstop, manager and a "one-man board of strategy." He had "proved himself inadequate to the job of coping with the mental urgencies and requirements of the series."

Terry, it continued, "managed rings around the twenty-six-year-old pilot of the Senators." While Terry consulted with his various veterans, Cronin turned his dugout into a dictatorship.

"Cronin lost the Series in the eleventh inning of the fourth game," the paper continued. "Victory was in their grasp, victory in the key game."[31]

Cronin, the *Washington Post* concluded, "had brought the criticism of the baseball world down upon his ears."[32]

A few days after the season's conclusion, Cronin was asked to defend the strategy, and defend it he did.

"As for the criticisms of our offensive strategy," Cronin said, "I regarded all the moves attempted during the series to be sound and I still do. If I had it all to do over, I'd do it the same way."[33]

In some ways, facts vindicate Cronin. Over the course of the 1933 season, Bolton had ten hits in seventeen pinch-hit at-bats, a blistering .588 mark and the best average in the American League that season. Rice, meanwhile, batted .259 in twenty-seven pinch-hitting appearances.[34]

Also, Rice would conclude his career with a .190 average as a pinch-hitter in 105 at-bats, second-worst among Hall of Famers to Early Wynn's .167 mark, and a hundredth of a percentage point worse than Walter Johnson, who didn't exactly forge his reputation in the batter's box.[35]

In those days before spreadsheets and other computer data, Cronin did not have the numbers at his immediate disposal as he looked for a batter to send into the key situation. But what he had done was watched his players from opening day up through the World Series. His decisions had been good for ninety-nine victories that season, along with another one in the World Series. Cronin faced a difficult decision, and went with the man who had come through for him that season rather than the hero of a postseason eight years past and the obvious sentimental choice. It would have been tough to fault him either way.

***

Seldom is the parting of ways of an organization and a loyal long-time ball player easy. There are, on occasion, those perfect situations where the stars align and the player's desired exit time parallels the team's usefulness for him. Ted Williams, the best example of a perfect exit, hit a home run in his last at-bat at Fenway Park, the last at-bat of his career.[36]

Others, just as outstanding in their heyday, haven't been as lucky. Willie Mays batted .211 for the 1973 New York Mets. Babe Ruth, trying to squeeze out one more season, batted .181 with the Boston Braves in 1935.[37] Ruth, at least, gave one last thrill to the city of his first major league stop, famously hitting three home runs in a game that summer.[38]

In the recent era, we've seen Michael Jordan part the Chicago Bulls in the middle of a championship run, returning to play with the Washington Wizards for two seasons, and making the playoffs in neither of them.[39] Steve Young of the San Francisco 49ers had completed his understudy duties before Joe Montana was ready to step aside, so Montana finished things up in Kansas City.

In early January of 1934, Griffith and Rice sat down for what must have been a gut-wrenching but necessary conversation about the outfielder's future. Soon after, Griffith drafted a letter to his long-time star. Like many a parting speech, Griffith's letter began in a clinical, no-nonsense manner before turning into all-out sentiment:

> In pursuance of my conversation with you in reference to your baseball future, at which time you expressed a desire to be given permission to deal for yourself in the event the Washington club decided not to retain your services, I wish to say to you that the Washington club is pleased to acquiesce in your request and here by grants you permission to deal with any club that you see fit.
>
> Sam, it is with deep regret that the time has arrived when your service with the Washington team is ended, but I hope our personal friendship will carry on for all time.
>
> "Old War Horse," I have no words that can express my deep appreciation of your wonderful playing, loyalty to service and the one hundred percent effort you put into your work for those long eighteen years when you were with the Washington club. You were ever-ready and willing to give your best, and oh, what the best was! Sam, I consider you one of the best ball players of all time, and Washington fans and myself are going to miss you, but you can be assured that wherever you go and whatever you do, the hearts of Washington fans and myself will be with you and pulling for your success.[40]

On January 8, after nineteen seasons and 2,889 base hits with the club, the Washington Senators released Sam Rice. He immediately pledged to find a place to play in 1934, swearing that this wasn't the end for him.[41]

"I may be old, as ballplayers go," said Rice, "but I'm not as old as Sam Rice goes. I can still play baseball for a lot of teams."[42]

Despite Griffith's best efforts, the local press jumped on the Washington organization, and particularly the owner himself, for its handling of Rice's release. After his two decades with the Senators, the public's sympathy was definitely with the player.

"Griffith graciously said that he was pleased to acquiesce in Rice's request for release," the *Washington Post* wrote, "but Rice asserts he never made any such request. The (forty-three)-year-old veteran says that he learned of his dismissal when a newspaperman called him and asked him if he had another job lined up.

"He doesn't have one, and he has less prospect of getting one, he says, than if Griffith had given him notice before the winter baseball meeting in Chicago."

The Post was cynical about Griffith's emotional letter.

"But if he has no job," the paper continued, "at least he has the fulsome good wishes of the club management, expressed in a letter from Griffith."[43]

Of course, Rice couldn't go on batting. 300 all his life. He knew, too, that forty-three-year-old legs don't get under fly balls as well as twenty-year-old legs. He knew, of course, that some day he would have to give way to a young rookie on the way up. But perhaps it would have been kinder if the pill had not been sweetened with so much verbal saccharine.

The situation might have been even more difficult today, or even just a few years after Rice's era. The Baseball Hall of Fame would open before the end of the decade, prompting writers to make a much closer examination of the game's statistical milestones. One of the numbers quickly established to separate the cream of baseball's crop was three-thousand career hits. Rice was handed his Washington walking papers 111 hits short. No one seemed to notice, with Rice's lifetime batting average noted in newspaper accounts of his release, but not his hit total. Had the circumstances occurred a few years later, one can only imagine the difficulties manager Joe Cronin would have faced. In what should have been a joyous time, the team's march to a third American League pennant, even more attention would have been paid to Rice's diminished role. While Cronin's primary objective was to secure a World Series berth, the spectacle of Rice sitting while his assault on history stalled at the hand of a longtime teammate would surely have drawn the ire of some critics, who had been so quick to jump on the young manager anyway for declining to use Rice in the key World Series situation.

15

REUNION IN CLEVELAND

Despite his release from the Senators, Rice wasn't ready to retire from the game, not after a season in a bit role with a franchise he had given nearly half his lifetime to. Not with the memory of sitting in the dugout in a World Series game, waiting for the nod that would never come, as his final recollection. The longing of that day, had Rice not found somewhere to play in 1934, might never be quenched. Luckily for him, an old friend was more than happy to give his career an extension.

Walter Johnson and Rice had grown close over the last few years, particularly as the two old Midwestern country boys moved back into the farming business. Even after baseball had ended for both of them, a smile would stretch across Johnson's face when he viewed the sight of Rice's familiar car turning into his property and winding up the driveway to his house. Recently named the manager of the Cleveland Indians, and in search of some outfield depth to bolster a possible pennant contender, Johnson had to also smile when he saw Rice's name among those available to him.

Johnson had taken over as Cleveland's manager in midsummer the season before, taking the place of another former Washington luminary, Roger Peckinpaugh.

"I know the club has some good talent and I believe it can be whipped into a winner," Johnson said upon taking the job.

And for the better part of the last decade, Cleveland had indeed been home to a winner, just not to the extent that one of baseball's most demanding—and unrealistic—fan bases demanded.

"It's a seasonal shout with Cleveland fans," wrote Shirley Povich. "They read all winter that the Indians are an improved ballclub and they yelp all spring that the Indians are the class of the league. Come summer, they don't want a pennant—that's impossible—they want the manager's scalp."[1]

Senators pitcher Walter Johnson. Rice was close with Johnson, with some of his own family tragedies during his illustrious career. (National Baseball Hall of Fame Library, Cooperstown, N.Y.)

Echoing that, *Philadelphia Record* writer Bill Pooly criticized the extended Cleveland baseball family, as well, sarcastically placing the word "experts" in quotation marks. He predicted a second-division finish.[2]

Tough place to play or not, Rice wasn't ready to hang up his jersey, and this looked like his best, if not only, option.

By early February, talks between Cleveland and Rice had grown serious, and the signing of his official contract appeared imminent. The Indians had been one of the teams Rice had victimized the most during his Washington days, batting .324 against Cleveland. So the Cleveland baseball public rejoiced at the mutual interest between the two parties, despite the fact Rice would turn forty-four years old less than two months before the season's start.

"The club might do much worse than have this cagey veteran on the bench as added protection against slumps and injuries," wrote one Indians beat writer. "There were times last season where he would have been invaluable."[3]

Rice accepted the offer of Cleveland general manager Billy Evans and signed his contract on February 13. Johnson thought it was the perfect situation for an aging veteran like Rice, the cooling effect of Lake Erie helping keep him fresh compared to the summer humidity in the District of Columbia.[4]

In the days long before the designated hitter extended American League careers, Rice would still have to defend his position. And right field at his new home would provide a unique challenge. The Indians had played the 1933 season at cavernous new Cleveland Stadium, which seated over seventy thousand. But the experiment had been short-lived and for 1934 they would move back into cozy League Park, their longtime home. Among the ballpark's quirks was a steel beam that protruded from the concrete wall in right. Well-hit balls were known to ricochet at crazy angles off the feature, and League Park, it was said, was the only park in the majors where left-fielders fielded doubles to right.[5]

Rice had been signed as to provide some depth to the team's lineup and to act as insurance in case any of the Cleveland regulars either didn't perform or went down with an injury. Heading into the season, the Indians looked pretty set in the outfield.

In left field the Indians had Joe Vosmik. He had suffered through an off year in 1933, but as a twenty-one-year-old rookie in 1931, Vosmik had batted .320 and driven in 117 runs, despite just seven home runs. Vosmik was a fan favorite in Cleveland, and his humble beginning as a member of the organization was a baseball fairy tale. In 1929, Evans decided to scout the city's amateur All-Star game at his team's stadium. While watching the game, Evans asked his wife if she was impressed with any of the players.

"That good looking blond Viking over there," she said, so Evans signed him up.

The Indians' center fielder, Earl Averill, had a background that was anything but humble. The Indians had purchased Averill from San Francisco of the Pacific Coast League a few years before paying the Seals $40,000. Instead of seizing the opportunity to show his stuff in the big leagues, Averill held out for $5,000. In fact, his Cleveland career would become marked by various holdouts and constant salary bickering. But also by production at the plate — Averill put together one of the most distinguished careers in franchise history, and his plaque eventually joined Rice's in the Hall of Fame.[6]

Finally, in Rice's preferred position, right field, the Indians had Dick Porter, who burst on the scene with a .350 second season in 1930.[7]

Yet on opening day against St. Louis, Rice was in the lineup, batting first and playing his customary right field. He doubled high against the right-field screen in his first at-bat with his new team and the Indians won 5–2.[8] He had another hit the next afternoon in a 2–0 loss.

But the hits would be hard to come by for a long time afterward, and then so would the playing time. After hitting safely in those first two games, Rice endured a 1-for-22 stretch. By May 13, his batting average had plummeted to .148, and he was pulled from the everyday lineup. Around Cleveland, people were calling Rice a bust.[9]

As spring began to turn into summer, the Indians battled on the fringes of the early scramble for first place in the American League, surging to a 20–12 record with a five-game winning streak while Rice sat on the bench, appearing occasionally to pinch-hit. But even in Rice's absence from the lineup, right field continued to be a black hole in the Cleveland lineup when it came to productivity. Johnson trotted out a chorus line of hopefuls. Porter, whose batting average had sunk nearly forty points in 1933 after four consecutive .300 seasons to begin his career, struggled and was eventually traded to the Boston Red Sox. Dutch Holland, acquired from Brooklyn in the offseason, didn't turn any heads in his attempt to secure the position, either. On June 5, Rice was inserted back into the lineup for another opportunity to seize the starting position. This time he would make the most of it.

From early June until early August, an approximately two-month span, Rice looked like the hit machine of his prime. Over the stretch, he batted .349. He had three four-hit games. At one point, he hit safely in seventeen consecutive games. In an August 2 loss to the Tigers, Rice went 2-for-4, and his batting average sat at .2996. Three days later, in a pinch-hitting appearance, Rice managed a base hit to nudge his average for the season to .302.

For a man who lived nearly his entire career over the .300 mark, this would be the final time he would find himself over that line during the course of a season.

"Sam Rice ... had started to hit so spectacularly," the *Sporting News* reported, "that there was no question about him remaining as the club's regular right fielder."

In the dead heat of summer at age forty-four, and after a putrid beginning that had to make Washington believe it had made a difficult but correct decision to let him walk away, Rice was hitting better than most men twenty years his junior. The Indians were so satisfied with him that they shipped a would-be replacement, Kit Carson, back to the minors after just eighteen at-bats.[10]

And then age finally began to catch up with him.

In early August, Rice suffered what was reported as a "charley horse" in one of his legs.[11] Holland took his place in right field in the meantime, but really the last two months of the season would see a parade of hopefuls given a shot at the position, as the Indians fell further from the lead pack and Johnson, Evans and Cleveland team president Alva Bradley began to look toward the future.

The future, it soon became evident, would not include a soon-to-be forty-five-year-old, hobbling "Man o' War."

Rice barely played in September, and the organization began to scout young outfielders in the minors, especially Indianapolis' Vernon Washington and Minneapolis' Ab Wright. With the big-league team, Bob Seeds and Milt Galatzer, two men in the prime of their late twenties, joined the scramble for playing time. The direction of the ballclub as it pertained to 1935 was fairly clear.[12]

Late in the season, Bradley made the managerial situation clear, as well. With Johnson under increasing heat from the fans and press, Rice got a front-row seat to how quickly the Cleveland baseball public could turn on someone. The situation came to a boil in July, during a loss to the Yankees. While a string of Indians pitchers blew a ninth-inning lead, fans began to chant for ace pitcher Mel Harder, and jeered Johnson as he trotted out everyone, it seemed, but the people's choice. The heat on the manager became so sweltering during the eighty-five-victory campaign — a ten-game improvement from the year before, by the way — that Bradley felt compelled to make an announcement. Johnson would be part of the organization in 1935.[13] Meanwhile, anyone watching would have to conclude that chances were slim to none that Rice would join him.

But with time running out on his long career, Rice had one more thrill left in the tank.

On September 18, against none other than the Washington Senators, Johnson penciled Rice's name onto his Indians lineup card. The start was the first for Rice since August 28, when he had led off, collected a base hit, then found himself lifted about midway through the game. His appearances in games had been sporadic and brief over the three weeks leading into this, the second game of a double header between American League also-rans. Rice had pinch-hit in a game against Boston in early September, then did the same three days in a row against Philadelphia, getting a base hit in the last two of those contests. Three days before the double header against Washington, Rice pinch-hit in a close loss to the Yankees, but did made an out.[14]

Many years later, Rice would reveal, with a pang of regret, that a leg injury had kept him out of most of the Indians' games over the last few weeks of the season.

"Everybody thought I was just being contrary," he said. "The truth is I had a bad leg. A doctor told me it could be serious if I insisted on playing."[15]

The lineup Joe Cronin sent out for the second game was probably scarcely recognizable to Rice. Long-time teammate Ossie Bluege led off for the Senators. Another staple of the 1930s Washington lineup, Buddy Myer, batted cleanup. But other than those two, most of the Senators' regulars took a seat. For example Pete Susko and John Stone, two 1934 additions to the Washington roster, batted second and third, respectively.

Finally, Luke Sewell of all people, the catcher for the 1933 pennant winners as well as many other teams during a long career behind the plate, occupied Rice's old ground in right field. It was one of just nine games Sewell would play in the outfield over his twenty-year career.[16]

A detailed account of the game, the second of the day in a relatively meaningless late September matchup, is not easy to come by. The *Washington Post*, for example, didn't even send a reporter on the trip, saving a few dollars by taking the Associated Press wire account.[17]

It is often wondered why Rice would let his career end thirteen hits short of one of baseball's most respected milestones. Perhaps, after the Indians had completed the 9–6 victory and the double header sweep, he never saw any manner in which he could more perfectly wrap things up, not even standing on first base while his three thousandth base hit was tossed back to the diamond.

Batting in the number two spot in the lineup behind Galatzer, Rice went to bat five times in the game. He had three hits, including the 498th and final double of his career. He scored a run. He also drove in a pair. Sure, these weren't the Washington Senators of his prime. Like Rice, Goslin had departed Washington after the season, and was tacking on three more high-quality seasons to his own Hall-of-Fame career in Detroit. Judge had earned scant playing time in his second year with the Boston Red Sox, and 1934 would also be his last in the majors. Peckinpaugh had not earned another major league managerial job after being fired in Cleveland the season before.

But these were still the Senators, clothed in the same uniform Rice had worn for nineteen glorious seasons. The men, though many of them were unfamiliar to him, regardless played for an organization still run by Clark Griffith, the man who had obtained Rice from a Virginia League team so many summers before as repayment of an outstanding debt, a repayment that had reimbursed Griffith with interest many times over.

Rice collected hits No. 2,985, 2,986 and 2,987 and then, as so many of his peers had been doing, stepped away from the game forever. He would never play in another major league game. Unlike many of his peers and teammates, he would never manage one, either.

The players retreated to their clubhouses. The fans exited League Park. The foul lines, the borders of Rice's canvas for all of those seasons in the shadow of Ruth, Hornsby and others, were now closed to him. One of the most unlikely Hall-of-Fame careers ever constructed had ended on a perfect note.[18]

16

LIFE ON THE FARM

Rice's official release from the Indians came soon after the start of the New Year.

Cleveland remained overstocked with outfielders, and general manager Billy Evans announced on January 4 that he was issuing Rice his unconditional release.

On the same day, the Indians let go of catcher Moe Berg, also a teammate of Rice's in Washington.[1] It's not known whether Rice and Berg had any relationship beyond sharing a uniform for a few years, but in some ways, they are baseball soul mates. Because of his mysterious off-the-field activities, Berg is widely considered one of the most intriguing players in the game's history. He spoke several languages, was involved in the CIA, and may or may not have acted as a spy for the U.S. government. Like Rice, Berg took many of his own secrets to the grave.[2]

Even during his long baseball career, Rice had indulged off the field passions, primarily golf. In retirement, Rice quickly found a new hobby on which to spend his time — chicken farming — which would also serve as his new livelihood.

On August 22, Elizabeth Stabler, a member of a prominent family in the town of Ashton, Maryland, sold forty-five acres of her family farm to Rice, and he and Edith moved into the tight-knit community about twenty miles due north of Washington.[3]

The town, which combined with the bordering town of Sandy Spring and several other tiny local villages to essentially form one community.

Ashton/Sandy Spring, one former resident explained, was the sort of community where if one got into trouble at school, his parents were well aware of the details by the time he came home in the afternoon.[4] And it was a place

Youth baseball players in Morocco, Indiana, play their games at Sam Rice Ballpark. (Randy Decker)

where Sam's wife Edith would fit in nicely. She was a graduate of Indiana's Earlham College, a place so tied into the religious Society of Friends sect that, to this day, its athletic teams are known as the Quakers. And Quakers were an extremely influential group in Ashton/Sandy Spring society.

"Sandy Spring's enduring strength," writes modern town historian Thomas Y. Canby, in fact, "the reason it survives as a state of mind, springs from values that we identify with it, values we are drawn to and wish to share in. And these values, these foundations, derive largely from our Quaker past."

In current times, the area faces many of the challenges of any modern suburban area, the same challenges when it comes to retaining a place's identity faced by all those towns one drives through on the way from Chicago to Rice's boyhood Indiana home.

Among them, writes a Canby are "the destruction of the farming way of life, a dilution of community ties and flavor, and gradual strangulation of road traffic."

But in the mid–1930s, farming was still king in the area and just as in baseball and golf, Rice wasn't content to toil in mediocrity in his latest venture, and he quickly built his new farm up to a very profitable level. By 1938, just three years after moving in, Rice had eliminated some of the more extraneous buildings on the site and dedicated as many acres as he could to buildings and equipment for a productive, profitable chick-hatching and chicken-raising operation.[5]

By 1943, Rice had twenty thousand chickens on his farm. He also lived just down the road, about five miles, from a very influential American at the time — United States Secretary of the Interior Harold L. Ickes. While Ickes used his platform to help right as best he could an embarrassing injustice, Rice also did his small part to help his neighbor and the wrongfully persecuted Americans Ickes had become an unlikely advocate for.[6]

Some background: While the U.S. south's dark legacy is of institutionalized racism against black Americans, the western United States cultivated for many years a deep division between white Americans and Asian-Americans. In 1905–06, the *San Francisco Chronicle* warned of "The Yellow Peril." The city removed Japanese pupils from white school and ordered them into segregated schools in the Chinatown section of San Francisco. In 1921, a group of white men in Turlock, California gathered fifty-eight Japanese-Americans and sent them on a train out of town.

Anti-Japanese sentiment in the United States, and specifically on the West Coast, came to a head on December 7, 1941, when twenty-five hundred Americans were killed in the Japanese attack on Hawaii's Pearl Harbor. The event famously brought the United States into World War II, and it also put Americans of Japanese ancestry under suspicion. Many military officials were loathe to admit their own intelligence-gathering shortcomings—instead, they announced suspicions that Japanese-Americans had been spying for their native land.

Assistant Secretary of War John McCloy was the first to recommend "restricted areas" in which Japanese-Americans would be cleared from and relocated. "The Constitution is just a scrap of paper to me," he said in defense of the idea. If the proposal sounds preposterous today, it sadly gained traction quickly during World War II.

On February 19, 1942, President Franklin D. Roosevelt signed into law Executive Order 9066, granting the military permission to exclude people from designated areas. The order didn't specifically mention people of Japanese ancestry, but people of Italian descent, whose homeland was also at war with the United States, avoided similar action primarily because of the popularity of New York Yankees star Joe Dimaggio.

By the time the newly created War Relocation Authority had run its course, as many as 112,000 Japanese-Americans had been forcefully evacuated from their West Coast homes and moved into government-created "relocation centers."[7]

Rice's neighbor and fellow chicken farmer Ickes had seen enough.

In the fall of 1942, Ickes first expressed an interest in bringing internees to work on his Maryland farm. He also tried unsuccessfully to persuade Roosevelt to make a statement encouraging others to do the same.

Not deterred, Ickes tried a different approach, appealing to Roosevelt's sympathy for the American farmer.

"The President ought to issue a proclamation to the country," Ickes said at a cabinet meeting, "saying it was in the interest of the country to employ the Japanese as farm labor. It would help the Japanese, too."[8]

His work began to pay off in April of 1943, as Ickes arranged to have seven previously interned Japanese-Americans relocated to work at his own 165-acre Headwaters Farm, as well as Rice's farm.[9] The group included four men, experienced poultry specialists, who were all graduates of the California State Polytechnic Institute. Three of the men were brothers, by the last name Kobayashi.

They had been living at a "Relocation Camp" in Arizona for the previous eight months.

"I interested myself in their relocation for two reasons," Ickes said. "First, because I believe we should do all we can to ease the burden that the war has placed upon this particular group of our fellow citizens. I do not like the idea of loyal citizens, whatever their race or color, being kept in relocation centers any longer than need be."

The second reason, Ickes continued, was that the war-caused labor shortage made good help hard to find.[10] And the Kobayashi brothers and company certainly qualified as good help for the two high-profile poultry farming neighbors.

"They're real Americans and they're smart," Rice said. "They've already shown me they're real poultry men."

Sam, explained his friend Bill Birely, believed Asians were genetically gifted in determining certain traits in baby poultry simply by touch.

"Their hands are so sensitive, they can determine the sex of a chick when it's born," he said. "One of the primary reasons he had them was because they were good at that."

Other farmers in the area were inspired by the actions of Rice — by the time the initial seven made their way from their camp in Poston, Arizona, to Maryland, twenty more local farmers had requested assistance from Japanese-American workers.

Rice probably wasn't attempting to make a political statement by bringing the workers aboard — he was far from a liberal, according to Birely.

"He and Edith were both strong Republicans," Birely said. "I would say they were not ultra-conservative. They were not liberal. They were sensible."

Edith Rice was more politically involved than Sam, a leader of the Women's Republican Club in Ashton/Sandy Springs.

"I don't think he took an interest in campaigning and things of that sort," Birely said. "That wasn't Sam's nature."[11]

Raising chickens gave Rice an advantage over many of his area's other farmers — his business was, for the most part, drought proof.

That allowed him to keep a steady income coming in the following spring, 1944, after a damaging drought had a devastating impact on many of the crops being raised in the Sandy Spring/Ashton area. While favorable weather across the nation allowed record harvests in some places, Rice's area was an exception. A June dry spell destroyed much of the wheat crop. And when a six-week drought hit, corn yields dropped to one-third to one-half of expected levels.

But all the while, Rice was able to hatch and sell 170,000 of his chicks in just nine months, while also selling thousands of eggs to the Army Medical Center. And just a couple of years before, he had installed two large diesel generators to his property, making his farm completely independent of the local power company.

No era in American history has been romanticized as much as the World War II era, when the country got back onto its feet economically while also helping to lead one of the most important military victories for Democracy in world history. But prosperity wasn't everywhere, not matter how the lens of history may distort things. Rice had grown up poor in the Midwest, but had been an astute, cautious businessman all the way back to the pre–Great Depression playing days, when Clark Griffith worried from year to year that he would take his money and run. Not everyone in his area was so lucky, though, as the Second World War dragged onward into 1944.

"How far have we advanced in ... sixty years?" a local historian wrote. "Honestly, your historian could not say it was very far. There are houses almost in sight of this meeting house in which you would not want to keep a pet dog, yet human beings go on from day to day enduring privations and hardships that we completely overlook or in our ignorance know nothing about. There are still those houses without the conveniences we know, with the same filthy surroundings and no sanitary comforts."[12]

After the turmoil of his youth, Rice's life had settled into a comfortable rhythm, mostly free of very much sadness outside of that which he already carried with him (Rice's surviving sister did die during his playing career).[13]

That changed a little bit in December of 1946, when Walter Johnson, one of Sam's closest friends in baseball and a man he had played both with and later for, died after being diagnosed a few months earlier with an inoperable brain tumor.[14]

Rice was one of eight members of the 1924 world champions selected to carry the World Series hero's casket to its final resting place. Assisting him was Ossie Bluege, Nick Altrock, Muddy Ruel, Joe Judge, Roger Peckinpaugh, Tom Zachary and team trainer Mike Martin.

"All are gray or balding or both," wrote famed sports writer Red Smith.

Johnson's services were held in the National Cathedral, an Episcopalian church in Washington, D.C., that contains the crypt of United States President

Woodrow Wilson. Rice was mourning the death of a friend in a structure containing the remains of a man who, thirty-two years earlier, had nearly sent Rice to his own demise in the ill-fated Veracruz mission.[15]

Like Rice, Johnson had suffered through immeasurable grief as a young man. In the winter between the 1921 and 1922 baseball seasons, Johnson's 2½-year-old daughter Elinor became ill with influenza. She died just before Christmas.

While Johnson was managing the Senators in 1930, son Eddie suffered through a throat infection that caused complications with his already weak kidneys, forcing him to miss most of his school year. Another son, Walter Jr., was hit around the same time by a drunk driver while roller skating, an accident that put him in the hospital for nearly two months and nearly resulted in amputation of one of his legs.

In late July of the ensuing season, Johnson's wife, Hazel, returned to Kansas from a road trip exhausted. She quickly became ill, and died two days later, never having been diagnosed with any particular disease.

"She had simply driven herself past the point of complete exhaustion," Johnson biographer Henry W. Thomas wrote.

In a span of nine years beginning in 1921, Johnson had lost six close relatives.

Rice's anguish had been delivered in one fell swoop in late April of 1912. Johnson's had been distributed over several years. And now he had been released from the pain.[16]

Did Johnson take Sam's secret to his grave?

It certainly seems possible. The two men were close, and everything ever written about Johnson indicates that he was a man of the highest character, someone who could be trusted to hold something in confidence. So respected was the pitcher in his Maryland community that once he entered politics after his baseball career, townspeople typically filled out a council ballot with four Democrats, the prevailing party of the area, and one Republican — Walter Johnson.[17]

Johnson shared with Rice an understanding of grief most people never know.

"I had a fine little family all my own, three boys and a little girl, and there was never a happier family," Johnson wrote in a letter. "There never was a happier, healthier, sweeter baby than our little girl. She took sick and died just before Christmas."

Then came the kicker.

"Only people," Johnson continued, "who have had the same experience know what that means to a home."

Barring a cache of correspondence stuffed in an attic box somewhere, we'll likely never know whether the two former teammates offered the kind of support that only such survivors can really share.

It would be an utter shame if they hadn't.

We also don't know, of course, with complete certainty how much Edith Rice knew about the burden her husband carried with him from the tragedy that turned his world upside down early in life, although I have speculated — fairly, I believe — that it would have been difficult for him to keep it from her. People in their community did know about Rice's background, revealed his friend Bill Birely.

"I knew about it," he said, "but we never discussed it, as I recall. It was such a horrible thing. He didn't want to talk about it and I certainly didn't want to remind him of it."[18]

From the time they were married in 1920, through three American League pennants, dozens upon dozens of golf tournaments and a prosperous farming venture after baseball, Sam and Edith had lived a relatively quiet, private existence. They did not have any children, so in early November of 1957, when Sam became a widow for the second time in his life, he was left again without any close relatives. Edith, who had arrived in Washington to work during World War I and met a fellow Hoosier, died suddenly at the couple's home.

Two years later, at age sixty-nine, Sam married for the third time. He and fifty-four-year-old Mary Kendall Adams, whose husband Herbert Adams had died at Christmastime in 1946. Herbert Adams had been a World War I veteran, just like Rice, and also a keen businessman — he owned the community's General Store.

When he married Mary in a tiny church ceremony, Rice stepped into the role of father for the first time since April of 1912. Mary had two daughters, and while Margaret was already out of the house by the time her mother married the famous baseball player, her younger daughter Christine was eighteen years old and still around. She was close to her stepfather, taking his last name and still living on the property in Silver Spring, Maryland, that he and Mary would move into before Sam's death.[19]

"Daddy was modest and hard-working," Christine told the Baseball Hall of Fame in an interview a few years ago. "He used to say, 'If you want to succeed, you have to concentrate and work hard.' I think he got those ethics at a young age. He used to say he would have played for a meal ticket. He was a sharp dresser and very conservative with his money. He was a fantastic father."

Sam clearly was a huge influence on his step daughter, who went on to earn two degrees, traveling through Europe and setting up activities for American enlisted men serving there, and later becoming a teacher.

"Daddy always told me that I could do anything a man could do," she said, "and that advice helped me get through many tough times."[20]

Unfortunately, upset about information divulged during a *Sports Illustrated* story written about Rice nearly twenty years after his death, Christine Rice politely declined to be interviewed for this book.

"To me he was perfect," she said, "and that's how I choose to remember him."[21]

Now that Rice had become a family man again, he withdrew from some of his old social circles.

"He had a very definite change of social life after that," said his friend Bill Birely. "I know people that had known him many, many years and they commented on how changed he was.

"We were really surprised that he married her. As an outsider looking in, it just didn't look like a match. But people don't know what goes on in people's hearts."

By the time the former Mary Adams and Sam were married, Rice had sold his chicken farm and taken up yet another hobby — another one dealing with birds, actually. He began racing homing pigeons during the 1950s, owning three hundred of the birds on the farmland he had left. The pigeons could reach speeds up to seventy-three miles per hour, and raced anywhere from two-hundred and fifty to six hundred miles.[22]

"He was one of the top breeders in the country," Christine Rice later said.

At the same time, Rice continued to excel in golf, and was a thirteen handicap at the age of eighty-four.[23]

He would travel around the country playing left-handed golf tournaments, joking with people that, "It pays the bills."[24]

Rice was proving to be a great competitor well into senior citizenship, but as the 1960s dawned and he neared age seventy, there was still a tremendous void — the Baseball Hall of Fame had been open for more than two decades, and yet he still was not a member. Those thirteen hits he never collected had turned the entrance of the Cooperstown shrine for him into a fortress doors.

17

THIRTEEN HITS

The photo is splashed across the nation's established paper of record, the *New York Times*. In it, the left-handed batter has just about finished the follow-through of a pure swing that has been replicated over thousands of at-bats over the course of a big-league career that stands at sixteen years and counting. Honed as it is, the swing has netted the man in the photo three batting titles — in 1927, 1934 and 1936, all with his previous team, the Pittsburgh Pirates.

By the time this photo is taken, Paul Waner is a Boston Brave.[1] A patch on his left sleeve, a red, white and blue shield worn by all major league teams of the era, is a subtle reminder that the photo was taken during a time when baseball was more diversion than national passion. The Second World War is underway.[2]

Waner, thirty-nine years old and his skills beginning to wane a bit, is one of the recognizable stars of the game left behind. And in this photo, his head is lifted and his eyes peer into center field, watching the trajectory of a line drive he has smacked into center field. Pittsburgh catcher Al Lopez — for Waner is facing his former team on this June afternoon — is in the frame, as well. His opened catcher's mitt awaits a ball that won't arrive. It appears that he, too, is watching Waner's liner make its way safely into center field.

Sure, the nation has more important matters to attend to in 1942. But Waner's hit is big news, and the *Times*, along with the rest of the nation's sporting press, treats it as such.

The photo is of Waner's three thousandth base hit.

With it, he has become just the seventh major leaguer to that point to reach the three-thousand milestone — the others are Ty Cobb (4,191), Tris Speaker (3,515), fellow Pittsburgh luminary Honus Wagner (3,430), Eddie Collins (3,313), Napoleon Lajoie (3,242) and Adrian "Cap" Anson (3,081).

Everyone present is well aware of the significance of Waner's milestone base hit. Home plate umpire Tom Dunn stops the game, receiving the ball from Pittsburgh outfielder Tommy Holmes and then personally presenting the man nicknamed "Big Poison" the three thousand-hit baseball. Before Waner even reaches first base, Pittsburgh players have emptied from the dugout to greet and congratulate their former teammate. The first to shake his hand is Pirates manager Frankie Frisch, a playing peer of Waner's who retired a few years earlier (the warm and fuzzy moment only last so long — Frisch will be ejected from this game, an eleven-inning affair that goes to the Pirates, for arguing balls and strikes).[3]

The fanfare over Waner's three-thousandth hit is illuminating for a couple of reasons. First of all, coming less than ten years after Rice retired just thirteen hits short of the milestone, the spectacle that attends the attainment of that particular mark seemed to have arrived to stay. In the more than sixty years hence, the exclusive three thousand-hit club has its own rich lore. Roberto Clemente's three thousandth was his final hit before he was killed tragically while flying supplies to earthquake-ravaged Nicaragua.[4] More recently, Rafael Palmeiro reached the mark just weeks before he was publicly disgraced by a positive steroid test — when the Baltimore Oriole smacked the historic hit and reveled in the on-field celebration, he was already aware that his violation was in the major league appeals process, that the clock was ticking.[5]

Second, the coverage of Waner's hit is strong evidence that the existence of the new Hall of Fame in Cooperstown had changed the way we recognize such accomplishments. Just six years after the Hall opened, three thousand was not longer an arbitrary number, but the accepted exclamation point on a career bound for bronze immortality.

Late in his life, and surely not for the first time, Rice was asked why he didn't try to hang on for his final thirteen steps into what would have become, in essence, automatic enshrinement.

"The truth of the matter is I did not even know how many hits I had," Rice said. "A couple of years after I quit, Clark Griffith told me about it, and asked me if I'd care to have a comeback with the Senators and pick up those thirteen hits. But I was out of shape, and didn't want to go through all that would have been necessary to make the effort. Nowadays, with radio and television announcers spouting records every time a player comes to bat, I would have known about my hits and probably would have stayed to make three thousand of them."[6]

Rice is correct — to a point. At the time of his release from the Indians, the last couple of players to reach the three thousand-hit mark were not noted, and it had been a decade since anyone reached the milestone. But that doesn't mean it hadn't drawn attention in the past. It had.

Honus Wagner's three thousandth hit, coming on June 9, 1914 against the Philadelphia Phillies, didn't draw the media, fan and fellow player celebrations Waner's milestone base hit would twenty-eight years later (a ritual repeated as each subsequent player has joined the club, including seven each in the 1970s and 1990s). But it certainly was noted at the time with a *New York Times* headline and a brief write-up that noted the pitcher (Erskine Mayer), type of hit (a "two-bagger") and crowd reaction ("He was applauded when he made the hit and again when he crossed the plate"). It also noted that Wagner was just the second major leaguer to collect three thousand hits. Cap Anson, whose career hit total and whether he indeed actually eclipsed the magic number has been a point of contention among historians for years, was the other.[7]

Later that summer, actually in the last week in the season, Cleveland's Napoleon Lajoie joined Anson and Wagner with number three thousand in front of the home crowd. He was presented the baseball at second base — like Wagner, his three thousandth had been a "two-bagger" — and his accomplishment was noted nationally.[8]

Ty Cobb's three thousandth hit in 1921 slipped the mind of the writers of the day. It doesn't appear to be noted in any report of the August 20 game against the Boston Red Sox.[9] Cobb's four thousandth hit, however, drew a small headline in the *New York Times* on July 19, 1927. Playing for the Philadelphia Athletics in the twilight of his career, Cobb, "who has broken and holds more records in big league baseball than any other man living or dead," according to the miniscule (but present) write-up, collected number four thousand in Detroit.[10]

Tris Speaker was the next after Cobb to join the three thousand club. He did it on May 17, 1925. In fact, Speaker's three thousandth came against the defending world champion Senators, with Rice in the lineup. Yet game stories note nothing about Speaker reaching the landmark — his dislocated knee, however, which had kept him out of the lineup over the previous few days, was a prominent subject in the news copy accounts of the game.[11] If Speaker was honored in any way, like Wagner and Lajoie had been years earlier, it doesn't appear to be mentioned anywhere. Since sports writers of the day rarely witnessed action that they didn't work into sometimes mind-numbing play-by-play game accounts, it seems fair to assume that Speaker's career-capping feat went off unnoticed.

An astute observer, if present that afternoon, could have probably saved Rice decades of heartache and aggravation bordering on bitterness. Had Speaker's hit been celebrated, even in the modest manner accorded to Wagner and Lajoie upon the occasion of their three thousandth hits, it's likely something Rice would have remembered. By 1925, he was already piling up hits at a nice, steady pace. Aware of the significance of the milestone, surely Rice would have been able to find a place to play for a handful of more games at the tail end of his career, maybe even convinced Cleveland to roll him out there on occasion if the franchise thought it was important to him, at least for as long as it would have taken for him to reach the mark.

And, presumably, the statistics-obsessed Baseball Writers Association of America would have rubber-stamped Rice's election to Cooperstown, instead of dragging out his election over more than two agonizing decades due to thirteen missing base hits.

If only.

Interestingly enough, Rice's proximity to three thousand hits was noted prominently in at least one major publication. In June of 1935, *Baseball Magazine's* Frank W. Koster penned a three-page article updating various players' approach at both three thousand and two thousand hits. In a story that must have been green lighted, written and even printed before Rice's release, the writer thought the forty-five-year-old's last thirteen hits would be little more than a formality.

"Veteran Sam Rice, of the Cleveland Indians, stands at the head of the van of actively engaged players in total hits," Koster wrote. "Sam has garnered the amazing total of 2,987 hits off American League hurling in his twenty years of play.

"...Whatever his fate may be, Sam should see enough activity this season to obtain the thirteen hits he needs to enter the exclusive and elusive 'three thousand' hit class."

The author also noted that Rogers Hornsby had 2,905 hits, but limited playing time in a dual player-manager role for the St. Louis Browns would probably impede his march.[12] Hornsby, a .359 career hitter at that point, had just twenty-three at-bats in 1934. He would play for three more years, but compile just twenty-five hits in that time, falling far short of the milestone. At least compared to Rice's eventual struggles to earn election, it wasn't really an issue as far as Hornsby's Hall of Fame election went — his seven batting titles, along with a .359 career batting average that to this day trails just Ty Cobb on the all-time list, ensured his election in 1942.[13]

Koster's story went on to update the hit total for any batter in either major league within striking distance of the two thousand-hit mark. Included on that list was Waner, who would of course go on to become the next three thousand-hit club member to great fanfare.[14]

Either Rice didn't read or he really didn't care. In 1935, they were simply numbers that sports writers and fans kicked around to have something to talk about. Milestones, and baseball statistics in general, wouldn't begin to assume the gravity we bestow on them to this day until the following year, when the building in Cooperstown, New York, would first swing open its doors.

* * *

The idea of a museum of baseball history first crossed the mind of Cooperstown local activist Alexander Cleland as he walked past workers in 1934 preparing a local field for a baseball "Centennial Celebration" for a couple of years down the road. Soon enough, items began pouring in to give Cleland's idea credibility, including a framed portrait of supposed baseball inventor Abner Doubleday and prints of several United States presidents throwing out the first ball at Griffith Stadium, items donated by Clark Griffith.

National League president Ford Frick, remembering a failed proposal to Congress back in the 1920s for a $100,000 baseball monument in Washington, D.C., to honor the game's greats, took the idea one step further, and suggested to Cleland that a "Hall of Fame" be opened in conjunction with a museum of nostalgic items.

"In the beginning," Frick wrote in his memoirs, "the Hall of Fame was a vision — and it came to pass."[15]

The early years of Hall of Fame voting essentially served as a trial period for various methods — though the results, of course, were permanent. The BBWAA held its first election early in 1936 and announced its first results on January 29. Though many of the rules for election have changed through the years, particularly during the first twenty years of balloting, one thing that has remained constant is the requirement that in the writers' vote, a player must receive seventy-five percent of votes cast to enter the Hall. With 226 votes cast in 1936, 170 were required for enshrinement, and five of the game's greatest names met the threshold and became the Hall of Fame's first class of inductees — Ty Cobb (222 votes), Babe Ruth (215), Honus Wagner (also 215), Christy Mathewson (205) and Walter Johnson (189). A year later, a committee consisting of the members of the Hall's executive committee selected five pioneers of the game — George Wright, Morgan G. Bulkeley, Ban Johnson, John McGraw and Connie Mack.

In 1938, his first year on the ballot, Rice received one vote from the BBWAA — one out of 262 cast. He wouldn't receive another one for ten years, when one of 153 writers was generous enough to give him a vote in the 1948 election.

Rice earned three votes the next year (1.96 percent), then one of 226 in 1951 (0.44 percent), one of 234 in 1953 (0.43 percent) and three of 234 (1.28 percent). In 1954, he received nine votes out of 252 cast (3.57 percent).[16]

Shirley Povich wrote probably the first stirring piece supporting Rice's candidacy in advance of the 1956 election. Assuming, correctly, that Hank Greenberg and Joe Cronin, who were the top voters not to gain election the year before, would be elected this time around, Povich was finally fed up. He wrote Greenberg's only talent was his muscles, as if leading the American League in home runs four times and RBIs four times should be detriments to his candidacy. Another point was legitimate—Rice's longevity far exceeded that of Greenberg, who played just thirteen seasons. Rice fell just shy of three thousand hits—Greenberg ended his career with a mere 1,628.

The Hall of Fame had been open for exactly two decades, and already one of its longest-lasting arguments was beginning to form — should voters place greater value on short-term brilliance, as Greenberg had displayed, or long-term consistency, Rice's forte.

Povich said he had kept his opinion to himself about Rice in the early days of the Hall of Fame, because he understood the waiting list to gain entrance was long at that point. But now, feeling that a flood of lesser players were about to start gaining entrance, he could stay silent no longer, particularly since Rice's vote totals had remained so low.

Povich's case may not have been clinical, but it certainly was passionate.

"Rice had what has become an increasing rarity among major league players; style," Povich said. "He was the popular conception of what a big leaguer should look like, how he should knock the dirt from his spikes, step into the batter's box, watch the near strikes go by with a sort of contempt for them, and whip his bat into the pitch that he did like."[17]

Perhaps swept up in the enshrinement buzz, Povich calmed the rhetoric by induction weekend, writing of Cronin and Greenberg that "the Hall of Fame is getting a pair of deserving guys."[18]

Local sports writers weren't the only ones trying to talk their younger colleagues into voting for Rice. Fred Lieb, the prolific baseball writer, penned a 1959 piece for *Sport* magazine entitled, "Thirteen Hits from the Hall of Fame."

"Ol' Sambo had the bad luck to miss the Hall of Fame by thirteen little hits," Lieb wrote.

After rattling off the names of the men who have reached the three thousand-hit milestone, Lieb continues, "Membership in the club has been tantamount to automatic admission to the Hall of Fame.... Had Rice made those extra thirteen hits, and beaten Waner to the distinction of being the seventh man to get three thousand hits, he would have become durably famous and would have made Cooperstown years ago. But who today, outside of baseball statisticians, remembers how many hits Rice had when he closed out his career some twenty-five years ago?"[19]

Rice certainly did, eventually lamenting the fact that he didn't reject his doctor's advice and battle through the leg injury for those final thirteen hits.

"I kept telling myself that it didn't really matter if I had 2,887 hits or three thousand hits," he said. "How can you go back? There's no way. Now, I wish I had stuck around for those thirteen hits. It just would have been a distinction."[20]

Rice's contemporary, Ty Cobb, also took up his cause in print, as well as behind the scenes: "Some others have been sadly overlooked," he said in an article about the election of his old teammate Sam Crawford. "Take old Sam Rice. Played for the Washington Senators twenty seasons. Look up his record. Lifetime batting average of .309 (actually .322). It's a shame they've passed him so many years."[21]

"Rice can be consoled that he is in Ty Cobb's private Hall of Fame," Povich wrote.

In what was becoming his annual drumbeat, Povich wrote a column supporting Rice's candidacy. In fact, he rewrote the same exact passage about Rice's style as a supporting factor.[22]

"This could be the time Sam Rice makes it," Post columnist Bob Addie, full of hope, wrote ten days before the 1960 ballots were due.

At the same time, perhaps offering a glimpse into the psychology of a Washington baseball fan, Addie seemed to be pleased just to see Senators on the ballot alongside greats from the more storied franchises like the Yankees and Cardinals.

"As you probably have noticed, there are a lot of former Washington stars on the eligible list," Addie wrote. "Many, of course, won't get a look-in. But it's nice to realize we did have some boys who were stars."[23]

As it turned out, the momentum that Rice had been gaining in recent elections carried him to a second-place finish on the 1960 BBWAA ballot — only Edd Roush finished with more votes (three more than Rice). Neither man, however, received enough votes for enshrinement. In fact, they were quite a way off. Roush's 146 votes, out of a record 269 cast (54.28), left him fifty-six votes shy. The 143 Rice received pushed him over the fifty percent threshold for the first time — his 53.16 percent total was a monster jump from the previous election two years earlier. But he was still far short of election, as was a third player, Eppa Rixey.[24]

Commissioner Ford Frick along with American League president Joe Cronin, frustrated perhaps at seeing his old Washington teammate rejected year after year, both called for an overhaul of the voting system. They felt the seventy-five percent requirement could possibly be "too harsh."

The *Post's* Povich, however, while expressing sadness that the doors still hadn't opened to Rice, wrote that this was the price that had to be paid for important selectivity.

"The steady rejection of the less-than-great has been a good thing for Cooperstown," Povich wrote.

He preached patience when it came to Rice, who he was sure would eventually gain entrance.

"It was good to slow up the voting and keep it carefully selective," Povich wrote.

It was a logical sentiment, but for one thing, Povich was afflicted by the mentality that the players of yesteryear were superior to those playing today.

"The game currently isn't producing the giant-type performers of the past," he said.[25]

Active players at the time the column was written included Mickey Mantle, Brooks Robinson, Ted Williams, Yogi Berra, Willie Mays, Ernie Banks, Roberto Clemente, Eddie Matthews, Hank Aaron, Stan Musial and Frank Robinson.[26]

Crusty *New York Daily News* columnist Jimmy Powers railed against the whipper-snappers of the BBWAA:

"The bat in use today compares with the bat of fifty years ago the way a hydrogen bomb compares with a World War I artillery shell," he whined. "And the modern fielder's glove is a trap from which only the most ingenious baseball can escape. Older stars had to possess certain manual skills. They were not blessed with self-operating booby traps."

The *Post*, in editorial form, also questioned the writers' credentials to vote on the Rices of the game.

"A certain irony resides in the fact that all three of these antique heroes long ago turned the age of sixty," the uncredited opinion piece states. "This means that in the days of their glory a considerable portion of the present membership of the Baseball Writers Association or America had been but barely weaned and some were still unborn."[27]

In March, Post columnist Addie had an opportunity to catch up with Rice at spring training. In probably the most revealing interview Rice ever consented to (players weren't quoted very often in the newspapers of his day), Rice was asked if he would have voted for himself, had he been granted a vote.

He began his answer modestly.

"People are always asking me if I was disappointed when I didn't get into the Hall of Fame," Rice said. "I wouldn't call it being disappointed. I think that a fellow would like to make the Hall of Fame because it means prestige. Everybody likes honors like that."

But, Rice continued, when he thinks of Cooperstown, he thinks of giants of his era like Walter Johnson, Ty Cobb, Tris Speaker, Grover Cleveland Alexander, Babe Ruth and Lou Gehrig.

"I think it's right that a fellow like Sam Rice was kept out," he continued.

That being said, Rice felt that the Hall had been "cheapened" in recent years by some of the players elected in. Specifically and apparently off the top of his head, Rice mentioned Hank Greenberg and Joe Cronin as two Hall of Famers that should not have been voted in, in his opinion (the same two players Post columnist Povich argued against in favor of Rice in his impassioned support piece a few years earlier). Greenberg was one-dimensional, Rice said. He didn't feel that his ability to hit for power was enough to overcome his lack of fielding ability and speed.

The mention of Cronin is telling. Cronin was Rice's teammate in the early 1930s, when Rice was wrapping up his career with the Senators. And, of course, he also served as his manager in Rice's last two seasons in D.C. Cronin, Rice told Addie, wasn't as good as many other shortstops he could think of. He credited Cronin with one of the best overall seasons he had seen from a shortstop, combining his fielding, overall hitting and hitting in the clutch, in the pennant season of 1933. He also gave Cronin credit for guiding the Senators to the American League pennant that season.

"But one year doesn't make a Hall of Famer," Rice continued.

He suggested a ten-year waiting period for Hall of Fame election, rather than the five-year waiting period that is still in place to this day.

As much as he feigned modesty, Rice clearly sided with players who had shown consistency in their careers over those who had been brilliant for a relatively brief period. Dizzy Dean, brilliant from 1932 through '36 but barely able to stay healthy after that, drew perhaps Rice's most pointed wrath. (Dean had been elected in 1953.)

"Dizzy Dean has no business being in the Hall," Rice said.

Rice concluded the interview by again playing humble.

"Don't feel sorry for Sam Rice," he said. "If he deserved to be in there, he would be."[28]

While Rice continued to be snubbed, Ty Cobb personally took up his cause, calling the failure to elect Rice a "terrible oversight."

"I know, I played against him," Cobb said. "You know about ball players when you play against them."

To close his column on the subject, Povich made what seems to be a challenge to his colleagues in the baseball writing business:

"On his forty acres at nearby Ashton, Maryland, Sam Rice could be wondering if baseball writers can read, and if so, what is keeping him out of Cooperstown?"[29]

Povich's urging had little effect — Rice drew eighty of 160 votes cast in the 1962 election (50.63 percent), the results announced in late January. He did finish third, behind electees Bob Feller and Jackie Robinson. Though at least the BBWAA was now actually electing players — the pair were the first elected by the organization since 1956 — it remained a tough crowd. The legendary Robinson received 77.5 percent, sneaking in just four votes over the number necessary for election.

Probably owing to the presence on the ballot of first-timers Robinson and Feller, Rice's percentage of the vote total actually fell slightly in '62 from the fifty-three percent he had garnered in the previous election two years before. But there was hope on the horizon — the next year, Rice's name would move from the BBWAA's ballot to that of the Old Timers' Committee, a precursor to today's Veteran's Committee. Finally, the please for Rice's election found sympathetic ears.[30]

Because the writers only voted every other year in the 1960s, the twelve-man Old-Timers' Committee cast the only ballot in 1963.

And as it turned out, all four of their selections — Eppa Rixey, Elmer Flick, John Clarkson and, finally, Sam Rice — were unanimous. Finally, Mr. 2,987 was a Hall of Famer.

Soon after the votes were tabulated, the calls began going out.

"You sure scraped the bottom of the cracker barrel," Eppa Rixey joked.

"Stop fooling," Elmer Flick said.

Calls started going out to find relatives of John Clarkson, the only deceased member of the class at the time of the vote.[31]

Meanwhile, an old teammate of Rice's was a member of the committee, and took the honors of calling him.

From his office, Joe Cronin, the manager of the 1933 pennant winners and a man Rice had reserved some of his harshest Hall of Fame commentary for, picked up the phone and called his former teammate.

While Rixey and Flick were prepared with one-liners, Rice was caught off guard by Cronin's call.

"That's very nice," Rice told him. "It's a thrill.... Thanks for calling, Joe."

The rumor Rice had finally been elected spread quickly around Washington, D.C., and the Maryland-Virginia area, so quickly that Rice's neighbors began bombarding the newspaper with phone calls before Rice had even received his official notification. Before long, Washington Post operators began simply answering the phone, "Yes, it's true. Sam Rice is in the Hall of Fame."

"You've got some fine telephone operators down there at the *Post*," Rice told *Post* columnist Bob Addie.

"To tell you the truth, I was stunned," he said after having a few weeks to reflect on the long-awaited honor. "My wife Mary had felt all along that I'd be elected. I was disgusted and had given up hope. I really was thrilled, but Cronin had caught me by surprise."[32]

So the group, minus one more in Rixey, who had died in the months between his election and induction, gathered on that rainy afternoon in Cooperstown. The Boston Red Sox and Milwaukee Braves played the annual little exhibition game.[33] And Rice finally held the plaque he had been waiting nearly thirty years for in his hand.

It read:

EDGAR CHARLES (SAM) RICE
WASHINGTON 1915–1933
CLEVELAND 1934

At bat 600 or more times eight different seasons. Had 200 or more hits in each of six seasons. Batted .322 for 20-year career and had 2,987 hits. Set AL record with 182 singles in 1925. Led AL in number of hits (216) in 1924 and 1926. Led AL in putouts for outfielders with 454 in 1920 and 385 in 1922.[34]

* * *

After the pageantry of his Hall of Fame induction, Rice returned to the golf course, where he continued to play almost every day. He lauded the invention of the electric golf cart.

"Now I can play eighteen and go home and cut the lawn," Rice said.

And he explained that he approached his golf game the same way he approached baseball — by utilizing the gifts nature gave him.

"I swing at a golf ball the same way I did at a baseball," Rice said, after a golfing partner commented on the consistent distances of his drives despite a smooth, steady swing. "Just try to hit it solidly."[35]

Rice and his family made the trip to Cooperstown every summer for that year's induction ceremony. It had taken Rice so long to earn election, he wanted to enjoy his new status.

"He was like a little kid," Christine Rice said. "All of the players would get together and swap stories. I think going back to Cooperstown was what kept him going so long."[36]

Like all of us, he couldn't go on forever. In 1974, Sam and Mary were forced to cancel a golf trip to Florida (they took many trips to Florida and Hawaii in Rice's later years).[37]

Rice had cancer, and by October, he was bedridden in a Maryland hospital.

"Ol' Sam is mighty weak," Rice told someone. "I dunno if I'll ever get out of here, but what's an old goat like me have to worry about? All I miss is playing golf and I don't know if I'm going to ever get out for that."

Age had taken a long time to catch up with Rice on the baseball field. It had taken an even longer time to catch up with him on the golf course. And now, at age eighty-four, age caught up with Sam Rice once and for all. Preceded in death by two wives, his parents, all of his siblings, the only two biological children he ever had, and most of his Washington teammates, Rice died at home on October 13, 1974. No longer would the memories of that horrible evening in 1912 haunt him, though judging from the productive and happy life he had forged for himself, Rice had come to terms with those events long before, at least as best as he could. He died having never breathed a word publicly about what had happened so many years before.[38]

Rice was cremated and his remains buried in Woodside Cemetery on Haviland Mill Road near Ashton.[39]

Rice's funeral was attended by, among others, Hall of Fame president Paul Kerr, to whom Christine Rice hand wrote a letter of appreciation.

"He loathed funerals of any nature," she wrote, expressing thanks that his friends celebrated his life rather than mourning his passing, "saw no need to wear dark colors or show tears. He would surely have been pleased about all the fondness shown as everyone remembered some nice event in his life."[40]

Christine may have been one of a diminishing handful of people still alive who knew why her stepfather "loathed" funerals—he had been to far too many of them in a shot span in his youth.

That secret would come out eventually, but in the meantime, Rice's more well-known secret came to the forefront.

A few years before, Sam had holed up in the Otsaga Hotel in Cooperstown, writing a letter to be sealed until his death. In it, he planned to reveal the truth about the catch.

"I used to ask him," Christine once recalled, "'Would you tell me if I asked you?' And he'd say with a little gleam in his eye, 'No.'"[41]

Fans waited for an answer to the nearly fifty-year-old question. But there was a problem. Less than two weeks after Rice's death, Cooperstown officials had not yet located the legendary letter. Distressingly, some were publicly beginning to wonder if one really existed, or whether it was the stuff of myth, like Ruth's called shot or Abner Doubleday inventing the game. Either they really believed that, or they were frightened that they had misplaced such an anticipated time capsule, and were trying to shield themselves from public embarrassment.

"Not a trace," said Hall of Fame director Ken Smith.

Smith wondered if perhaps the letter didn't end up in the possession of his predecessor as director of the Hall of Fame, Lee Allen. Allen retired in 1969. The problem was that he had since died.

"I do know that Lee Allen was always prodding Rice to leave some sort of a secret letter about the catch with the Hall of Fame," Smith said. "But we have never been able to retrieve much from Allen's estate, or from his widow."

The most troubling comment came from Cliff Kachline, the Hall of Fames official historian, who practically dismissed the letters existence as a morsel of baseball gossip.

"That Sam Rice letter has been a rumor for a long time," he said, "but we never had any solid evidence there was one."

Others were more optimistic than Kachline.

"We're still looking high and low," Jack Redding, the museum's librarian told Povich.

Mary Rice was the most adamant about the letter's existence. Not only did she swear that her late husband had penned such a document, but she said she had read it herself. Perhaps wary of the skepticism about whether Sam had caught the ball, including a claim by old teammate Ossie Bluege that Rice had told him he didn't catch it, she also claimed to know its general contents.

"There was a letter," she said. "Sam showed it to me several years ago after he was elected to the Hall of Fame in (1963). He turned it over to somebody up there. I read it. It was a to whom it may concern thing. In it, Sam wrote that he did make the catch."[42]

They were all, it turned out, looking in the wrong place. It wasn't in Cooperstown after all. Rice's letter, which indeed did exist, was stashed away in an office file in Manhattan, a needle tucked away in the world's largest haystack. Of all the paper fluttering on Wall Street on that day in early November, 1974, only one captured the rapt attention of baseball buffs. As it turned out, Rice didn't give the letter to Lee Allen after all. He had entrusted it to Kerr, the president of the Hall of Fame. Kerr's office was at Thirty Wall Street in New York City. And somehow, even though he had attended Rice's funeral, he had missed the preceding furor over the missing letter.

All that mattered, though, was that the letter had been found safe and sound. Kerr preceded over the revealing of its contents. In a ceremony infused with the gravity of a will reading, he slit the envelope open and read it to those gathered.[43]

The letter was dated Monday, July 26, 1965, and hand written in cursive:

> It was a cold and windy day, the right field bleachers were crowded with people in overcoats and wrapped in blankets, the ball was a line drive headed for the bleachers towards right center, I turned slightly to my right and had the ball in view all the way. Going at top speed and about 15 feet from (the) bleachers jumped as high as I could and back handed and the ball hit the center of pocket in glove (I had a death grip on it). I hit the ground above five feet from a barrier about four feet high in front of the bleachers with all my breaks on but couldn't stop so I tried to jump it to land in the crowd but my feet hit the barrier about a foot from top and I toppled over on my stomach into first row of bleachers, I hit my Adams apple on something which sort of knocked me out for a few seconds but (Earl) McNeely arrived about that time and grabbed me by the shirt and pulled me out. I remember trotting back toward the infield still carrying the ball for about halfway and then tossed it towards the pitcher's mound. (How I have wished many times I had kept it.)
> At no time did I lose possession of the ball.
> Sam Rice[44]

* * *

So it seemed that the book on Rice's life had been closed. However, Rice's obituaries, of course, were incomplete.

17. Thirteen Hits

And for nearly a decade after his death, recollections of Rice stayed that way. The last time, at least that can be found, the tornado had been written about was by the *Chicago Tribune* political writer during the 1925 World Series, and of course even then the story seemed to fall on mostly deaf ears, buried as the pertinent information was in the piece.

Then John Yost became interested in Rice's life story.

In the early 1980s Yost, a local freelance journalist working for the weekly *Newton County Enterprise,* located in Rice's home county in Indiana, happened upon a list of former major leaguers who had Indiana connections. Noticing Rice's name on the list, he decided to write up a nuts-and-bolts piece about Rice's accomplishments for the paper.

After it had run, Yost was about town running some errands when an older local complimented him on the article.

"Saw your piece about Sam Rice," he said to Yost. "Terrible tragedy."

Yost, however, was unaware of any tragedy, and pressed the man for more information. Some time around World War I, the man told the writer, Rice's family had been killed by a storm that ravaged the area. Yost decided to investigate further, combing through every copy of the *Kentland Democrat* newspaper published from 1913 through 1919, hoping that in one of those issues, the story of the Rice family tragedy would leap from an old, yellowed page.

But it was all wasted time. Yost didn't find anything about a storm killing Sam Rice's family, so he gave up the search, dismissing the information as either not factual or lost to history.

He had pretty much forgotten the search for Rice's past when Yost was given a box of pre–World War I newspapers by somebody who knew about his interest in local history. Those sat on the corner of his desk, however, for close to two years before finally his office announced an upcoming spring cleaning.

Yost began sifting through the old papers and suddenly it was staring out at him, an article from April of 1912, documenting in gut-wrenching detail the tragedy that had occurred in nearby Donovan, Illinois, at the Gard farm, seventy-one years before.

Yost began work on a new story for the weekly Enterprise, and he contacted the Baseball Hall of Fame, which at first was skeptical about the authenticity of Yost's find.

"They were so reluctant to endorse this as the real thing, which it was," says Yost, who knew what he had found.[45]

By early January of 1984, officials there realized that Yost's version of the Rice early history was the correct one, and information flowed back and forth.

"Many thanks for the material you sent me which I received today," Yost wrote in a letter to Cooperstown. "One added piece of information that I have learned is that Charles Rice, the father of Edgar Rice, died a week later of injuries suffered in the tornado, and also of an apparent loss of the will to live."[46]

Rice's revised story made its way to D.C. fairly quickly. A few months after Yost broke it for the first time, the *Washington Post*, by that time bereft of a baseball team to cover year-in and year-out, ran the Rice story as part of its 1985 season-opening coverage.

"He was a man heavy of mind," wrote Shirley Povich, "beset by a sadness that few could know.... As Rice, in his major league years, stood at the plate facing the great pitchers of his time, how many times was it replayed in his mind, that terror Sunday of 1912? The unknowing thousands, millions, who watched him perform for those twenty years with the grace of a big leaguer born, could hardly relate to the sadness within him. They were the innocents. Sam Rice made his sorrow private."[47]

Then, in 1993, Rice's tale received national reading audience.

Sports Illustrated writer Steve Wulf, in a special edition of the magazine dedicated to sports history, dug into Rice's story.

"The Rice bronze may be the most inadequate in Cooperstown," he wrote. "...No plaque could tell of the tragedy and triumph of Sam Rice."

Shirley Povich told Wulf that Rice was "a bit of a loner." And Christine Rice told him about the revealing of his secret family tragedy, which he apparently had kept from Mary.

According to Rice's stepdaughter, a newspaper reporter was interviewing Rice in the 1960s, probably about his Hall of Fame election, with Mary standing near.

"The writer suddenly asked him about the tragedy in Indiana," Christine Rice told Wulf. "And that was the first my mother had ever heard about it."[48]

Perhaps the reporter never put Rice's background into print, because as far as is currently known, no story about the tornado ever saw the light of day until Yost's piece in 1984, another 21 years after Rice's enshrinement into Cooperstown.

Epilogue

A few days before I turned in the manuscript for this book, I spoke for a few minutes with Randy Decker, the town manager for Morocco, Indiana. I was heartened to hear that Rice's hometown had not forgotten about their Hall of Famer. The blue welcoming sign still stands just off of U.S. 41, Decker told me. The town's youth baseball and softball complex is now named "Sam Rice Park." Thanks to the work of local banker and Rice buff Jeff Iseminger, the complex will be graced, by the time of this book's publication, with a black stone monument to the town's most famous former resident (but not the only Hall of Famer — Morocco's own Dick Potts was recently elected to the National Late Model Dirt Track Hall of Fame, a tremendous honor in a state that loves its auto racing).[1]

It has been difficult to keep the memory of the Washington baseball greats alive, in large part because for more than thirty years, there wasn't a home fan base to carry the torch. The original Washington Senators, Sam Rice's Washington Senators, left town for Minnesota after 1960, where they still exist as the Minnesota Twins. From the time the 1933 World Series wrapped up until the time the franchise boxed up its belongings, the Senators finished with a .500 record or better just five times, never again reaching the postseason. The closest they came was 1945, when the Senators won three out of five against the front-running Detroit Tigers to draw nearly even atop the American League standings. But even then, interest in the franchise among the locals had waned — less than six thousand spectators showed up for the final game of the five-game series. The Tigers pulled away by just a game and a half over the season's final week.

That team moved out after the 1960 season, and the new Senators moved in the next spring, posted four consecutive one hundred–loss seasons, then moved out after the 1971 season to Arlington, Texas, where they became the Texas Rangers.[2] A widespread belief was born that baseball just wasn't meant to succeed in D.C.

Then on April 14, 2005, after a thirty-four-year absence, baseball once again returned to Washington, D.C. For once, the District was the beneficiary of a franchise relocation, not the victim of it. The Montreal Expos, an organization on life support for several years, moved into Washington's RFK Stadium, and gracious D.C. fans numbering more than 2.7 million filled the seats that summer. Not only that, but the Nationals, the name of the new team and actually the official name of Rice's Senators for most of the years of the team's existence, spent a lot of the summer in first place before fading.[3]

Will the existence of the new Nationals start a revival of interest in some of the previous franchise's greats? Will this be the time that baseball in Washington finally succeeds, both on the field and at the cash register? It's difficult to say. But those questions helped inspire me to get into print a biography on Sam Rice, that's for sure.

It is difficult to study Rice and not wonder what went through his mind in all those years following the awful tragedy on Gard farm. Was he at peace? Hopefully. Was he tortured by the fact that he was playing minor-league baseball at the time? By the idea that, as many survivors felt, he "should have been there"? That's certainly a strong possibility. But ultimately, I think, the message is this—Rice overcame tragedy to put together a Hall-of-Fame baseball career, to marry happily twice, to start a very prosperous chicken farm, and to find great success in two hobbies, golf and homing pigeon racing.

Rice's ashes are buried near his former home in Ashton/Sandy Spring, Maryland. It is unknowable what level of peace he found in the sixty-two years that followed the tornado. But there is this comfort always: He has found it now.

APPENDIX:
SAM RICE BY THE NUMBERS

Rice on All-Time Leaders (as of Opening Day, 2007)

Batting average: 49th (.322). Games: 71st (2,404). At-Bats: 49th (9,269). Runs: 55th (1,514). Hits: 27th (2,987). Total bases: 75th (3,955). Doubles: 47th (498). Triples: 14th (184). Singles: 14th (2,271). Times on Base: 57th (3,751). Sacrifice Hits: 74th (214). At-Bats per Strikeout: 12th (33.7). Outs: 69th (6,638). Source: Baseball Reference.com

BBWAA Hall of Fame Voting

Year	Votes	Pct.
1938	1	0.38
1948	1	0.83
1949	3	1.96
1950	1	0.60
1951	1	0.44
1952	1	0.43
1953	3	1.14
1954	9	3.57
1955	28	11.16
1956	45	23.32
1958	90	30.83
1960	134	53.16
1962	81	50.63

Source: BaseballHallofFame.org

Career Batting Stats

Year	Team	G	AB	R	H	2B	3B	HR	RBI	BB	SO	Avg.	OBP	Slg.	SB-CS	G at Pos.
1915	Wash.	4	8	0	3	0	0	0	0	0	1	.375	.375	.375	0	P-4
1916	Wash.	58	197	26	59	8	3	1	17	15	13	.299	.352	.386	4	P-5, LF-4, RF-42
1917	Wash.	155	586	77	177	25	7	0	69	50	41	.302	.360	.369	35	RF-155
1918	Wash.	7	23	3	8	1	0	0	3	2	0	.348	.400	.391	1	RF-6
1919	Wash.	141	557	80	179	23	9	3	71	42	26	.321	.376	.411	26	RF-141
1920	Wash.	153	624	83	211	29	9	3	80	39	23	.338	.381	.428	63–30	CF-153
1921	Wash.	143	561	83	185	39	13	4	79	38	10	.330	.382	.467	26–12	CF-137, RF-4
1922	Wash.	154	633	91	187	37	13	6	69	48	13	.295	.347	.423	20–9	CF-154
1923	Wash.	148	595	117	188	35	18	3	75	57	12	.316	.381	.450	20–8	RF-147
1924	Wash.	154	646	106	216	39	14	1	76	46	24	.334	.382	.443	24–13	CF-34, RF-123
1925	Wash.	152	649	111	227	31	13	1	87	37	10	.350	.388	.442	26–11	CF-29, RF-133
1926	Wash.	152	641	98	216	32	14	3	76	42	20	.337	.380	.445	44–23	CF-44, RF-120
1927	Wash.	142	603	98	179	33	14	2	65	36	11	.297	.336	.408	19–6	LF-1, RF-138
1928	Wash.	148	616	95	202	32	15	2	55	49	15	.328	.379	.438	16–3	LF-1, RF-147
1929	Wash.	150	616	119	199	39	10	1	62	55	9	.323	.382	.424	16–8	RF-147
1930	Wash.	147	593	121	207	35	13	1	73	55	14	.349	.407	.457	13–8	CF-15, RF-133
1931	Wash.	120	413	81	128	21	8	0	42	35	11	.310	.365	.400	6–5	LF-10, CF-11, RF-85
1932	Wash.	106	288	58	93	16	7	1	34	32	6	.323	.391	.438	7–4	LF-10, CF-14, RF-48
1933	Wash.	73	85	19	25	4	3	1	12	2	7	.294	.326	.447	0–2	LF-8, CF-10, RF-23
1934	Cle.	97	335	48	98	19	1	1	33	28	9	.293	.351	.364	5–1	LF-13, RF-65
Totals		2,404	1,514 9,269	2,987	498	184	34	1,078	708	275	.322	.374	.427	351–143	P-9, LF-47, CF-601, RF-1,657

Source: Palmer & Gilette, *The Baseball Encyclopedia*

Career World Series Stats

Year	Team	G	AB	R	H	2B	3B	HR	RBI	BB	SO	Avg.	OBP	Slg.	SB-CS
1924	Wash.	7	29	2	6	0	0	0	1	3	2	.207	.281	.207	2-0
1925	Wash.	7	33	5	12	0	0	0	3	0	1	.364	.364	.364	0-0
1933	Wash.	1	1	0	1	0	0	0	0	0	0	1.000	1.000	1.000	0-0
Totals		15	63	7	19	0	0	0	4	3	3	.302	.333	.302	2-0

Source: Baseball-Reference.com.

Career Pitching Stats

Year	Team	W-L	G	GS	CG	IP	H	R	HR	HP	BB	SO	ERA
1915	Wash.	1-0	4	2	1	18	13	8	0	0	9	9	2.00
1916	Wash.	0-1	5	1	0	21.1	18	10	0	0	10	3	2.95
Totals	1-1		9	3	1	39.1	31	18	0	0	19	12	2.52

Source: Palmer & Gilette, *The Baseball Encyclopedia*.

Chapter Notes

Preface

5. *The Sporting News*, March 9, 1963, "Rice Lacked Color, But Not Diamond Skills."
6. Personal interview with William C. Birely, November 30, 2006.

Prologue

1. Stewart O'Nan, ed., *The Vietnam Reader*.
2. *New York Times*, August 10, 1963.
3. Palmer & Gilette, *The Baseball Encyclopedia*.
4. *New York Times*, August 10, 1963.

Chapter 1

1. Knowledge of the layout of Lake and Newton counties, particularly the geography of U.S. 41, comes from the author's upbringing in nearby Griffith, Indiana, as well as my six years working as a sports writer at The Times of Northwest Indiana in nearby Munster, Indiana.
2. Palmer & Gilette, *The Baseball Encyclopedia*.
3. *Kentland (Ind.) Democrat*, April 26, 1912. A great deal of what is known about Rice's family as well as the tornado that took their lives comes from the definitive existing article on the events, headlined, "Fierce Tornado Visits Newton and Adjoining Counties."
5. Born, Gerald, "The Cyclone of 1912." The local historian's account of the tornado that took Rice's family's life was published in the *Morocco Sesquincentennial Historical Collection*.
5. *Kentland (Ind.) Democrat*, April 26, 1912.
6. Sam Rice, "How the U.S. Navy Made Me a Ball Player," *Baseball Magazine* (August 1920).
7. *Newton County (Ind.) Enterprise*, June 7, 1984. Ten years after Rice's death, Morocco historian and part-time journalist for the local weekly newspaper John Yost unearthed the secret of Rice's early adulthood. Yost's work, as far as we know, marked the first time a word about Rice's family tragedy appeared in print for 69 years.
8. *Chicago Tribune*, October 13, 1925, "'Rango' Rice Just a Regular Guy from Watseka, Illinois."
9. *Kentland (Ind.) Democrat*, April 26, 1912.
10. Reed Browning, *1924: Baseball's Greatest Season*.
11. "Country Boys in the Big Leagues," *Literary Digest* (April 18, 1925).
12. *Galesburg (Ill.) Evening Mail*, April 11, 1912. The minor-league team in Galesburg was covered on a daily basis by the local newspaper.
13. *Kentland (Ind.) Democrat*, April 26, 1912.
14. Transaction card, *Sam Rice Hall of Fame Player File*.
15. *Galesburg (Ill.) Evening Mail*, April 11, 1912.

16. *Galesburg (Ill.) Evening Mail*, April 15, 1912.
17. *Galesburg (Ill.) Evening Mail*, April 17, 1912.
18. *Galesburg (Ill.) Evening Mail*, April 21, 1912.
19. *Kentland (Ind.) Democrat*, April 26, 1912.
20. Born, "The Cyclone of 1912."
21. *Newton County (Ind.) Enterprise*, June 7, 1984.
22. *Kentland (Ind.) Democrat*, April 26, 1912.
23. Born, "The Cyclone of 1912."
24. *Galesburg (Ill.) Evening Mail*, April 21, 1912.
25. *Kentland (Ind.) Democrat*, April 26, 1912.
26. *Newton County (Ind.) Enterprise*, June 7, 1984.
27. *Kentland (Ind.) Democrat*, April 26, 1912.
28. Born, "The Cyclone of 1912."
29. *Galesburg (Ill.) Evening Mail*, April 22 & 23, 1912.
30. *Newton County (Ind.) Enterprise*, June 7, 1984.
31. *Galesburg (Ill.) Evening Mail*, April 22, 1912.
32. *Newton County (Ind.) Enterprise*, June 7, 1984.
33. *Kentland (Ind.) Democrat*, April 26, 1912.
34. *Newton County (Ind.) Enterprise*, June 7, 1984.
35. *Galesburg (Ill.) Evening Mail*, May 6, 1912.
36. *Galesburg (Ill.) Evening Mail*, May 12, 1912.

Chapter 2

1. *Newton County (Ind.) Enterprise*, June 7, 1984.
2. Rice, "How the U.S. Navy Made Me a Ballplayer."
3. John S.D. Eisenhower, *Intervention! The United States and the Mexican Revolution, 1913–1917*.
4. Rice, "How the U.S. Navy Made Me a Ballplayer."
5. Eisenhower, *Intervention!*
6. *New York Times*, May 9, 1914, "Senate Eulogy to Dead: Mr. Lewis Pays a Tribute to the Men Who Fell at VeraCruz."
7. August Heckscher, *Woodrow Wilson*.
8. Kendrick A. Clements, *The Presidency of Woodrow Wilson*.
9. Heckscher, *Woodrow Wilson*.
10. Rice, "How the U.S. Navy Made Me a Ballplayer."
11. Society of American Baseball Research member Stephen Able of Indianapolis scoured articles about the Goobers in the *Petersburg (Va.) Daily Progress* and was the first to detail Rice's minor-league performance.
12. *New York Times*, April 9, 1915, "Yankees All Mussed Up: Petersburg Routs American Leaguers in Last Game in South."
13. *Petersburg (Va.) Daily Progress*, April 17, 1915.
14. Able, "Sam Rice" SABR Baseball Bio Project.
15. *Washington Post*, March 27, 1933, "High-Priced Rookie Is Gone Forever, Says Clark Griffith; Nats' Owner Recalls Bargains; Once Bid for Ty Cobb."
16. Shirley Povich, *The Washington Senators: An Informal History*. Until his death in 1998, Povich was considered the pre-eminent Washington baseball historian, covering the beat as a columnist at the Washington Post for many decades. His book on the Senators was published by Putnam in 1954, part of an intended series of team histories to be written about every team in the major leagues.
17. Palmer & Gilette, *The Baseball Encyclopedia*.
18. *Washington Post*, July 30, 1915, "Griffith Buys Outfielder Kopp of Canadian Team; Newcomer Will Report Here at Once for a Trial."
19. Palmer & Gilette, *The Baseball Encyclopedia*.

Chapter 3

1. *Washington Post*, May 8, 1963, "Rice Where He Belongs."
2. *Petersburg (Va.) Daily Progress*, July 24, 1915.
3. *Petersburg (Va.) Daily Progress*, July 29, 1915.
4. Baseball-Reference.com
5. *Washington Post*, July 31, 1915, "Gallia and Sisler Likely Opponents on the Slab Today."
6. Povich, *The Washington Senators*.
7. *Washington Post*, August 8, 1915, "Nationals Have Traveled at .656 Clip Since July 9"; Murphy, the reliable Web site Baseball-Reference.com reports, batted .231 in 68 games with Philadelphia in 1915. But after coming over to the White Sox, he batted. .315 the rest of the way.
8. BaseballAlmanac.com
9. *Washington Post*, August 11, 1915, "Notes About Nationals."
10. *Washington Post*, September 8, 1915.
11. Guy Waterman, "The Upstart Senators of 1912–1915." (*The National Pastime*, 1993).

Waterman lists the eight men he describes as "The Cinderella Eight":

"DAN MOELLER, RF — rookie, lifetime .243 hitter;
"KID FOSTER, 3B — rookie, owner of the longest streak of homerless at-bats in major league history (3,278 ABS without a homer!);
"CLYDE MILAN, CF — the one established player of proven competence;
"CHICK GANDIL, 1B — sophomore, and another genuinely good player, later to earn ill repute in the Black Sox scandal;
"HANK SHANKS, LF — rookie, .253 lifetime average with no power;
"RAY MORGAN, 2B — rookie, .254 lifetime without power;
"GEORGE McBRIDE, SS — veteran .218 lifetime hitter, though acknowledged a superb defensive shortstop;
"JOHN HENRY, C — sophomore, .207 lifetime average with two career home runs (in almost 2,000 at-bats). Actually, while Henry caught most games every year, the club deployed three catchers. Eddie Ainsmith, another sophomore, always handled Walter Johnson's starts. Third-stringer Biff Williams also saw substantial time behind the plate."

12. *Washington Post*, September 11, 1915.
13. Baseball-Reference.com.
14. *Washington Post*, September 12, 1915.
15. Palmer & Gilette, *The Baseball Encyclopedia*.
16. Information about the escalation of major league salaries and the formation of the Federal League comes from author John Heyler's book, *The Lords of the Realm*, the definitive reference for the business history of baseball; Victory totals for Connie Mack's Philadelphia Athletics between 1914 and 1915 come from Palmer & Gilette, *The Baseball Encyclopedia*.
17. *Washington Post*, October 27, 1915.
18. Heyler, *The Lords of the Realm*.
19. Palmer & Gilette, *The Baseball Encyclopedia*.
20. Thomas, *Baseball's Big Train*.
21. Baseball-Reference.com
22. Phillip Lowry, *Green Cathedrals*. The dimensions of Griffith Stadium, like those at most ballparks, were altered from time to time during its existence. But during Rice's playing days, a home run down the left-field line usually took a whopping 400-plus foot shot. Center field was over 420 feet, while a portion of right field was guarded by a 30-foot fence that helped turn back a lot of would-be home runs.
23. Able, "Sam Rice" SABR Baseball Bio Project biography.
24. Povich, *The Washington Senators*.
25. *Washington Post*, June 5, 1916.
26. Palmer & Gilette, *The Baseball Encyclopedia*.
27. *Washington Post*, June 5, 1916.
28. Povich, *The Washington Senators*.
29. *Washington Post*, June 5, 1916.
30. Able, "Sam Rice" SABR Baseball Bio Project biography.
31. BaseballAlmanac.com.
32. *Washington Post*, June 28, 1916.
33. *Washington Post*, July 18, 1916.
34. Baseball-Reference.com.
35. *Washington Post*, July 18, 1916.
36. *Washington Post*, July 19, 1916.
37. *Washington Post*, August 22, 1916.
38. *Washington Post*, September 22, 1916. Rice returned to the outfield on September 21 in a 3–2 loss to the Cleveland Indians. He had a single, double and triple in the game, and scored both of his team's runs.
39. Palmer & Gilette, *The Baseball Encyclopedia*.
40. *Washington Post*, November 28, 1916.
41. Rice, "How the U.S. Navy Made Me a Ballplayer."
42. Bill James, *The New Historical Baseball Abstract*.
43. Palmer & Gilette, *The Baseball Encyclopedia*.
44. Robert Creamer, *Babe: The Legend Comes to Life*.
45. Information in this section comes from both James' *The New Historical Baseball Abstract* and Palmer & Gilette, *The Baseball Encyclopedia*.
46. Cort Vitty, "Buzz Arlett," SABR Baseball Bio Project.
47. James, *The New Historical Baseball Abstract*.
48. Palmer & Gilette, *The Baseball Encyclopedia*.
49. *Washington Post*, April 1, 1917.
50. Mark Gauvreau Judge, *Damn Senators: My Grandfather and the Story of Washington's Only World Series Championship*.
51. Thomas, *Baseball's Big Train*.
52. *The Times of Northwest Indiana*, October 24, 2004.
53. *Washington Post*, February 4, 1933.
54. Byron Farwell, *Over There: The United States in the Great War, 1917–1918*.
55. Baseball-Reference.com.
56. *Washington Post*, August 19, 1917.

Chapter 4

1. Baseball-Reference.com.
2. *Washington Post*, December 26, 1917.
3. *Washington Post*, February 22, 1918.
4. *Washington Post*, March 3, 1918.
5. Rice, "How the U.S. Navy Made Me a Ballplayer."

6. *Washington Post*, April 4, 1918.
7. Creamer, *Babe*.
8. Palmer & Gilette, *The Baseball Encyclopedia*.
9. Thomas, *Baseball's Big Train*.
10. Creamer, *Babe*.
11. Cpt. J. Lindsay Hoyt, "History of the 68th Regiment, C.A.C.," http://freepages.military.rootsweb.com/~cacunithistories/68thcac.htm (September 21, 2001).
12. *Chicago Tribune*, February 17, 1919.
13. *Washington Post*, May 31, 1918.
14. *Washington Post*, June 20, 1918.
15. *Washington Post*, June 21, 1918.
16. *Washington Post*, June 24, 1918.
17. *Washington Post*, June 25, 1918.
18. *Washington Post*, June 24, 1918.
19. Hoyt, "History of the 68th Regiment, C.A.C."
20. Josh Leventhal, *The World Series*.
21. Palmer & Gilette, *The Baseball Encyclopedia*.
22. Leventhal, *The World Series*.
23. *Washington Post*, August 6, 1918.
24. Hoyt, "History of the 68th Regiment, C.A.C."
25. Stephen A. Pope and Elizabeth-Anne Wheal, *The Dictionary of the First World War*.
26. *Washington Post*, January 5, 1919.
27. *Washington Post*, January 17, 1919.
28. Hoyt, "History of the 68th Regiment, C.A.C."
29. *Washington Post*, January 31, 1919.
30. Hoyt, "History of the 68th Regiment, C.A.C."
31. *Washington Post*, January 30, 1919.
32. *Washington Post*, February 22, 1919.
33. *Washington Post*, February 18, 1919.
34. *Washington Post*, March 3, 1919.
35. Washington Post, March 23, 1919.
36. Palmer & Gilette, *The Baseball Encyclopedia*.
37. *The Sporting News*, May 1, 1919.
38. *Washington Post*, May 30, 1919.
39. *Washington Post*, July 25, 1919.
40. *Washington Post*, August 16, 1919.
41. Palmer & Gilette, *The Baseball Encyclopedia*.
42. *Washington Post*, August 16, 1919.
43. *Washington Post*, September 5, 1919; *The Sporting News*, September 25, 1919.
44. Palmer & Gilette, *The Baseball Encyclopedia*.
45. *Washington Post*, October 23, 1919.
46. Palmer & Gilette, *The Baseball Encyclopedia*.
47. Thomas, *Baseball's Big Train*.
48. Palmer & Gilette, *The Baseball Encyclopedia*.
49. Thomas, *Baseball's Big Train*.
50. Palmer & Gilette, *The Baseball Encyclopedia*.
51. *Washington Post*, October 23, 1919.
52. Eliot Asinof, *Eight Men Out*. The story of the 1919 "Black Sox" has been explored by many historians, but Asinof was the first to take it on in an in-depth manner, and his exploration of the events remains the most comprehensive, definitive account of the scandal, even as subsequent histories have helped add new research to the familiar tale.
53. Povich, *The Washington Senators*.

Chapter 5

1. William Curran, *Big Sticks*.
2. *Washington Post*, April 16, 1920.
3. *Washington Post*, April 23, 1920.
4. Morris A. Bealle. *The Washington Senators: An 87-year History of the World's Most Incurable Fandom*.
5. BaseballAlmanac.com.
6. Rice's statistics tracked through box scores published in *The Sporting News* in April and May of 1920.
7. BaseballAlmanac.com.
8. Box scores published in *The Sporting News* in June of 1920.
9. *Washington Post*, June 30, 1920.
10. Palmer & Gilette, *The Baseball Encyclopedia*.
11. Baseball-Reference.com.
12. The American League's top five in batting average was published on a regular basis in the *Washington Post* throughout the summer of 1920.
13. *The Sporting News*, August 5, 1920. Rice's batting average tracked using box scores published in same publication throughout the summer.
14. *Washington Post*, August 6, 1920.
15. BaseballAlmanac.com.
16. Box scores from *The Sporting News*.
17. *Washington Post*, July 18, 1920.
18. *Washington Post*, July 30, 1920.
19. *Washington Post*, June 27, 1920.
20. *Washington Post*, July 26, 1920.
21. *Washington Post*, August 25, 1920.
22. *Washington Post*, August 27, 1920.
23. *Washington Post*, July 2, 1920.
24. Palmer & Gilette, *The Baseball Encyclopedia*.
25. *Washington Post*, October 24, 1920.
26. Steve Wulf, "The Secrets of Sam" (*Sports Illustrated*, July 19, 1993); Personal interview with William C. Birely, Nov. 30, 2006.
27. *Washington Post*, December 18, 1920.
28. Baseball-Reference.com.
29. *Washington Post*, December 19, 1920.

30. The Yankees' victory total is from Palmer & Gilette, *The Baseball Encyclopedia*. Interested readers can find the thrilling account of the dramatic three-team pennant race in Mike Sowell's book *The Pitch That Killed*, which frames the pennant race against the tragedy of Cleveland shortstop Ray Chapman's death from a beanball thrown by New York's Carl Mays.
31. Palmer & Gilette, *The Baseball Encyclopedia*.
32. The details of Griffith's abdication of the managerial position with the Senators come from Shirley Povich's book *The Washington Senators*. The details of his won-loss record as a manager and his pennant history come from Baseball-Reference.com.
33. Rice's performance tracked through box scores published in *The Sporting News* in April of 1920.
34. *Washington Post*, April 27, 1921.
35. BaseballAlmanac.com.
36. Yankees home run total comes from Baseball-Reference.com.
37. *Washington Post*, June 13, 1921.
38. *Washington Post*, June 14, 1921.
39. BaseballAlmanac.com.
40. Details about Rice's five-hit game are from the *Washington Post*, July 25, 1921; The Senators performance over the previous days comes from BaseballAlmanac.com.
41. BaseballAlmanac.com.
42. *Washington Post*, August 3, 1921.
43. *Washington Post*, August 6, 1921.
44. Rice's performance during the streak culled from box scores published in *The Sporting News* in August of 1921.
45. Povich, *The Washington Senators*.
46. *Washington Post*, August 13, 1921.
47. Rice's participation taken from box scored published in *The Sporting News* in September 1921.
48. BaseballAlmanac.com.
49. Palmer & Gilette, *The Baseball Encyclopedia*.
50. Baseball-Reference.com.

Chapter 6

1. *Washington Post*, June 28, 1921.
2. Curran, *Big Sticks*.
3. Baseball-Reference.com.
4. Clark Griffith, "Why Managers Should Encourage Basestealing," (*Baseball Magazine*).
5. F.C. Lane, "Is Base Stealing Doomed?" (*Baseball Magazine,* June 1921).
6. Rice, "How the U.S. Navy Made Me a Ballplayer."
7. "Sad Decline of Base-Thievery in Baseball," (Literary Digest, August 2, 1924).

8. David E. Kyvig, *Daily Life in the United States, 1920–1940*.
9. *Washington Post*, December 13, 1921.
10. *Washington Post*, December 30, 1921.
11. *Washington Post*, December 31, 1921; O'Rourke's batting average from Palmer & Gilette, *The Baseball Encyclopedia*.
12. *Washington Post*, January 1, 1922.
13. *Washington Post*, January 6, 1922.
14. *Washington Post*, December 7, 1921.
15. Palmer & Gilette, *The Baseball Encyclopedia*.
16. *Washington Post*, January 24 and 25, 1922.
17. *Washington Post*, January 26, 1922.
18. *Washington Post*, March 6, 1922.
19. *Washington Post*, March 28, 1922.
20. Thomas, *Walter Johnson*.
21. *Washington Post*, April 12, 1922.
22. Goslin's signing was reported in the February 23 *Washington Post*; On February 28, The *Washington Post* commented positively on his spring training performance, particularly his ability to drive the ball out of the ballpark in batting practice; Walter Johnson's performance in the previous year along with the makeup of the rest of the roster comes from Baseball-Reference.com.
23. *Washington Post*, April 24, 1922.
24. Thomas, *Walter Johnson*; Baseball Almanac.com.
25. *Washington Post*, May 26, 1922.
26. Baseball-Reference.com; Rice's batting average tracked in 1922 through use of box scores published in *The Sporting News*.
27. *Washington Post*, August 12, 1922.
28. Baseball-Reference.com.
29. *Washington Post*, September 10, 1922; Baseball-Reference.com.
30. *Washington Post*, September 10, 1922.
31. Thomas, *Walter Johnson*.
32. *Washington Post*, January 7, 1923.
33. Povich, *The Washington Senators*.
34. Thomas, *Walter Johnson*.
35. Povich, *The Washington Senators*.
36. Baseball-Reference.com.
37. Povich, *The Washington Senators*.
38. *Washington Post*, March 19, 1923.
39. *The Sporting News*, March 3, 1927.
40. Palmer & Gilette, *The Baseball Encyclopedia*.
41. BaseballAlmanac.com.
42. *Washington Post*, July 12, 1923.
43. *Washington Post*, September 5, 1923.
44. Bealle, *The Washington Senators*.
45. *Washington Post*, September 6, 1923.
46. *Washington Post*, September 9, 1923.
47. Bealle, *The Washington Senators*.
48. Baseball-Reference.com; BaseballAlmanac.com.

49. Bill Rainer and David Finoli, *The Pittsburgh Pirates Encyclopedia*.
50. *The Sporting News*, July 12, 1928.
51. *Washington Post*, November 2, 1923; Palmer & Gilette, *The Baseball Encyclopedia*.
52. *Washington Post*, December 12, 1923.
53. Palmer & Gilette, *The Baseball Encyclopedia*.

Chapter 7

1. *Washington Post*, January 18, 1924.
2. *Washington Post*, February 28, 1924.
3. *New York Times*, March 4, 1924.
4. *Washington Post*, January 7, 1924.
5. *Washington Post*, February 6, 1924.
6. *Washington Post*, January 7, 1924.
7. *Washington Post*, January 19, 1924.
8. "Is Golf Threatening the Future of Baseball?" *Literary Digest* (August 5, 1922).
9. "Is Golf Supplanting Baseball?" *Literary Digest* (October 2, 1926).
10. "Golf vs. Baseball as a Paying Profession," *Literary Digest* (April 9, 1921).
11. "Is Golf Supplanting Baseball?"
12. *New York Times*, March 4, 1924.
13. *Washington Post*, July 27, 1924.
14. Reed Browning, *1924: Baseball's Greatest Season*.
15. Povich, *The Washington Senators*.
16. *Washington Post*, March 29, 1924.
17. *Washington Post*, April 3, 1924.
18. Browning, *1924*.
19. *Washington Post*, May 3, 1924.
20. Browning, *1924*; Details about Rice's whereabouts in the outfield come from Baseball-Reference.com.
21. BaseballAlmanac.com.
22. *Washington Post*, May 31, 1924.
23. *Washington Post*, June 1, 1924.
24. BaseballAlmanac.com.
25. *Washington Post*, June 23, 1924.
26. Browning, *1924*.
27. Povich, *The Washington Senators*; Baseball-Reference.com.
28. *Washington Post*, August 24, 1924.
29. Browning, *1924*; BaseballAlmanac.com.
30. *Washington Post*, August 28, 1924.
31. *Washington Post*, August 29, 1924.
32. *Washington Post*, August 30, 1924.
33. Washington Post, August 31, 1924.
34. *Washington Post*, September 1, 1924.
35. *Washington Post*, September 23, 1924.
36. Thomas, *Walter Johnson*; Baseball Almanac.com.
37. Thomas, *Walter Johnson*; The Sporting News, October 2, 1924.
38. Thomas, Walter Johnson. In Thomas' book, Lefler is credited with driving in the runs in the clinching victory two days later. But according to box scores of the time running in the October 2, 1924, *Sporting News*, Lefler's contribution came in Saturday's victory, not Monday's. Lefler's career statistics, as well as his Duke background, come from Baseball-Reference.com. The Web site Baseball Library.com reports that Lefler became an attorney after he was finished with baseball.
39. Browning, *1924*.
40. *Washington Post*, September 30, 1924.
41. Palmer & Gilette, *The Baseball Encyclopedia*.

Chapter 8

1. Browning, *1924*.
2. F.C. Lane, "A Review of the Recent Scandal," *Baseball Magazine* (December, 1924).
3. Browning, *1924*.
4. Lane, "A Review of the Recent Scandal."
5. Eliot Asinof, *Eight Men Out*.
6. Lane, "A Review of the Recent Scandal."
7. Asinof, *Eight Men Out*.
8. Mark Gauvreau Judge, *Damn Senators*.
9. Retrosheet.org.
10. Judge, *Damn Senators*.
11. Retrosheet.org; Palmer & Gilette, *The Baseball Encyclopedia*.
12. Thomas, *Walter Johnson*.
13. Judge, *Damn Senators*.
14. Browning, *1924*.
15. Thomas, *Walter Johnson*.
16. Judge, *Damn Senators*.
17. Baseball-Reference.com.
18. Thomas, *Walter Johnson*.
19. Judge, *Damn Senators*.
20. Browning, *1924*.
21. Retrosheet.org.
22. Browning, *1924*.
23. Retrosheet.org.
24. Browning, *1924*.
25. Judge, *Damn Senators*.
26. Thomas, *Walter Johnson*.
27. BaseballHallofFame.org.
28. Thomas, *Walter Johnson*.
29. Judge, *Damn Senators*.
30. Thomas, *Walter Johnson*.
31. Browning, *1924*.
32. Thomas, *Walter Johnson*.

Chapter 9

1. Thomas, *Walter Johnson*.
2. Browning, *1924*.
3. Browning, *1924*; Judge, *Damn Senators*.
4. *New York Times*, October 10, 1924.
5. *Washington Post*, October 10, 1924.

6. Judge, *Damn Senators*.
7. *Washington Post*, October 11, 1924.
8. Judge, *Damn Senators*.
9. F.C. Lane, "Fred Marberry, King of Relief Hurlers," *Baseball Magazine* (December, 1924).
10. Judge, *Damn Senators*.
11. *Washington Post*, October 11, 1924.
12. Thomas, *Walter Johnson*.
13. Judge *Damn Senators*.
14. "Washington's Big Day in Baseball," *Literary Digest* (October 25, 1924).
15. Thomas, *Walter Johnson*.
16. Retrosheet.org.
17. Thomas, *Walter Johnson*.
18. Retrosheet.org.
19. Judge, *Damn Senators*.
20. Jim Reisler (ed.). *Guys, Dolls and Curveballs: Damon Runyon on Baseball*.
21. Thomas, *Walter Johnson*.
22. "Washington's Big Day in Baseball," *Literary Digest*.
23. *Washington Post*, October 11, 1924.
24. "Washington's Big Day in Baseball," Literary Digest.
25. Judge, *Damn Senators*.
26. Thomas, *Walter Johnson*.
27. Retrosheet.org.
28. "The Castoff Who Became a Star," *Baseball Magazine* (October, 1927).
29. Finoli & Ranier, *The Pittsburgh Pirates Encyclopedia*.
30. Retrosheet.org.
31. Thomas, *Walter Johnson*.
32. Retrosheet.org.
33. Thomas, *Walter Johnson*.
34. Retrosheet.org.

Chapter 10

1. *Washington Post*, November 30, 1925.
2. *Washington Post*, October 12, 1924.
3. *Washington Post*, October 30, 1924.
4. *The Sporting News*, November 6, 1924.
5. *Washington Post*, November 16, 1924.
6. *Washington Post*, December 3, 1924.
7. *The Sporting News*, April 30, 1925.
8. Ray Robinson, *Iron Horse: Lou Gehrig in His Time*.
9. *The Sporting News*, June 25, 1925.
10. Robinson, *Iron Horse*.
11. *The Sporting News*, June 18, 1925.
12. *The Sporting News*, July 2, 1925.
13. *The Sporting News*, June 25, 1925.
14. Rice's batting average tracked through box scores published in *The Sporting News*.
15. *Washington Post*, August 21, 1925; BaseballAlmanac.com.
16. Povich, *The Washington Senators*.
17. *Washington Post*, September 20, 1925.
18. Baseball-Reference.com.
19. *The Sporting News*, August 20, 1925.
20. Baseball-Reference.com.
21. *The Sporting News*, September 10, 1925.
22. *The Sporting News*, September 17, 1925.
23. David Finoli & Bill Ranier, *The Pittsburgh Pirates Encyclopedia*.
24. Povich, The Washington Senators.
25. Finoli & Ranier, *The Pittsburgh Pirates Encyclopedia*.

Chapter 11

1. Thomas, *Walter Johnson*.
2. Finoli & Ranier, *The Pittsburgh Pirates Encyclopedia*.
3. Baseball-Reference.com.
4. Thomas, *Walter Johnson*.
5. Baseball-Reference.com.
6. Thomas, *Walter Johnson*.
7. Baseball-Reference.com.
8. Retrosheet.org.
9. Finoli & Ranier, *The Pittsburgh Pirates Encyclopedia*.
10. "'Oil Smith,' the Pirates' Colorful Catcher," *Baseball Magazine* (June, 1927).
11. Retrosheet.org.
12. *New York Times*, October 11, 1925.
13. Thomas, *Walter Johnson*.
14. David Cicotello, "Cy Rigler," (*SABR Baseball Bio Project*).
15. Thomas, *Walter Johnson*.
16. *New York Times*, October 11, 1925.
17. *Pittsburgh Gazette-Times*, October 11, 1925.
18. Thomas, *Walter Johnson*.
19. Curran, *Big Sticks*.
20. Allen & Meany, *Kings of the Diamond*.
21. Transcript of Rice interview in "The Last Out" graciously provided by SABR member Andrew Sharp.
22. *The Sporting News*, March 6, 1930.
23. Allen & Meany, *Kings of the Diamond*.
24. *Pittsburgh Gazette-Times*, October 11, 1925.
25. *Pittsburgh Gazette-Times*, October 12, 1925.
26. *Pittsburgh Post*, October 11, 1925.
27. *Pittsburgh Gazette-Times*, October 12, 1925.
28. Thomas, *Walter Johnson*.
29. Retrosheet.org.
30. F.C. Lane, "Fred Marberry, King of Relief Hurlers," *Baseball Magazine* (December, 1924).
31. Cicotello, "Cy Rigler."
32. "After the Ball is Over or Swift-Foot Sam's Sensational Catch," *Baseball Magazine* (December, 1925).

33. Creamer, *Babe*.
34. Thomas, *Walter Johnson*.
35. Retrosheet.org.
36. Finoli & Ranier, *The Pittsburgh Pirates Encyclopedia*.
37. Retrosheet.org.
38. Palmer & Gilette, *The Baseball Encyclopedia*.
39. Retrosheet.org.
40. Thomas, *Walter Johnson*.
41. *Washington Post*, October 13, 1925.
42. Retrosheet.org.
43. *New York Times*, October 14, 1925.
44. Retrosheet.org.
45. *Washington Post*, October 14, 1925.
46. Retrosheet.org.
47. Thomas, *Walter Johnson*.
48. Retrosheet.org.
49. Retrosheet.org.
50. Thomas, *Walter Johnson*.
51. Thomas, *Walter Johnson*.
52. Thomas, *Walter Johnson*.
53. *Washington Post*, October 16, 1925.
54. Thomas, *Walter Johnson*.
55. *New York Times*, October 16, 1925.
56. *The Sporting News*, September 17, 1925.
57. Thomas, *Walter Johnson*.
58. Baseball-Reference.com.
59. Barry Levenson, *The Seventh Game*.
60. *Chicago Tribune*, October 13, 1925.

Chapter 12

1. Thomas, *Walter Johnson*: "In front of 25,000 frozen fans on a wintry April 13, 1926, in Washington, Walter Johnson's 20th season in the major leagues began."
2. Palmer & Gilette, *The Baseball Encyclopedia*.
3. *Washington Post*, April 14, 1926.
4. *The Sporting News*, June 3, 1926.
5. Baseball-Reference.com. Johnson went 15–16 after 20–7 season in 1925. He served up 13 home runs in 1925 after surrendering seven long balls in 1924. Ruether had posted a 3.87 ERA in 1925, and a 4.84 ERA in 1926 in 23 Washington appearances.
6. Thomas, *Walter Johnson*.
7. Thomas, *Baseball's Big Train*. Johnson's clubhouse speech took place on August 30, after a 12–6 victory in New York over the Yankees. The author sources it to a newspaper clipping of unknown origin discovered in a family scrapbook.
8. *The Sporting News*, June 17, 1926.
9. *The Sporting News*, August 26, 1926.
10. *The Sporting News*, August 12, 1926.
11. *The Sporting News*, July 1, 1926; Palmer & Gilette, *The Baseball Encyclopedia*.
12. Brad Snyder, *In the Shadow of the Senators*. Snyder's chapter on Griffith explains in detail Griffith's role in maintaining baseball's color line, his eagerness to sign Cuban players, and why those seemingly contradictory actions both made sense in the context of Griffith pursuing his own self-interest.
13. *The Sporting News*, July 22, 1926.
14. Rice's hitting streak and his numbers during the course of the streak come from issues of *The Sporting News* published in June, 1926.
15. Povich, *The Washington Senators*.
16. Palmer & Gilette, *The Baseball Encyclopedia*.
17. Povich, *The Washington Senators*; Thomas, *Baseball's Big Train*. The details of Judge's line drive off Johnson's leg have been taken from both books.
18. Palmer & Gilette, *The Baseball Encyclopedia*.
19. Al Stump, *Cobb*.
20. Palmer & Gilette, *The Baseball Encyclopedia*.
21. Povich, *The Washington Senators*; Baseball-Reference.com. Myer drew 48 walks in 133 games with Boston after the trade. Back with the Senators by them, he drew 102 walks in 1934 and 96 more in 1935. His 1934 total put him fourth in the American League, behind only sluggers Jimmie Foxx (111), Lou Gehrig (109) and Babe Ruth (104).
22. Palmer & Gilette, *The Baseball Encyclopedia*.
23. Povich, *The Washington Senators*.
24. *The Sporting News*, May 26, 1927.
25. *Washington Post*, April 12, 1927.
26. *Washington Post*, May 5, 1927.
27. *Washington Post*, May 7, 1927.
28. *Washington Post*, May 4, 1927.
29. Baseball-Reference.com.
30. Details regarding Rice's early-season 1927 slump have been reconstructed from Washington Senators box scores published in *The Sporting News*.
31. *Washington Post*, May 18, 1927.
32. *Washington Post*, May 26, 1927.
33. *The Sporting News*, June 2, 1927.
34. Charles C. Alexander, *Breaking the Slump*.
35. Information taken from box scores appearing in *The Sporting News*.
36. *Washington Post*, July 24, 1927.
37. *Washington Post*, July 25, 1927.
38. Palmer & Gilette, *The Baseball Encyclopedia*; Box scores appearing in *The Sporting News*.
39. Palmer & Gilette, *The Baseball Encyclopedia*.
40. Thomas, *Baseball's Big Train*: "Tris

Speaker was another veteran who wasn't going to let an injury, a sprained wrist in his case, keep him from participating in the historic game. His doctor doubted the wrist would be strong enough for Speaker to play until later in the week, but the outfielder had other plans. 'If it is possible, I certainly will be in that game,' he told Frank Young of the *Post*, 'and if my injury has not healed enough to let me go the route, I am going to ask Harris to let me play one inning anyway, just so I can say that I was in it.'"

41. *Washington Post*, October 20, 1927.
42. Palmer & Gilette, *The Baseball Encyclopedia*. Reference for both Gaston and Goslin's 1927 statistics.
43. *Washington Post*, October 19, 1927.
44. *Washington Post*, October 20, 1927; Palmer & Gilette, *The Baseball Encyclopedia*.
45. *Washington Post*, December 3, 1927.
46. *Washington Post*, December 25, 1927; *Washington Post*, January 20, 1928; *Washington Post*, January 21, 1928.
47. *Washington Post*, January 26, 1928; Palmer & Gilette, *The Baseball Encyclopedia*.
48. *Washington Post*, December 3, 1927.
49. BaseballAlmanac.com.
50. *The Sporting News*, August 2, 1928; *The Sporting News*, August 9, 1928.
51. *The Sporting News*, August 9, 1928.
52. Computed using box scores from *The Sporting News*.
53. *Washington Post*, September 14, 1928.
54. *The Sporting News*, September 20, 1928.
55. *The Sporting News*, September 13, 1928; *The Sporting News*, September 20, 1928.
56. *The Sporting News*, September 20, 27, October 4, 1928.
57. *The Sporting News*, January 12, 1928.
58. *The Sporting News*, May 17, 1928.
59. *The Sporting News*, April 26, 1928.
60. Palmer & Gilette, *The Baseball Encyclopedia*.
61. Baseball-Reference.com.
62. Povich, *The Washington Senators*.
63. Palmer & Gilette, *The Baseball Encyclopedia*.
64. Povich, *The Washington Senators*.
65. Thomas, *Baseball's Big Train*.
66. *Washington Post*, November 26, 1928.
67. *Washington Post*, January 21, 1929. Article about Rice and others, titled "Some Ball Players Play Mean Golf," was written by former New York Giants pitcher Al Demaree.
68. *Washington Post*, February 4, 1929.
69. *Washington Post*, February 4, 1929; Palmer & Gilette, *The Baseball Encyclopedia*. Griffith's comments regarding Rice's status in the outfield come from the Post article titled "1929 Contract Signed by Rice." Rice's 1928 statistics are taken from The Baseball Encyclopedia.
70. *Washington Post*, March 26, 1929.
71. *The Sporting News*, May 2, 1929.
72. *The Sporting News*, August 22, 1929.
73. *Washington Post*, May 18, 1929.
74. Palmer & Gilette, *The Baseball Encyclopedia*. Paschal was born October 13, 1895. In 1929, he batted just .208 in 72 at-bats, with two home runs. In his career year of 1925, Paschal had not only hit 12 home runs in 247 at-bats, but also batted .360 and stole 14 bases. He never lived up to that potential, however.
75. *The Sporting News*, September 5, 1929.
76. Alexander, *Breaking the Slump*: "Branch Rickey continued to scheme to enlarge the Cardinals' farm system. By the start of the 1938 season, it would consist of thirty minor-league franchises that the Cardinals either owned outright or maintained working agreements with — not to mention a number of subrosa hookups that had come under Commissioner Landis's suspicious eye. All told, the Cardinals controlled 732 players. Nobody before or after would have as extensive a system as Rickey built in St. Louis."
77. *The Sporting News*, October 10, 1929.
78. *The Sporting News*, June 13, 1929.
79. *The Sporting News*, October 10, 1929.
80. *The Sporting News*, July 25, 1929.
81. *The Sporting News*, September 12, 1929.
82. *The Sporting News*, July 11, 1929.
83. *The Sporting News*, October 3, 1929.
84. Palmer & Gilette, *The Baseball Encyclopedia*.
85. *The Sporting News*, June 13, 1929.
86. Rice's 1929 batting average tracked through box scores published in *The Sporting News*.
87. Palmer & Gilette, *The Baseball Encyclopedia*.
88. Barnard and Evans information taken from *The Sporting News*, October 10, 1929; World Series results for 1929 taken from Baseball-Reference.com.

Chapter 13

1. Carole Bryan Jones, *Teach Yourself Twentieth Century, U.S.A.*
2. Leventhal, *The World Series*.
3. Jones, *Teach Yourself Twentieth Century, U.S.A.*; Personal interview with William C. Birely, November 30, 2006.
4. *Washington Post*, March 3, 1930. The free-spirited Goslin and Clark Griffith battled over the outfielder's salary throughout the winter and spring, and by early March, Griffith was seriously listening to trade offers for him.

The granting of permission to Rice to train early at Hot Springs was reported in the *Washington Post*, November 24, 1929.

5. *The Sporting News*, October 24, 1929.
6. *The Sporting News*, April 17, 1930.
7. Rice's performance tracked through box scores published in *The Sporting News* in April and May of 1930. The daily results and schedule for the Senators and Athletics from BaseballAlmanac.com.
8. *The Sporting News*, July 10, 1930.
9. Rice's performance tracked through box scores published in The Sporting News. Eight complete games by Washington pitchers reported in *The Sporting News*, July 3, 1930. Athletics and Senators games and the two teams' relationship to each other in the American League standings comes from Baseball Almanac.com.
10. *Washington Post*, June 24, 1930.
11. *The Sporting News*, July 3, 1930.
12. Rice's batting performance tracked through box scores published in *The Sporting News* in 1930.
13. *The Sporting News*, November 13, 1930. As far as Rice's reported stomach problems, the publication had this to say: "Last summer, although he wound up with a highly credible average of .350, he was handicapped by a stomach attack that left him weak and under par and was unable to obtain the essential time off for needed rest periods."
14. *The Sporting News*, July 17, 1930; Palmer & Gilette, *The Baseball Encyclopedia*.
15. Palmer & Gilette, *The Baseball Encyclopedia*.
16. Lawrence S. Ritter, *The Glory of Their Times*.
17. The General Electric ad ran, presumably, several times, including *The Sporting News*, May 22, 1930. Griffith's quotes on the matter come from *The Sporting News*, September 11, 1930.
18. "Famous First Night Games," Baseball Almanac.com.
19. *The Sporting News*, September 4, 1930.
20. *The Sporting News*, October 30, 1930.
21. Palmer & Gilette, *The Baseball Encyclopedia*.
22. The Goslin-for-Manush trade occurred on June 14, 1930, and was reported in the *Washington Post*, June 15, 1930. The trade was an enormous deal to Washington baseball fans— the Post, for example, constantly updated Goslin's performance with St. Louis throughout the rest of the summer, and frequently looked at how the trade had shaped up for both teams. The Red Barnes-for-Dave Harris trade had taken place the day before the trade of Goslin, on June 13, and was reported in the *Washington Post*, June 14, 1930. Statistical splits of the players taken from Baseball-Reference.com.
23. Povich, *The Washington Senators*. The strategy seemed to work. Judge ended up hitting .326 in 1930, the highest batting average of the 36-year-old's long career (Palmer & Gilette, *The Baseball Encyclopedia*).
24. Rice's performance tracked through box scores and American League hitting leaders published in *The Sporting News* throughout the summer of 1930.
25. Baseball-Reference.com ranks play performances at each age, though it takes some mathematical computation to eliminate players who batted less than the amount required to qualify for a league batting title — the Web site's cutoff is seventy-five games.
26. "Facts & Figures on Players with 200-hit Seasons," *Baseball Digest* (December 2005).
27. "Oldest Players to Hit a Home Run," *Baseball Digest* (August 2006); Baesball Reference.com.
28. Baseball-Reference.com.
29. *The Sporting News*, October 9, 1930.
30. *Washington Post*, September 21, 1930.
31. *Washington Post*, April 26, 1931.
32. *Washington Post*, April 28, 1931.
33. *Washington Post*, May 14, 1931.
34. "Steals of Home," *Sam Rice Baseball Hall of Fame Player File*.
35. BaseballAlmanac.com. Ty Cobb holds the career record for documented steals of home with fifty-four.
36. *Washington Post*, June 8, 1931.
37. *Washington Post*, June 21, 1931.
38. *Washington Post*, July 10, 1931.
39. Baseball-Reference.com.
40. *Washington Post*, October 12, 1931.
41. *Washington Post*, October 24, 1931.
42. Reynolds statistics from Palmer & Gilette, The Baseball Encyclopedia. Griffith's take on Reynolds' injuries from the *Washington Post*, January 10, 1932.
43. *Washington Post*, February 4, 1932.
44. Alexander, *Breaking the Slump*.
45. *Washington Post*, April 14, 1932.
46. *Washington Post*, April 2, 1932.
47. *Washington Post*, April 14, 1932.
48. *Washington Post*, April 17, 1932.
49. *Washington Post*, May 5, 1932.
50. *Washington Post*, May 8, 1932; *Washington Post*, May 9, 1932.
51. *Washington Post*, July 20, 1932.

Chapter 14

1. Thomas, *Walter Johnson*.
2. *Washington Post*, October 5, 1932.

3. *Washington Post*, October 8, 1932.
4. Povich, *The Washington Senators*.
5. *Washington Post*, January 29, 1933.
6. Washington Post, March 1, 1933.
7. *Washington Post*, March 7, 1933.
8. *Washington Post*, March 16, 1933; Palmer & Gilette, *The Baseball Encyclopedia*.
9. *Washington Post*, March 15, 1933.
10. Jeff Merron, "Put Up Your Dukes," (*ESPN.com*, Page 2 column).
11. Povich, *The Washington Senators*.
12. *Washington Post*, April 26, 1933.
13. *The Sporting News*, May 11, 1933.
14. *Washington Post*, May 11, 1933.
15. *Washington Post*, August 15, 1933.
16. BaseballAlmanac.com.
17. *Washington Post*, August 29, 1933.
18. *Washington Post*, August 28, 1933.
19. Povich, *The Washington Senators*.
20. Lee Allen and Tom Meany, *Kings of the Diamond*.
21. Palmer & Gilette, *The Baseball Encyclopedia*.
22. Allen and Meany, *Kings of the Diamond*.
23. Retrosheet.org; Povich, *The Washington Senators*.
24. Povich, *The Washington Senators*.
25. Retrosheet.org.
26. Retrosheet.org.
27. Povich, *The Washington Senators*.
28. Retrosheet.org.
29. Povich, *The Washington Senators*.
30. Retrosheet.org.
31. *The Sporting News*, October 12, 1933.
32. *Washington Post*, November 7, 1933.
33. *The Sporting News*, Ocotber 19, 1933.
34. *Washington Post*, November 7, 1933.
35. Allen Lewis, "How Hall of Famers Performed as Pinch-Hitters," *Baseball Digest* (June, 1992).
36. John Updike, "Hub Fans Bid Kid Adieu," *The New Yorker* (October 22, 1960). Updike wrote the definitive account of Williams' last game from the vantage point of a fan sitting in the stands. The story is also available in the *anthology Best Sports Writing of the Century* published by Houghton-Mifflin.
37. Palmer & Gilette, *The Baseball Encyclopedia*.
38. Creamer, *Babe*.
39. Michael Leahy, *When Nothing Else Matters: Michael Jordan's Last Comeback* is the definitive version of Jordan's ultimately unsuccessful comeback attempt and the fallout from it. Leahy was assigned by the *Washington Post* to follow Jordan's comeback as his primary beat for two seasons.
40. *Washington Post*, January 9, 1934.
41. Rice's hit total with the Senators tabulated using Palmer & Gilette, *The Baseball Encyclopedia*.
42. *Washington Post*, January 9, 1934.
43. *Washington Post*, January 10, 1934.

Chapter 15

1. Thomas, *Walter Johnson*.
2. *The Sporting News*, February 22, 1934.
3. *The Sporting News*, February 1, 1934.
4. *The Sporting News*, February 22, 1934.
5. Phillip Lowry, *Green Cathedrals*.
6. Russell Schneider, *Tribe Memories: The First Century*.
7. Palmer & Gilette, *The Baseball Encyclopedia*.
8. *Washington Post*, April 18, 1934.
9. *The Sporting News*, May 24, 1934.
10. *The Sporting News*, August 2, 1934; Also, Rice's batting average and spot in the lineup tracked using box scores from *The Sporting News* throughout the summer of 1934.
11. *The Sporting News*, August 9, 1934.
12. *The Sporting News*, September 6, 1934.
13. *The Sporting News*, July 26, 1934.
14. Game details from box scores published in *The Sporting News* throughout September, 1934.
15. *The Washington Post*, March 1, 1963, "Rice Grateful for Vote," by Bob Addie.
16. Washington's lineup from *The Sporting News*, September 20, 1934; Details about Sewell's career from Baseball-Reference.com.
17. *Washington Post*, September 19, 1934.
18. *The Sporting News*, September 24, 1934.

Chapter 16

1. *Cleveland Plain Dealer*, January 5, 1935.
2. Nicholas Dawidoff, *The Catcher Was a Spy: The Mysterious Life of Moe Berg*. The "Library Journal" review of Dawidoff's Berg biography states, "Dawidoff has done a lot of research on a fascinating subject but draws few conclusions, and his overall theme seems to be the impenetrability of his subject. In the end, Berg remains a mystery." That sounds awfully familiar.
3. *The Annals of Sandy Spring, Volume V*. The timeline of Rice's life after baseball can be found by perusing these periodical books put out by motivated record-keepers, beginning all the way back in the eighteenth century. Births, deaths, marriages and divorces, weather, real estate transactions—there isn't much that didn't make its way into the *Annals*.
4. The anecdote comes from Rice's stepdaughter Margaret Robinson, who was extremely

helpful but politely requested that she not be quoted in the text of this book.
   5. *The Annals of Sandy Spring, Volume V and VI.*
   6. *New York Times*, April 16, 1943, "Internees Hired by Ickes for Farm."
   7. David K. Fremon, *Japanese-American Internment in American History.*
   8. Greg Robinson, *By Order of the President: FDR and the Internment of Japanese Americans.*
   9. Associated Press, April 18, 1943, "New Farmhands For the Ickes Acres: Japanese Internees."
   10. *New York Times*, April 16, 1943, "Internees Hired by Ickes for Farm."
   11. Associated Press, April 18, 1943, "Internees Hired by Ickes for Farm"; Personal interview with William C. Birely, November 30, 2006.
   12. *The Annals of Sandy Spring*, Volume V.
   13. Rice, "How the U.S. Navy Made Me a Ball Player."
   14. Thomas, *Walter Johnson.*
   15. Red Smith, *Red Smith on Baseball: The Game's Greatest Writer on the Game's Greatest Years.* Smith's column on Walter Johnson's funeral was written in December of 1946 and is titled, "The Big Train and His Buddies."
   16. Thomas, *Walter Johnson.*
   17. Smith, *Red Smith on Baseball.*
   18. Thomas, *Walter Johnson*; Personal interview with William C. Birely, November 30, 2006.
   19. *Annals of Sandy Spring*, Volume VI.
   20. Dan Holmes, "Seventh Inning Stretch with Chris Rice: Daughter of Hall of Fame Outfielder Sam Rice Talks About Her Father and Her Trips with Him to Cooperstown." The article is from the *BaseballHallofFame.org* Web site.
   21. Personal interview with Christine Rice. Ms. Rice initially did not respond to several mailed and phone call requests to speak about her stepfather for this biography. I finally reached her one afternoon in the weeks before the project's completion. She was certainly polite, and even explained that people had encouraged her to write her own book about Sam Rice in the past, an idea she had decided against. She was, she said, unhappy about the way a *Sports Illustrated* story published about Sam thirteen years before had turned out, an article that had quoted her extensively and one in which author Steve Wulf had visited her at the family property, and had decided not to speak to writers about Sam any more.
   22. *Washington Post,* October 23, 1956, "Homer, Sweet Homer" by George Dixon in his "Washington Scene" column; Personal interview with William C. Birely, November 30, 2006.
   23. Holmes, "Seventh Inning Stretch with Chris Rice."
   24. Personal interview with Margaret Robinson.

Chapter 17

   1. *New York Times*, June 20, 1942, "Waner of Braves Gets Three Thousandth Hit."
   2. Marc Okkonen, *Baseball Uniforms of the Twentieth Century.*
   3. *New York Times*, June 20, 1942, "Waner of Braves Gets Three Thousandth Hit."
   4. David Maraniss, *Clemente: The Passion and Grace of Baseball's Last Hero.* Maraniss's book, published in 2006, stands as the definitive biography of Clemente.
   5. *Washington Post*, August 2, 2005, "Palmeiro Suspended For Steroid Violation."
   6. Lee Allen and Tom Meany, *Kings of the Diamond.*
   7. *New York Times*, June 10, 1914, "Wagner's Three-Thousandth Hit: Wonderful Batting Record of Old Pirate for Seventeen Years."
   8. *New York Times*, September 28, 1914, "Yankees Get Even Break With Naps: Lajoie Major League Hit Record Reaches Three Thousand."
   9. The date of Cobb's three thousandth hit comes from BaseballHallofFame.org, as do all of the dates of players reaching the milestone; The *New York Times* and *Washington Post* game stories come from the editions of those newspapers dated August 21, 1921.
   10. *New York Times*, July 19, 1927, "Ty Cobb Gets His Four Thousandth Hit."
   11. *Washington Post*, May 18, 1925, "Tom Zachary Bests Uhle in Duel; Old Tom Gets Superb Support With Three Double Plays; Speaker Returns to Game and Gets Trio of Hits. Nats Beat Indians, Winning Five in Row."
   12. Frank W. Koster, "On the Track of Three Thousand Clouts." *Baseball Magazine* (June, 1935).
   13. Palmer & Gilette, *The Baseball Encyclopedia.*
   14. Koster, "On the Track of Three Thousand Clouts."
   15. Jim Reisler, *A Great Day in Cooperstown.*
   16. "History of BBWAA Hall of Fame Voting," BaseballHallofFame.org. The full URL address for this database is listed in this book's bibliography.
   17. *Washington Post*, January 10, 1956, "This Morning... With Shirley Povich."
   18. *Washington Post*, July 23, 1956, "This Morning... With Shirley Povich."

19. Fred Lieb, "Thirteen Hits from the Hall of Fame," *Sport* (June, 1959).
20. *Washington Post*, March 1, 1963, "Rice Grateful for Vote."
21. *Washington Post*, February 5, 1957, "Ty Cobb Says Rice Earned Hall of Fame."
22. *Washington Post*, February 7, 1957, "This Morning... With Shirley Povich."
23. *Washington Post*, January 12, 1960, "Bob Addie's Column."
24. "History of BBWAA Hall of Fame Voting," BaseballHallofFame.org.
25. *Washington Post*, February 5, 1960, "This Morning... With Shirley Povich."
26. Baseball-Reference.com.
27. *Washington Post*, February 7, 1960, "Veterans in Limbo."
28. *Washington Post*, March 11, 1960, "Rice Won't Vote Himself in Hall of Fame."
29. *Washington Post*, January 2, 1962, "This Morning... With Shirley Povich."
30. "History of BBWAA Hall of Fame Voting," BaseballHallofFame.org.
31. *The Sporting News*, February 9, 1963, "Game Salutes Four New Shrine Immortals."
32. *Washington Post*, March 1, 1963, "Rice Grateful for Vote."
33. *The Sporting News*, September 17, 1963, "Red Sox Homers Defeat Braves at Doubleday Field."
34. Steve Wulf, "The Secrets of Sam," *Sports Illustrated* (June 19, 1993).
35. *Washington Post*, October 24, 1965, "Rice Still Lines Drives, But It's a Different Game."
36. Dan Holmes, "Seventh Inning Stretch With Chris Rice."
37. Personal interview with Margaret Robinson. Robinson recalled her mother and Sam calling off a trip because Sam was sick.
38. *Washington Post*, October 14, 1974, "'Sam' Rice, Hall of Famer Who Played for Senators."
39. Letter, dated December 2, 1998, from Bob Lord to Hall of Fame senior researcher Scot Mondore (*Baseball Hall of Fame Sam Rice Player File*).
40. Letter from Chris Rice to Paul Kerr (*Baseball Hall of Fame Sam Rice Player File*).
41. Wulf, "Secrets of Sam."
42. *Washington Post*, October 25, 1974, "Rice Leaves Them Guessing on Mystery Catch; Hall Fails to Turn Up Rice Letter."
43. *Washington Post*, November 5, 1974, "Sam Rice's Secret Is Out — He Made the Catch in '25; Sam Rice Letter Says He Made Catch."
44. A copy of Rice's letter is in the *Baseball Hall of Fame Sam Rice Player File*.
45. I spoke with Yost initially for my article about Sam Rice that ran in *The Times of Northwest Indiana*, October 24, 2004, "Mr. 2,987."
46. Letter from Yost to the Baseball Hall of Fame, dated January 9, 1984 (*HOF Sam Rice Player File*).
47. *Washington Post*, April 8, 1985, "Sam Rice: Very Model of a Major Leaguer."
48. Wulf, "Secrets of Sam."

Epilogue

1. Personal interview Randy Decker.
2. Baseball-Reference.com.
3. Baseball-Reference.com

BIBLIOGRAPHY

Books

Alexander, Charles C. *Breaking the Slump: Baseball in the Depression Era* (New York: Columbia University Press, 2002).
Allen, Lee and Meany, Tom. *Kings of the Diamond.* (New York: G.P. Putnam's Sons, 1965).
Annals of Sandy Spring. *Volumes V & VI.* (Sandy Spring, MD: Sandy Spring Museum, 2002).
Asinof, Eliot. *Eight Men Out* (New York: Holt, Rinehart and Winston, 1963).
Bealle, Morris A. *The Washington Senators: An 87-year History of the World's Most Incurable Fandom.* (Washington, D.C.: Columbia Publishing Company, 1947).
Browning, Reed. *1924: Baseball's Greatest Season.* (Amherst, Mass.: University of Massachusetts Press, 2003).
Clements, Kendrick A. *The Presidency of Woodrow Wilson* (Lawrence, KS: The University Press of Kansas, 1992).
Creamer, Robert. *Babe, The Legend Comes to Life* (New York: Simon and Schuster, 1974).
Curran, William. *Big Sticks: The Batting Revolution of the Twenties* (New York: William Morrow and Company, Inc., 1990).
Dawidoff, Nick. *The Catcher Was a Spy: The Mysterious Life of Moe Berg* (New York: Pantheon, 1994)
Eisenhower, John S.D. *Intervention!* (New York: W.W. North & Company, 1993).
Farwell, Byron. *Over There: The United States in the Great War, 1917–1918.* (New York: WW. North & Company, 1999).
Fremon, David K. *Japanese-American Internment in American History.* (Springfield, N.J.: Enslow Publishers, Inc., 1996).
Green, Harvey. *The Uncertainty of Everyday Life: 1915–1945.* (New York: HarperCollins, 1993).
Halberstam, David (ed.). *Best American Sports Writing of the Century.* (New York: Houghton Mifflin, 1999).
Heckscher, August. *Woodrow Wilson.* (New York: Charles Scribner's Sons, 1991).
Helyar, John. *Lords of the Realm.* (New York: Villard, 1994).
James, Bill. *The Bill James Historical Baseball Abstract.* (New York: Villard Books, 1985).
James, Bill. *The New Bill James Historical Baseball Abstract.* (New York: Free Press, 2003).
James, Bill. *Whatever Happened to the Hall of Fame?* (New York: Simon and Schuster, 1995).

Jones, Carole Bryan. *Teach Yourself Twentieth Century U.S.A.* (Chicago: Contemporary Books, 2005).
Judge, Mark Gauvreau. *Damn Senators.* (San Francisco: Encounter Books, 2003).
Kyvig, David E. *Daily Life in the United States, 1920–1940.* (Chicago: Ivan R. Dee, 2002, 2004).
Levenson, Barry. *The Seventh Game.* (New York: McGraw-Hill, 2004).
Leahy, Michael. *When Nothing Else Matters: Michael Jordan's Last Comeback.* (New York: Simon & Schuster, 2004).
Leventhal, Josh. *The World Series.* (New York: Tess Press, 2005).
Lowry, Philip J. *Green Cathedrals.* (Reading, Mass.: Addison-Wesley Publishing Co., Inc., 1992).
Maraniss, David. *Clemente: The Passion and Grace of Baseball's Last Hero.* (New York: Simon & Schuster, 2006).
Okkonen, Marc. *Baseball Uniforms of the Twentieth Century.* (New York: Sterling Publishing Co., Inc., 1991).
O'Nan, Stewart (ed.), *The Vietnam Reader.* (New York: Anchor Books, 1998).
Palmer, Pete & Gilette, Gary, *The Baseball Encyclopedia.* (New York: Barnes & Noble Books, 2004).
Pope, Stephen A. and Wheal, Elizabeth-Anne. *The Dictionary of the First World War.* (New York: St. Martin's Press, 1995).
Povich, Shirley. *The Washington Senators, An Informal History.* (New York: G.P. Putman's Sons, 1954).
Rainer, Bill and Finoli, David. *The Pittsburgh Pirates Encyclopedia.* (Champaign, Ill.: Sports Publishing, L.L.C, 2003).
Reisler, Jim. *A Great Day in Cooperstown.* (New York: Avalon, 2006).
Reisler, Jim (ed.). *Guys, Dolls and Curveballs: Damon Runyon on Baseball.* (New York: Carroll & Graf, 2005).
Ritter, Lawrence S. *The Glory of Their Times: The Story of the Early Days of Baseball Told by the Men Who Played It.* (New York: Morrow, 1966).
Robinson, Greg. *By Order of the President: FDR and the Internment of Japanese Americans.* (Cambridge, Mass: Harvard University Press, 2001).
Robinson, Ray. *Iron Horse: Lou Gehrig in His Time.* (New York: W.W. North, 1990).
Schneider, Russell. *Tribe Memories: The First Century.* (Hinckley, Ohio: Moonlight Publishing, 2000).
Smith, Red. *Red Smith on Baseball: The Game's Greatest Writer on the Game's Greatest Years.* (Chicago: Ivan R. Dee, 2000).
Snyder, Brad. *Beyond the Shadow of the Senators.* (New York: McGraw-Hill, 2003).
Sowell, Mike. *The Pitch That Killed.* (New York: MacMillan Publishing Company, 1989).
Stump, Al. *Cobb: A Biography.* (Chapel Hill, N.C.: Algonquin Books, 1994).
Thomas, Henry W. *Walter Johnson: Baseball's Big Train.* (Washington D.C.: Phenom Press, 1985).

Articles

"After the Ball is Over or Swift-Foot Sam's Sensational Catch," *Baseball Magazine* (December, 1925).
Associated Press, "New Farmhands for the Ickes Acres: Japanese Internees," *Unknown Orgin, Sam Rice Baseball Hall of Fame Player File* (April 18, 1943).
Cicotello, David, "Cy Rigler," SABR Baseball Biography Project.
"Country Boys in the Big Leagues," *Literary Digest* (April 18, 1925).
"Editorial Comment," *Baseball Magazine* (December, 1924).
"Facts and Figures on Players With Two Hundred-Hit Seasons," *Baseball Digest* (December, 2005).
"Golf vs. Baseball as a Paying Profession," *Literary Digest* (April 9, 1921).
Griffith, Clark. "Why Managers Should Encourage Basestealing," *Baseball Magazine* (December 1924).
"History of BBWAA Hall of Fame Voting," http://www.baseballhalloffame.org/history/hof_voting/default.htm.

Holmes, Dan, "Seventh Inning Stretch with Chris Rice: Daughter of Hall of Fame Outfielder Sam Rice Talks About Her Father and Her Trips with Him to Cooperstown," http://www.baseballhalloffame.org/history/2004/040613.htm.
Hoyt, Cpt. J. Lindsay. "History of the 68th Regiment, C.A.C.," http://freepages.military.rootsweb.com/~cacunithistories/68thcac.htm (September 21, 2001).
"Is Golf Supplanting Baseball?" *Literary Digest* (October 2, 1926).
"Is Golf Threatening the Future of Baseball?" *Literary Digest* (August 5, 1922).
Kofoed, J.C. "The Star of the World's Series," *Baseball Magazine* (December, 1924).
Koster, Frank W. "On the Track of Three Thousand Clouts." *Baseball Magazine* (June, 1935).
Lane, F.C. "A Review of the Recent Scandal," *Baseball Magazine* (December, 1924).
Lane, F.C. "Fred Marberry, King of Relief Hurlers," *Baseball Magazine* (December, 1924).
Lane, F.C. "Is Base Stealing Doomed?" *Baseball Magazine* (June, 1921).
Lewis, Allen. "How Hall of Fame Players Performed as Pinch-Hitters," *Baseball Digest* (June 1992).
Lieb, Fred. "Thirteen Hits from the Hall of Fame," *Sport* (June, 1959).
Merron, Jeff. "Put Up Your Dukes," ESPN.com Page 2 column (Date unknown).
" 'Oil' Smith, the Pirates' Colorful Catcher," *Baseball Magazine* (June, 1927).
"Oldest Players to Hit a Home Run," *Baseball Digest* (August, 2006).
Phelon, W.A. "Washington," *Baseball Magazine* (December, 1924).
Rice, Sam. "How the U.S. Navy Made Me a Ball Player," *Baseball Magazine* (August 1920).
"Sad Decline of Base-Thievery in Baseball," *Literary Digest* (August 2, 1924).
"Steals of Home, 1915–1934, Edgar (Sam) Rice, Washington A.L.," *Sam Rice Baseball Hall of Fame Player File.*
Updike, John. "Hub Fans Bid Kid Adieu," *The New Yorker* (October 22, 1960).
Ward, John J. "A Brilliant But Obscure Baseball Star," *Baseball Magazine,* (October, 1926).
Ward, John J. "How Sam Rice Broke the Outfield Record," *Baseball Magazine,* (June, 1921).
Ward, John J. "Major League Stars of 1920," *Baseball Magazine,* (March, 1921).
Ward, John J. "The Man Who Gave Washington Their Punch," *Baseball Magazine* (December, 1924).
"Washington's Big Day in Baseball," *Literary Digest* (October 25, 1924).
Waterman, Guy. "The Upstart Senators of 1912–1915," *The National Pastime,* (1993).
Wulf, Steve. "The Secrets of Sam," *Sports Illustrated,* (June 19, 1993).

Newspapers

Chicago Tribune; Cleveland Plain-Dealer; Galesburg (Ill.) Evening Mail; Kentland (Ind.) Democrat; Newton County (Ind.) Enterprise; New York Times; Petersburg (Va.) Daily Progress; Pittsburgh Post; Pittsburgh Gazette Times; The Sporting News; The Times of Northwest Indiana; Washington Post.

Documents

Several personal letters, including Rice's famous 1925 World Series catch letter, were found in the Baseball Hall of Fame's Sam Rice Player File.

Helpful websites

BaseballAlmanac.com; BaseballHallofFame.org; Baseball-Reference.com; ESPN.com; Retrosheet.org; TheBaseballIndex.org.

Personal Interviews

Randy Decker; Dorothy (Judge) McDonough; Christine Rice; Margaret Robinson; John Yost.

Index

Aaron, Hank 205
Adams, Babe 120
Adams, Christine *see* Rice, Christine
Adams, Herbert 196
Adams, Margaret 196
Adams, Mary Kendall *see* Rice, Mary
Addie, Bob 204–07
Africa 54
Ainsmith, Eddie 40–43
Alabama 14, 174
Alcohol *see* Drinking and baseball
Aldridge, Vic 119, 122–23, 136, 138
Alexander, Grover Cleveland 41, 48, 205
Alexandria, Virginia 60
All-Star Game, First 133
Allen, Lee 209–10
Alma Temple 169
Almeida, Rafael 146
Altoona, Pennsylvania 131
Altrock, Nick 132, 169, 194
American Association 118
American League (founding) 23–25
Anderson, E.A. 19
Anson, Adrian "Cap" 198, 200
Archbald, B.L. 14
Arkansas 18
Arlett, Buzz 36–37
Arlington, Texas 214
Armistice 47
Army 40–50
Army Medical Center 194
Ashman, R.I. 131
Ashton, Maryland 190, 193–94, 206, 209, 214
Atlanta Crackers 158
Australian wool 67

Averill, Earl 185–86
Ayers, Doc 33
Aztec 38

Babson, Roger 160
Badger, Charles T. 18
Baker, Frank 44
Baker, J. Franklin 71
Baker, Secretary of War Newton 39, 41–43
Ball Players Protective Association 25
Baltimore Orioles 37, 96, 199
Banks, Ernie 205
Barber, Turner 30
Barnard, E.S. 159
Barnes, Colonel T.C. 48
Barnes, Jim 83
Barnes, Red 156–57, 159, 165
Barnes, Virgil 100, 106–107
Barnhart, Clyde 120, 132, 136
Barrow, Ed 54, 56
Bartren, Thomas 15
Baseball Writers Association of America 6, 201–02, 204–06
Bentley, Jack 96–98, 101, 109
Berg, Moe 190
Berra, Yogi 205
Biddle, Kittie 60
Bigbee, Carson 120, 140
Biloxi Golf Club 173
Biloxi, Mississippi 162
Binghampton, New York 51
Birely, Bill 3, 60, 162, 193, 196–97
Bishop, Max 144
"Black Sox" scandal 52–53, 85, 92–94, 129, 147

Black Tuesday 160, 162
Bluege, Ossie 38, 85, 96–97, 99, 107, 121–122, 137, 139, 148, 155, 177–78, 188, 194, 210
Bodie, Ping 61
Boehling, Joe 33–34
Boken, Bob 173
Bolton, Cliff 179–80
Born, Gerald 9
Boston Braves 75, 89, 126, 180, 198
Boston Red Sox 6, 24, 27, 30, 36, 43–44, 46, 49–50, 54, 57–58, 63, 65, 72, 76, 86, 89–90, 99, 118, 121, 126, 148–49, 152, 158, 162–63, 167–68, 186–88, 200, 207
Bradley, Alva 187
Bressler, Rube 36
Bright's disease (Ross Youngs) 101
Brooklyn Dodgers 92, 120, 124, 155, 166, 186
Brown, Lloyd 172
Bryan, Secretary of State William Jennings 21
Bulkeley, Morgan W. 202
Bulova (clock) 169
Burlington (Central Association team) 15
Burns, Edward 67
Busch, Heine 22
Bush, Donie 75–78, 80, 85, 167
Bush, Illinois 14
Bush, Joe 89, 145
Butzow, Frank 142–43

Cain, Cullen 83
Caldwell, Charlie 116
California State Polytechnic Institute 193
Camp Grant 48
Campus, Illinois 14
Canavan, Bernie 142
Canby, Thomas Y. 191
Cantillon, Joe 33
The Capitol (building) 111
Carey, Max 69, 120, 122, 126, 132, 136, 139
Carson, Kit 187
Cassell, Bob 173
"The Catch" (1925 World Series) 128–34, 136–37, 141–42, 149, 170, 179, 209–10
Cedar Lake, Indiana 7
"Centennial Celebration" 202
Central Association 11, 15
Chance, Frank 78–79
Chapman, Ben 173–75
Chapman, Ray 68, 122
Charlotte, North Carolina 157
Charlottesville, Virginia 33
Chase, Hal 93–94
Chattanooga (Southern League team) 158
Chavez, Endy 141
Cherrydale, Virginia (town) 111
Chesbro, Jack 68
Chicago Bulls (NBA) 180
Chicago Colts 23
Chicago Cubs 32, 46, 119, 155, 159–60

Chicago Excelsiors 53
Chicago, Illinois 7
Chicago White Sox 24, 29–30, 32, 34, 36, 39, 52, 58–59, 61–62, 65, 78–79, 85, 87, 89, 114, 147, 163, 168–69, 173, 175
Chicken farming 190–94, 197, 214
Chouinard, Felix 32
Cicotte, Eddie 92
Cincinnati Reds 6, 24, 93–94, 115, 119, 146
"Cinderella Eight" 30
Clarke, Fred 118, 120
Clarkson, John 5–6, 207
Cleland, Alexander 202
Clemente, Roberto 199, 205
Cleveland Indians 30–31, 34–36, 50, 61, 63–64, 68, 74, 76, 87, 115, 117, 147, 149, 159–60, 167, 172, 175, 183–190, 200–01, 208
Cleveland Stadium 185
Cobb, Ty 2, 30–31, 51, 59, 74, 82, 84, 121, 147–48, 152, 165, 198, 200–02, 204–06
Collins, Eddie 59, 65, 78–79, 85, 198
Comiskey, Charles 24–25, 78
Comiskey Park 56, 133
Congress Hotel 78
Coolidge, President Calvin 107, 110, 115
Coolidge, First Lady Grace 107
Cooney, Johnny 37
Cooper, Wilbur 119
Coveleski, Stan 115, 122–24, 136
Crawford, Sam 204
Cronin, Joe 171–72, 175–80, 182, 188, 202–07
Cross, Harry 128
Crowder, Alvin 165, 176–77
Crowder, General Enoch 41
Cuba 146
Curran, William 56
Curtis, Byrn 153
Cuyler, Kiki 77, 120–122, 124, 132, 136, 140

Daniels, Josephus 21
Darcy, G.W. 67
Dauss, George 33
"Dead Ball Era" 68
Dean, Dizzy 206
Decker, Randy 213
Detroit Pistons 174
Detroit Tigers 30, 33–34, 42, 59, 61, 64, 75–76, 82–87, 120–121, 135, 147, 149, 153–54, 163, 168–69, 172, 186, 188, 200, 213
Devlin, Art 120
Dickey, Bill 173
Dimaggio, Joe 192
Dolan, Cozy 92–93
U.S.S. *Dolphin* 17
Donovan, Illinois 12–13, 60, 211
Doubleday, Alexander 202, 209
Doyle, Chilly 131–32
Dressen, Charley 179
Dreyfuss, Barney 77, 118–119, 132, 139
Drinking and baseball 119

Index

Dublin, Ireland 114
Dugan, Joe 61
Dugan, John A. 74
Duke University 89
Dumont, George 51
Dunn, Tom 199

Earlham College 191
Eastern League 88
Eaton, Paul W. 162
Eberts, Ducky 11–12, 15
The Economist (magazine) 21
Eddington, Arthur 54–55
Ehmke, Howard 89
Einstein, Albert 54
Eisle, Nebraska 9
Elk Boys Band 169
Engel, Joe 50–51, 85, 158
England 46, 114
Eopolucci, John I. 38
Europe, Baseball Winter Tour of 114
Evans, Billy 102, 159, 185, 187, 190
Evans, Joe 61
Evansville, Indiana 133
Evers, Johnny 47
Everton Field 114
Executive Order 9066 192

Faber, Red 41
Farming (among major leaguers) 10
Federal League 31–32, 117
Felix, Gus 127
Feller, Bob 6, 206
Fenway Park 56–57, 180
Ferguson, Alec 118, 124, 126–128, 136
Ferrell, Wesley 167
Fisher, Thomas A. 60
Fletcher, Art 92
Fletcher, Admiral Frank 18, 20
Flick, Elmer 5, 207
Florida 112, 208
Forbes Field 136–137, 140
Forest City Club 52
"The Forgotten Man" (song) 175
Fort Terry 44
Foxx, Jimmie 157, 176
France 46–48, 114, 121
Franco, Julio 165–66
Frazee, Harry 57, 72
"Freak deliveries" 70
Frick, Ford 202, 204
Frisch, Frankie 98–99, 106, 108–110, 199
Fullerton, Hugh 94

Galatzer, Milt 187–88
Galesburg, Illinois/Galesburg Pavers 11–12, 15, 81
Gallia, Bert 29, 33
Gambling in baseball 52–53, 147
Gandil, Chick 29

Gard Family Farm 12–13, 211, 214
Garner, U.S. Vice President John 174
Gaston, Milton 152, 169
Gehrig, Lou 88, 116–117, 149, 154, 166, 176, 205
General Electric 164
Germany 47
Gharrity, Pat 51, 63
Giant Manufacturing Co. 164
Giddy, Leonard 9
Gilmore, Grover 32
Gleason, Kid 85
Golf 3, 80–85, 112, 153, 155, 162, 166–67, 173, 190–191, 197, 208, 214
Gomez, Vernon 174
Gooch, Johnny 135
Gorman, U.S. Senator Arthur Pue 53
Goslin, Leon "Goose" 10, 73, 78, 84–86, 88, 96–97, 99–100, 111–112, 117, 127, 135, 137, 139, 144, 148–49, 152, 154, 159, 162, 164–66, 172, 177, 188
Gowdy, Hank 100, 103, 107, 109–110
Grandpaps of the Potomac 165
Grantham, George "Boots" 119–120, 128136
Gray, Martin 12–13, 15
Great Depression 23, 160, 162, 168–69, 171, 173, 176, 194
Greenberg, Hank 202–03, 205–06
Gregg, Vean 67
Griffith, Clark 23–31, 34–35, 37–38, 40–42, 47–52, 58, 61–65, 69, 71–75, 77–79, 82–85, 87, 89–90, 93, 102, 108, 112, 115, 118–119, 132, 139, 145–48, 152–53, 155–58, 162, 164–65, 167–69, 171–73, 181, 188, 194, 199, 202
Griffith Stadium 33
Grimes, Burleigh 120
Grimm, Charlie 119

Hagen, Walter 83
Hall, Frank 169
Hall of Fame 1–3, 5–6, 182, 186, 188–89, 196–97, 199, 201–10, 212–14
Hamilton Hotel 169
Hammond, Indiana 7
Harder, Mel 187
Harper, Harry 33
Harris, Dave 163, 165, 167, 176, 178
Harris, Joe "Moon" 50, 118, 121, 135, 137, 144
Harris, Stanley "Bucky" 51, 61, 71–72, 77–79, 85–88, 90, 96–100, 102–110, 112, 115, 117–118, 121, 124, 126–127, 135–137, 139–141, 144, 148–49, 151, 153–55, 169, 171–72, 175
Harrison, James 140
Hartford (Eastern League team) 88
Haviland Mill Road 209
Hawaii 208
Headwaters Farm 193
Heckscher, August 20
Heilman, Harry 149

Index

Henry, John 42
Heydler, John 66, 93–94
Highland, Indiana 7
Hinojosa, Col. Ramon 17
Holland, Dutch 186–87
Holmes, Tommy 199
Home runs, concern about proliferation of 56
Hoover, U.S. President Herbert 169
Hornsby, Rogers 56, 152, 166, 189, 201
Hot Springs, Arkansas 40, 162
Hot Springs, Virginia 21
Hoyt, Captain J. Lindsay 43, 46–48
Hubbell, Carl 176–78
Huerta, Victoriano 17, 20
Huggins, Miller 61–63, 82–83, 88, 116
Huntsinger, Walter 114

Ickes, Harold L. 192–93
Indian Spring (golf course) 153, 167, 169
Indiana Pacers 174
International League 37, 152
Iroquois, Illinois 9, 14–15, 129
Iseminger, Jeff 214

Jackson, Joe 41, 52, 59, 74
Jackson, Travis 98–99, 107
James, Bill 69
Jamieson, Charles 37, 44, 61
Japanese internment 192–93
Jasper County, Indiana 14
Jennings, Hughie 114
Jersey City (International League team) 152
Johnson, Byron Bancroft "Ban" 24–25, 32, 41, 47–48, 67, 93, 141, 202
Johnson, Charles 13
Johnson, Eddie 195
Johnson, Elinor 73, 195
Johnson, Hazel 94, 195
Johnson, Paul 54
Johnson, Walter 1, 10, 27–28, 33, 36, 42, 59–61, 73–75, 85–86, 88–90, 94–95, 100–104, 106–108–110, 121–22, 124, 134–35, 137–42, 144–47, 151–52, 155–58, 160, 163–67, 170–72, 180, 183–84, 187, 194–96, 202, 205
Johnson, Walter, Jr. 195
Jones, Frank 53
Jones, Sam 158
Jordan, Michael 180–81
Judge, Dorothy 38
Judge, Joe 26, 28, 30, 37–38, 48, 51, 61, 72, 84–85, 90, 95, 97–98, 107–108, 122–23, 127, 137–38, 146, 155, 158, 165–68, 188, 194
Judge, Mark Gauvreau 2
Juiced ball *see* Rabbit ball

Kachline, Cliff 209
Kansas City Chiefs 181
Kavanaugh, Marty 33

Kay Jewelry Co. 169
Kelly, George 95, 98, 100, 105–106, 108
Kendal, Rute 9
Kendall, Mary *see* Rice, Mary
Kerr, Paul 209–10
King George 115
Klem, Bill 133
Knights of Columbus 47
Knox College 11
Kobayashi brothers 193
Konetchy, Ed 58
Kopp, Merlin 25–26
Koster, Frank W. 201
Kremer, Ray 126–27, 137, 139
Kuhel, Joe 168, 178

Lacy, Sam 146
Lajoie, Napoleon 198, 200
Lake Erie 185
Landis, Kennesaw Mountain 32, 87, 92–94, 111, 129–31, 133–34, 138–39, 141, 147–48
Lane, F.C. 66, 69, 92, 94, 106
Lardner, Ring 136
"The Last Out" 130
League Park (Cleveland) 185, 189
Lefler, Wade 89
Le Havre, France 46
Leicestershire 45–46
Leigh, Doc 17, 21–23
Leonard, Dutch 147
Levenson, Barry 142
Lewis, Duffy 36, 61
Lewis, Senator J. Hamilton 20
Lewis, Army Sgt. Ralph 131
Lieb, Fred 101, 111, 130, 203
Lindstrom, Freddy 96, 98, 105, 107, 109
Liverpool, England 114–115
London, England 114–115
Long Island, New York 44
Lopez, Al 198
Louisiana 16
Louisville Colonels 118
Louisville, Kentucky 16
Louisville Slugger 164
Lowell, Indiana 7
Luque, Dolph 6

Maass, General Gustavo 19
Mac, Bernie 2
Mack, Connie 29, 31, 61, 79, 83, 86, 148, 202
Madero, Francisco 17
Mantle, Mickey 205
Manush, Heinie 154, 165, 172, 179
Maranville, Rabbit 41, 118–119
Marberry, Fred "Firpo" 10, 89, 98–100, 106–107, 127–28, 132, 167
Margin, U.S. Senator Thomas S. 22
Marriage: to Beulah Stam 10; to Edith Owens 60
Marsans, Armanda 146

Index

Martin, John D. 158
Martin, Mike 34, 194
Martin, Pat 51
Martin, "Speed" 155
Mathewson, Christy 94, 122, 202
S.S. *Matsonia* 48
Matthews, Eddie 205
Matthews, Wid 87
Mayer, Erskine 200
Mayo, Admiral Henry Thomas 17–18
Mays, Carl 68
Mays, Willie 141, 180, 205
McAleer, Jimmy 24, 27
McBride, George 62–65, 71–72
McCarthy, Alex 32
McCloy, John 192
McGraw, John 51, 82–83, 93, 95–97, 105–106, 126–27, 176, 202
McHale, Marty 76
McInnis, Stuffy 31, 74, 120, 136
McKechnie, Bill 119–120, 122, 126, 128, 131, 133–134, 136–139
McNally, Mike 71
McNeely, Earl 87, 89, 95–97, 103–105, 108–110, 127, 145, 147–48, 152–53, 210
M.E. Church South 60
Meadows, Lee 121
Menosky, Mike 47–48
Meusel, Bob 61, 88–89, 127, 129
Meusel, Irish 105–108, 110
Mexico 17–21
Michigan 18
Michigan, University of 35
Milan, Clyde 28, 45, 59, 64, 69, 72–77
Miller, Fred 44
Miller, Ralph 99–101, 108–109
Milwaukee Braves 207
Minnesota 16
Minnesota Twins 213
Mr. 3000 (movie) 2
Moeller, Danny 35
Mogridge, George 73, 85, 89, 100, 105–106
Molitor, Paul 165–66
Monmouth, Illinois 11–12
Mont Royal (ocean liner) 114
Montana, Joe 181
Montreal (International League team) 152
Montreal, Canada 114
Montreal Expos/Washington Nationals 2, 214
Moore, Eddie 120, 122–23, 126, 132, 137, 139
Moriarty, George 137
Morocco, Indiana 7, 9, 191, 213
Morris, Frizzy 9
Morrison, Johnny 138
Murphy, Eddie 29
Musial, Stan 205
Myer, Buddy 148, 173, 175, 177, 188

NASCAR 68
National Cathedral 194

National Late Model Dirt Track Hall of Fame 213
National League 24–25
National League Championship Series 141
The Natural (movie) 10
Navin, Frank 169
Navy 16–22, 40, 47, 114, 124
NBA 174
Nehf, Art 95–96, 103, 105, 107–108, 114
Neville, W.C. 19
U.S.S. *New Hampshire* 16–21
New Jersey 18
New London, Connecticut 45
New York Giants 51, 69, 91–111, 114, 119–120, 124, 126–27, 132, 142, 152, 176–180
New York Mets 180
New York Yankees 22, 24, 34, 42, 44, 49, 57–58, 61–63, 68, 71–77, 86, 87–89, 91, 96, 116–117, 126–27, 134, 145, 149–51, 154, 157–58, 166, 169, 172–75, 187, 192, 204
Newark, New Jersey 155, 164
Newmeyer, Louise *see* Rice, Louise
Newton County, Indiana 7, 14, 90
Nicaragua 199
Niehaus, Al 119
Night baseball 164
Norfolk, Virginia 16–17, 21
Nosker, Grace 15

O'Connell, Jimmy 92–93
Ogden, Curly 87, 105–106, 111
Ohio 128
Old Timers' Committee 207
Oldham, Red 140
Optimist Club 168–69
O'Rourke, Frank 72
O'Shea, Con 9
Otsaga Hotel 209
Ott, Mel 179
Owens, Brick 139
Owens, Edith *see* Rice, Edith

Pacific Coast League 36–37, 87, 185
Palmeiro, Rafael 199
Palmero, Emilio 146
Paoli, Indiana 12
Paris, France 114
Paschal, Ben 157
Pearl Harbor 192
Peckinpaugh, Roger 71–73, 85–86, 89, 96, 98–101, 103, 121–22, 139–40, 183, 188, 194
Pennock, Herb 88, 169
Perry, Scott 61
Petersburg, Virginia/Petersburg Goobers 17, 21–23, 27, 33, 70
Pfirman, Cy 134
Philadelphia Athletics 6, 26, 29–31, 36, 40, 44, 59–63, 71–72, 78–79, 86–87, 117, 144–45, 149, 152, 157, 159–60, 163–64, 165, 167–69, 171–72, 187, 200

Philadelphia Phillies 92, 200
Pigeon racing 3, 197, 214
Pipp, Wally 63, 116
Pittsburgh Pirates 36, 69, 77–78, 118–143, 151, 198–99
Polo Grounds 51, 57, 63, 98–101, 176–77
Pooly, Bill 184
Popular Mechanics 67
Porter, Dick 186
Poston, Arizona 193
Potts, Dick 214
Povich, Shirley 24, 53, 143, 148, 168, 170, 175, 177, 183, 202–06, 209, 212
Powers, Jimmy 205
Prairie Dell Cemetery 15
Pratt, Del 44
Prince of Wales 115

Quakers 191
Quinn, Jack 165–66

Rabbit ball 66–68
Radio, advent of commercial 71
"Rango" (origins of nickname) 9
Reach (baseball manufacturer) 67
Red Cross 46
Redding, Jack 209
Reeves, Bobby 154
Regester, Rev. Dr. E.V. 60
Reisling, Doc 26
Rensselaer, Indiana 14
Reynolds, Carl 167–68, 172–73
RFK Stadium 2, 214
Rice, Bernadine 9, 13–15
Rice, Bernie 11, 13, 15
Rice, Beulah 9–13, 15, 60
Rice, Charles 9, 12–15
Rice, Christine 196–97, 208–09, 212
Rice, Edith 38, 60, 155, 170, 190–91, 193, 196
Rice, Ethel 11, 13, 15
Rice, Genevieve 9, 13–14
Rice, Grantland 96, 108
Rice, Louise 9, 12–15
Rice, Mabel 9
Rice, Mary 60, 196–97, 207–08, 210, 212
Rice family misfortune 12
Richardson, William Miller 58
Richmond, Virginia 65
Rickey, Branch 157
Rigler, Charley "Cy" 128–33, 136–137
Rigney, Topper 148
Ring, Jimmy 94
Rixey, Eppa 5–6, 204, 207
Roanoke (Virginia League team) 22
"Roaring Twenties" 54
Robinson, Brooks 205
Robinson, Frank 205
Robinson, Jackie 6, 206
Robinson, Joseph 175
Rockwell, Norman 56

Rogers, Will 148
Rolen, Scott 141
Rome, Italy 114
Rommell, Eddie 144
Rommelof, Ed 169
Rondeau, Henri 35
Roosevelt, President Franklin D. 192–93
Ross Co. 169
Rothstein, Arnold 52
Roush, Eddie 10, 204
Ruel, Muddy 85, 95, 102, 108–111, 114, 122, 140, 158, 194
Ruether, Walter "Dutch" 115, 124, 145
Runyon, Damon 102, 109
Russell, Jack 172
Russell, Reb 36
Ruth, Babe 1–2, 36–37, 43, 47, 54–57, 59–61, 63, 67, 74, 84, 87–88, 100, 112, 116–117, 129, 134, 137, 149, 151, 157, 166, 176, 180, 189, 202, 205, 209
Ryan, Blondy 179
Ryan, Rosy 100

Sacramento (Pacific Coast League team) 87
St. John, Indiana 7
St. Louis Browns 24, 35, 56, 59, 65, 75–77, 87, 106, 117, 145, 151–52, 154, 162, 164–66, 172, 186, 201
St. Louis Cardinals 42, 120, 134, 157, 176, 204
Sam Rice Ballpark 191
"Sam Rice Day" 168–70
San Diego, California 155
San Francisco 49ers (NFL) 181
San Francisco Seals (Pacific Coast League) 185
Sandberg, Rev. O.G. 15
Sands, Heinie 92
Sandy Spring, Maryland 190, 193–94, 214
Sarazen, Gene 83
Sawyer, Carl 30
Schacht, Al 110, 147, 169
Schererville, Indiana 7
Schliebner, Dutch 76
Schriver, Bill 24
Schulte, Fred 172, 175, 178–79
Schultz, Robert 14
Schumacher, Hal 177
Scientific American 67
Scott, Everett 116
Scott, Jack 120
Scott, Jim 32
Seeds, Bob 187
Selective Service Act 38, 49
Sewell, Luke 173, 178, 188
Seybold, Sock 56
Shanks, Howard 35, 40
Shaw, Joe 29
Sheehan, Tom 119
Sherdel, Willie 134

Shibe Field 55, 160
Shires, Art 165
Silver Spring, Maryland 196
Simmons, Al 149, 176
Simpson, Jim 130
Sisler, George 35–37, 59, 69, 74, 106
Small, Robert 140
Smart family (Charles, Anna, Cassie, Iolene, John) 14
Smith, New York Governor Al 57
Smith, Chester L. 131
Smith, Earl (Washington outfielder) 65
Smith, Earl "Oil" 121, 126–137, 140, 179
Smith, Elmer 61
Smith, Ken 209
Smith, Red 194
Smith, Russ 11–13
Society of Friends *see* Quakers
Soden, A.H. 25
South Atlantic League 73
South Carolina 18
Southern Association 151
Southern League 158, 179
Southworth, Billy 96
Spalding (baseball manufacturer) 67, 164
Spalding, A.G. 52
Speaker, Tris 31, 59, 61, 63–64, 84, 117, 147–49, 151–53, 166, 198, 200, 205
Speece, By 10
Spitballs 68
Sports Illustrated 60
Sportsman Park 55
Springfield, Illinois 143
Stabler, Elizabeth 190
Stallings, George 75
Stam, Beulah *see* Rice, Beulah
Standard Oil 32
Staten Island 46
Statz, Arnold 155
Stewart, Walter 172, 177
Stolen bases (decline of) 68–70
Stone, John 188
Street, Gabby 24, 42
Strunk, Amos 31
Studebaker automobiles 162, 169
Suffolk (Virginia League team) 23
Sullivan, Ted 105
Susko, Pete 188
Sutherland, Elizabeth 154
Swanson, U.S. Senator Claude A. 22
Swedish Cemetery 15

Tampa, Florida 146, 152, 158
Tampico, Mexico 17–18, 20
Taylor, Tommy 99
Terry, Bill 95, 103, 105–106, 108, 176–79
Texas Rangers 214
Thomas, Henry W. 1–2, 139, 195
Thomas, Tommy 177
Thorne, Mr. 82

Three-thousand hits 2, 198–201, 203
Tobin, Jack 56, 145
Tornado 1, 11–14, 20–21, 41, 49, 60, 81, 90, 129, 142–43, 168, 195, 208, 211–12, 214
Town and Country golf club 82
Traynor, Pie 120–121, 132, 139
Treaty of Versailles 47
Tucker, Ollie 151

Union Cigar 162
U.S. Bureau of Standards 67
U.S.-Mexico military tension 17–21
U.S. 30 7
U.S. 41 7

Veach, Bobby 122
Veracruz, Occupation of 1, 18–21, 45, 49, 124, 195
Veterans Committee 207
Vietnam War 5
Virginia League 3, 17, 21–22, 65, 70, 188
Vosmik, Joe 185

Wagner, Earl 119
Wagner, Honus 118, 120–121, 198, 200, 202
Walker, Gerald 174
Walker, Tilly 61
Wall Street 160, 210
Walter Reed Hospital 169
Waner, Paul 198–201, 203
Wanniger, Peewee 116
War Relocation Authority 192
Wardman Park Hotel 111
Washington, Vernon 187
Washington Golf and Country Club 84
Washington Monument 23–24
Washington Senators: purchase of Rice 23
Washington Wizards (NBA) 180–81
Watseka, Illinois 9, 10–12, 31, 40, 142
Watson, Mule 100
Weaver, Buck 32, 92
Weaver, Monte 175, 178
Webster, Ray 9
West, Sammy 151, 156–57, 163, 172
Western League 24
White, Devon 141
White House 111
Whitehill, Earl 172–74, 176–77
Whiting, Indiana 7
Wilhelm the Second, Kaiser 47
Williams, Ted 180, 205
Willisville, Illinois 14
Wilson, First Lady Ellen 21
Wilson, Hack 95, 98, 101, 105–106, 108
Wilson, President Woodrow 17–18, 38, 41, 47, 194–95
Women's Republican Club 193
Wood, "Smokey" Joe 65, 147
Woodside Cemetery 209
"Work-or-fight" order 42–43

World Series (1909) 118, 120; (1914) 75; (1918) 46–47; (1919) 52, 115; (1920) 71, 147; (1924) 2, 91–112, 114, 124, 142, 147, 152; (1925) 118–143, 149, 170, 211; (1927) 77, 151; (1928) 134; (1929) 160; (1933) 176–180; (1954) 141; (1992) 141; (2004) 57; (2005) 52
World War I 5, 38–50, 121, 167, 196, 205, 211
World War II 5, 192, 194, 198
Wright, Ab 187
Wright, George 202
Wright, Glenn 77, 120–122, 128
Wrigley Field 160

Wulf, Steve 212
Wynn, Early 180

Yde, Emil 135
"The Yellow Peril" 192
Yost, John 90, 211–12
Young, Frank H. 88, 149
Young, Steve 181
Youngs, Ross 96, 101, 106–108
Ypiranga 18

Zachary, Tom 10, 51, 97–98, 103–105, 124, 136, 145, 151, 194

www.ingramcontent.com/pod-product-compliance
Ingram Content Group UK Ltd.
Pitfield, Milton Keynes, MK11 3LW, UK
UKHW041938140426
5217IPUK00014B/549